WEAPONS
OF THE AMERICAN
REVOLUTION
...AND ACCOUTREMENTS

AMERICAN

by Warren Moore

WEAPONS
OF THE
REVOLUTION
...AND ACCOUTREMENTS

PROMONTORY PRESS

NEW YORK

Copyright © 1967 by Warren Moore
All Rights Reserved.
ISBN 0-88394-027-2
Library of Congress
Catalog Card Number: 73-92816
Published by arrangement with Funk & Wagnalls,
A Division of Reader's Digest Books, Inc.

Printed in the United States of America

FOREWORD

It is always interesting to know the qualifications of an author and, when the author is also a collector, to know why he has chosen a particular field. Warren Moore tells me that when he was twelve years old, he was attracted by some flintlock pistols in a locksmith's shop. This fascination with the flintlock has stayed with him, and over the years since then he has succeeded in acquiring a fine collection of firearms and other weapons of the Revolutionary War period. An early purchase was an English holster pistol by Hadley that he bought in New Orleans on his honeymoon in 1947; and later that year he bought a pistol blunderbuss by mail from Glode Requa, a leading dealer in firearms. In 1950 Warren, who is an engineer, was transferred by his company from Atlanta to New York. After living in Riverdale for three years, he moved to Ramsey, New Jersey, which is only a few miles from the home of Glode Requa. Thus, intentionally or otherwise, Warren, who visited Requa frequently and who met the active collectors in his shop, expanded both his interest in firearms and his collecting activities. Today his collecting has slowed down, since Revolutionary War weapons—his specialty—are to be found only on rare occasions.

The present book includes some 700 illustrations; about two-thirds of the illustrated objects are in the author's collection, while the remainder are from about twenty other sources—museums and collector-friends. I point this out mainly to note that he is intimately familiar with his subject, having had the opportunity to scrutinize each item and, in the case of firearms, to dismount them to study mechanical features. The book is divided into five main sections—Pistols, Shoulder Weapons, Edged Weapons, Engraved Powder Horns, and Accoutrements (Pole Arms, Bayonets, Saddle Holsters, Gorgets, and Military Headgear). Cannon, which on occasion played an important role in the war, are not included, since they deserve special consideration.

The close relationship between American and European firearms gives the American historian and collector a logical interest in European firearms. European arms have been used here since the days of exploration, and European techniques and design are at the basis of all early American firearms. In 1609 the French explorer Samuel de Champlain supplied the first firearms used in Indian warfare. German and other European rifles brought by immigrants from their homelands influenced the development of American rifles. A brace of pistols that belonged to George Washington, now in the museum at West Point, bear London proof marks and the name of the London gunsmith Hawkins. A pair of Scottish pistols by T. Murdoch were Washington's legacy to Lafayette. A pair of Alexander Hamilton's pistols were made at St. Etienne by Jalabert Lamotte, and the fowling piece of John Jay, who negotiated the peace in 1783, was made in Paris (the Hamilton and Jay firearms are in the Metropolitan Museum of Art). It has been recorded that the first shot of the American Revolution was fired at Lexington by Major Pitcairn from a Scottish all-steel pistol. Pitcairn's pistols, carried throughout the war by Captain Parker, are now in the old Hancock-Clark House at Lexington, Massachusetts.

Two distinct types of flintlock weapons were used in the Revolutionary War—the smooth-bore musket of New England and the rifle of the central and southern colonies. The majority of New England's early gunsmiths came from England and naturally adopted the musket which was in general use there. The Pennsylvania Dutch immigrants brought rifles with them from Germany, and it is these German and other contemporary European rifles that influenced the development of the American rifle. In the early eighteenth century there were various types of German rifles, and Fleming's *Teutsche Jäger* (1719) illustrates several kinds of hunting guns—wheellock and flintlock, rifle and smooth bore, with short or long barrel. A single plate of the same book shows a long rifle for stalking big game, a short rifle for shooting wild boar, the *Schrottbüchse*, or "rifle-gun," with straight grooves from which ball as well as shot could be fired, and a shot gun with long barrel. The features of such firearms depended on their intended use, and because they were handmade, they varied considerably. Thousands of long-barreled hunting rifles were made in Germany in the 1700s; the immigrant-gunsmiths who settled in America were familiar with them, and on them, rather than on the German short rifle, they based the Pennsylvania rifle.

At the beginning of the Revolution, John Adams wrote from Philadelphia of "a peculiar kind of musket, called a rifle," and told that ten companies of riflemen were to be recruited from Pennsylvania, Maryland, and Virginia—companies Washington was soon to be awaiting at Cambridge. Washington knew of the skill of the backwoods riflemen because it was to them that the few Englishmen who escaped at Braddock's defeat on the banks of the Monongahela in 1755 owed their lives.

The Pennsylvania rifle's principal value was that most of the men who used it were trained marksmen. In Europe, since only the privileged could hunt, there were comparatively few marksmen, but in America the entire country was a hunting ground, and a man's life often depended on his ability to shoot accurately. Powder and lead were not plentiful, and when firing at an enemy, a man usually had only one chance to hit, because the muzzle-loading rifle is not a rapid-fire piece. The elusive and accurate riflemen comprised a valuable arm of the American forces, and they were particularly formidable in broken or wooded country.

During most of the war the British Army had no riflemen to provide a similar harassing and protective screen. Therefore, to counteract the American riflemen, the British hired from the Landgrave of Hesse a body of Jaegers (hunters) who were armed with rifles. Their rifle had a short barrel rifled with six or seven grooves, and it used an oversize bullet that was driven in with a mallet and ramrod. Its rate of fire was only about one shot a minute, as compared with the two or three shots of the Pennsylvania rifle. One of these Jaeger rifles is illustrated in the book. In the patch box is a German newspaper clipping of 1776 referring to the British attack on Charleston; it also mentions a conspiracy to assassinate George Washington and other American leaders. Charleston withstood attacks from the British in 1776 and in 1779, but was captured in 1780 from the land side by Sir Henry Clinton. Jaegers were particularly important in the siege of Charleston, and rendered valuable service elsewhere.

Major Patrick Ferguson of the 71st Highlanders invented a breech-loading rifle in 1776. Some of these were used in the battle of King's Mountain—October 7, 1780, the turning point of the war at the South —in which Ferguson was defeated and slain. A breech-loader, although not of American origin, has become American because its first appearance as a weapon of war was on the battlefields of America; this was the first use of a breech-loading rifle on this continent or any other.

That the Colonists were unprepared and without munitions in 1775 is an undisputed fact. They acquired their early meager supplies by seizure or by capture in combat until other ways and means to obtain them were found. In 1776 Congress sent Benjamin Franklin to Paris to seek all possible aid from the French government. The royal arsenal at Charleville was authorized to sell thirty thousand Model 1763 Charleville muskets, thus ending the American shortage of firearms. In March, 1777, a ship bearing twelve thousand muskets arrived at Portsmouth, New Hampshire; another, carrying eleven thousand muskets, docked in Philadelphia.

American engraved powder horns have a human interest aspect that keeps history alive. When in the course of the Seven Years' War, Spain made an alliance with France, England declared war on Spain and sent an expedition against Havana. This expedition was the last in which Americans served overseas under the British flag. By the Peace of Paris in 1763 Spain ceded Florida to the British in exchange for Cuba. After the Treaty of Paris it was necessary for the British to garrison an extensive line of forts — the forts represented on these powder horns. In 1765 Grenville, Chancellor of the Exchequer, thought that the thirteen colonies should share the costs of this defense, so he proposed to levy a stamp tax, which led to the first symptoms of alienation between America and the mother country. These powder horns belong to a time, much like the present, when every man was liable to be called for military service and when every armed man had one.

To motorists on the New York highways following the Hudson and Mohawk rivers, or along Lakes George, Champlain, and Ontario, the many signposts commemorating forts and battles associated with early Colonial times and with the American Revolution are familiar sights. These sections of the state are replete with historical interest. The Hudson and Mohawk valleys were of great military importance during the eighteenth century and their two rivers were the high roads. Britain chose the Hudson-Champlain Valley as the route offering the greatest strategic possibilities for a quick suppression of the rebellion. Her aim was to isolate New England, where the rebellion was the most active and capable of the longest resistance. The plan called for a double advance along the Hudson in which the army of Burgoyne, moving southward from Canada, would effect a junction at Albany with the army of Sir William Howe, moving northward from New York City; they were to be joined by the army of General Barry St. Leger, moving eastward along the Mohawk from Oswego on Lake Ontario. The turning point of American fortune came in October, 1777, at the Battle of Saratoga. The complete defeat of Burgoyne's expedition—the surrender of thirty-five hundred fighting men at Saratoga—was one of the great battles of the world, since it changed a little group of colonists into a nation.

During the Revolutionary War military pistols and infantry swords were rare and somewhat ineffective. Staff weapons played little active part in actual fighting, although the spontoon was carried by many officers in the American armies. In the early years of the war, because of the lack of firearms—a deficiency which all the industry of our ingenious gunsmiths could not suddenly supply—a pike was used (the staff fourteen feet long, the spear eighteen inches, thin and light). Accounts testify that a great many of these weapons were made by Josiah Wood, at a cost of about £3 per 100 pikes, and delivered by him at the average of 100 to 150 per month.

The extent to which pistols were in use in the Colonies as the day of the American Revolution drew near may be grasped from the contemporary account in Frothingham's *Siege of Boston*, in which 634 pistols are listed as having been turned in by Boston householders when the British General Gage assured them they might leave the city if the arms were surrendered. Military pistols were made at the Rappahannock Forge, which was established by an act of the Virginia Assembly in June, 1775, near Fredericksburg. It manufactured small-arms from the date of its founding until May 30, 1781, when it was dismantled to prevent capture and destruction by a British raiding party.

In the eighteenth century gentlemen's steel sword hilts and elegant *couteaux de chasse* (hunting swords, or "hangers") mounted in silver were being made in America. These were used by the Colonial officers of British provincial forces in the French and Indian War and continued in use throughout the eighteenth century. In a letter dated January 27th, 1775, Horace Walpole refers to the manufacture of swords in America: "I forgot to tell you that the town of Birmingham has petitioned the Parliament to enforce the American Acts, that is, make war; for they have a manufacture of swords and muskets." In due course Americans developed their own sword-making industry. Lewis Prahl of Philadelphia received sixty and seventy shillings, respectively, for horsemen's swords that he made in 1781. In 1776 the Connecticut silversmith Deodat Williams advertised that he made ". . . officers' silver mounted hangers with either lions, eagles, painters [panthers] or plain heads, etc." We have already referred to the Hessians in the service of the British. I have seen in the Springfield Armory a Hessian officer's sword with blade inscribed FRIEDRICH II^{te} LANDGRAFF ZU HESSEN; it was presented by George Tiemann to the Ordnance Museum in Washington, D.C., on April 17, 1876. The plain severity of the military guns is in striking contrast to the officers' pistols and swords which are often silver-mounted and veritable works of art.

Warren Moore tells me that his aim in writing this book is to present basic information mainly to the novice who is interested in the equipment of the Revolutionary War. He modestly hopes that the experienced collector and student will also find something that has not already come to his attention. A significant merit of the book is that only a few of the illustrations have previously been published. On turning the page, the reader, novice or scholar will be in good hands, for the author has included much of the knowledge that he acquired in discussing his subject with fellow members of the American Society of Arms Collectors and the Company of Military Historians.

STEPHEN V. GRANCSAY
Curator Emeritus, Department of Arms and Armor,
The Metropolitan Museum of Art
Fellow of the Company of Military Historians

New York, July, 1967

*The Company
of Military Historians
through its Review Board
is honored to sponsor*
Weapons of
the American
Revolution
*as an accurate and useful
reference work in American
military history.*

F. B. NIHART

*Colonel, USMC (Ret.)
President*

Review Board

ROBERT LEE KLINGER

ROBERT L. MILLER

HERMANN W. WILLIAMS, JR.

HENRY I. SHAW, JR.,
Editor-in-Chief

CONTENTS

PISTOLS

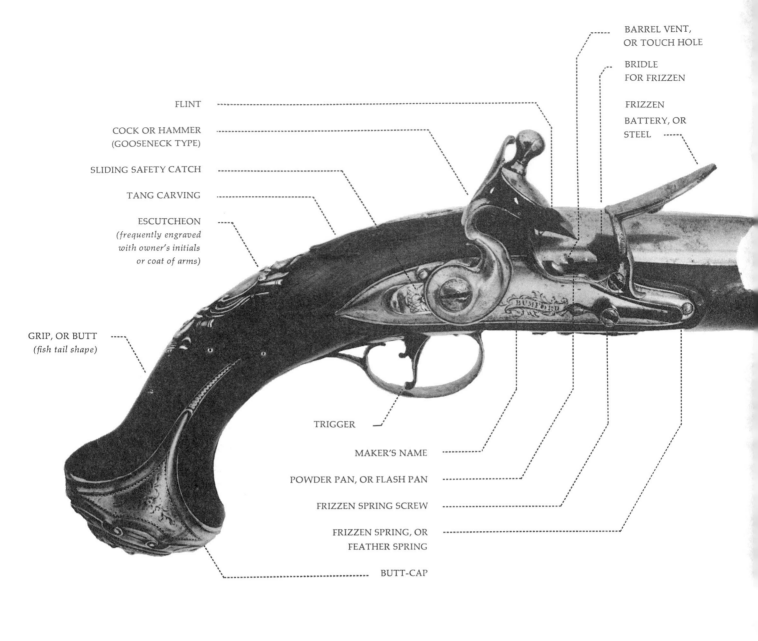

FLINT

COCK OR HAMMER
(GOOSENECK TYPE)

SLIDING SAFETY CATCH

TANG CARVING

ESCUTCHEON
(frequently engraved
with owner's initials
or coat of arms)

GRIP, OR BUTT
(fish tail shape)

BARREL VENT,
OR TOUCH HOLE

BRIDLE
FOR FRIZZEN

FRIZZEN
BATTERY, OR
STEEL

TRIGGER

MAKER'S NAME

POWDER PAN, OR FLASH PAN

FRIZZEN SPRING SCREW

FRIZZEN SPRING, OR
FEATHER SPRING

BUTT-CAP

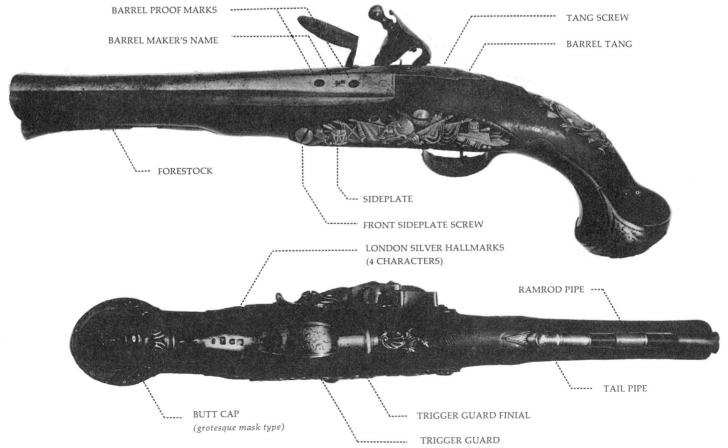

BARREL PROOF MARKS

BARREL MAKER'S NAME

TANG SCREW

BARREL TANG

FORESTOCK

SIDEPLATE

FRONT SIDEPLATE SCREW

LONDON SILVER HALLMARKS
(4 CHARACTERS)

RAMROD PIPE

TAIL PIPE

BUTT CAP
(grotesque mask type)

TRIGGER GUARD FINIAL

TRIGGER GUARD

NOMENCLATURE OF THE FLINTLOCK PISTOL

A TYPICAL SILVER-MOUNTED OFFICER'S
MUZZLE LOADING HOLSTER PISTOL
MADE IN LONDON BY I. BUMFORD IN 1761

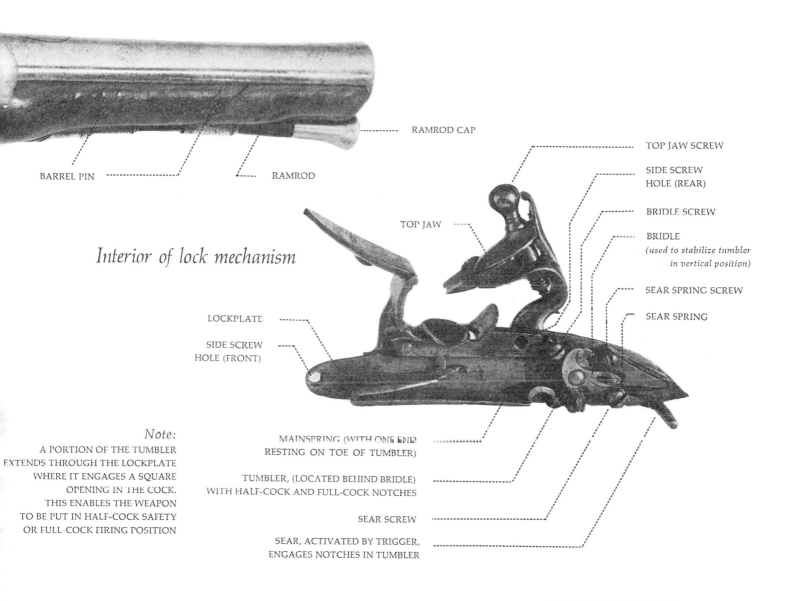

RAMROD CAP

BARREL PIN

RAMROD

TOP JAW SCREW

SIDE SCREW
HOLE (REAR)

BRIDLE SCREW

BRIDLE
(*used to stabilize tumbler
in vertical position*)

SEAR SPRING SCREW

SEAR SPRING

TOP JAW

Interior of lock mechanism

LOCKPLATE

SIDE SCREW
HOLE (FRONT)

Note:
A PORTION OF THE TUMBLER
EXTENDS THROUGH THE LOCKPLATE
WHERE IT ENGAGES A SQUARE
OPENING IN THE COCK.
THIS ENABLES THE WEAPON
TO BE PUT IN HALF-COCK SAFETY
OR FULL-COCK FIRING POSITION

MAINSPRING (WITH ONE END
RESTING ON TOE OF TUMBLER)

TUMBLER, (LOCATED BEHIND BRIDLE)
WITH HALF-COCK AND FULL-COCK NOTCHES

SEAR SCREW

SEAR, ACTIVATED BY TRIGGER,
ENGAGES NOTCHES IN TUMBLER

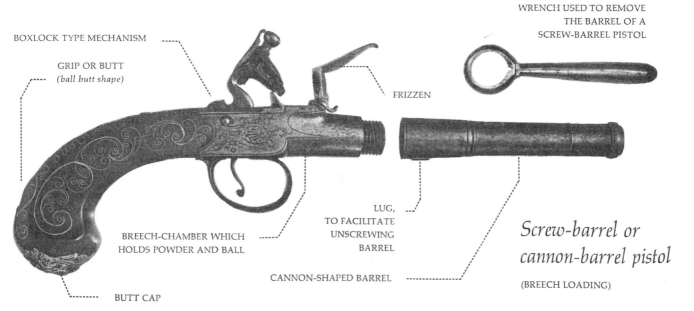

BOXLOCK TYPE MECHANISM

GRIP OR BUTT
(*ball butt shape*)

WRENCH USED TO REMOVE
THE BARREL OF A
SCREW-BARREL PISTOL

FRIZZEN

BREECH-CHAMBER WHICH
HOLDS POWDER AND BALL

LUG,
TO FACILITATE
UNSCREWING
BARREL

CANNON-SHAPED BARREL

BUTT CAP

*Screw-barrel or
cannon-barrel pistol*

(BREECH LOADING)

HOW TO LOAD
AND FIRE A FLINTLOCK

*These drawings illustrate
the principal steps in the use of
a typical flintlock.*

1, 2, 3 *Shooter pours desired quantity
of relatively coarse-grained
propellent powder into muzzle from large main flask.
Then he starts patched ball
(patch of thin cloth makes
for tight fit, accurate shot), and
rams it down until it is seated
atop the powder firmly but without
crushing grains.*

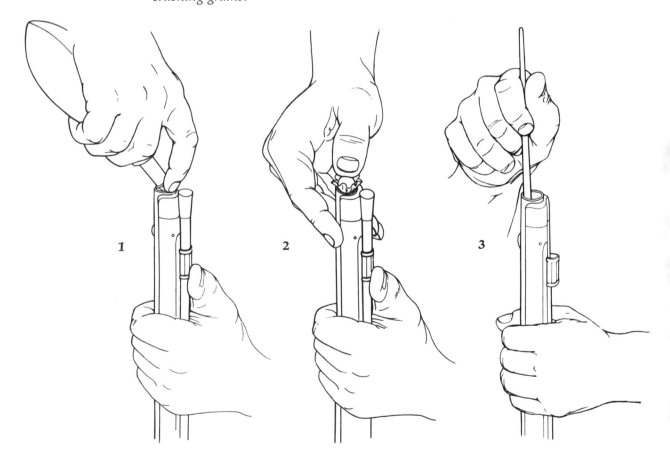

4 *The charge loaded,
he returns the ramrod, opens the flashpan
and half-cocks the gun.*

5 *About every fifth shot he frees the touchhole of carbon
to avoid a flash-in-the-pan.*

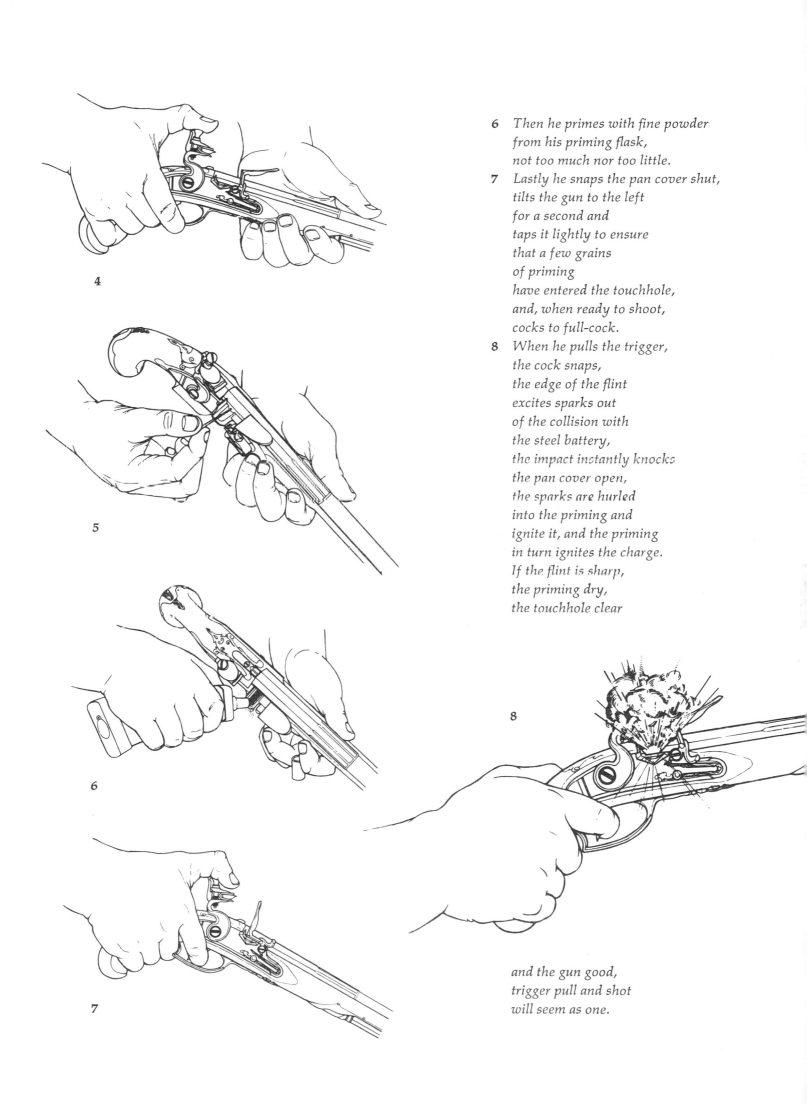

6   Then he primes with fine powder
     from his priming flask,
     not too much nor too little.
7   Lastly he snaps the pan cover shut,
     tilts the gun to the left
     for a second and
     taps it lightly to ensure
     that a few grains
     of priming
     have entered the touchhole,
     and, when ready to shoot,
     cocks to full-cock.
8   When he pulls the trigger,
     the cock snaps,
     the edge of the flint
     excites sparks out
     of the collision with
     the steel battery,
     the impact instantly knocks
     the pan cover open,
     the sparks are hurled
     into the priming and
     ignite it, and the priming
     in turn ignites the charge.
     If the flint is sharp,
     the priming dry,
     the touchhole clear

and the gun good,
trigger pull and shot
will seem as one.

Pistols used during the American Revolution utilized the flintlock form of ignition. Almost all of them were referred to as holster pistols, a designation which stemmed from the fact that these arms were carried in a pair of leather saddle holsters mounted on a horse. During the Revolution pistols were used by officers of all branches of the service; the only enlisted men who carried them were the horse soldiers and sailors. There were no strict regulations to guide the officer in selecting his pistols and, when ordering a pair from a gunsmith, he chose them in a style which suited his own taste. Though they were usually about the same size, no two matched pairs had decorations exactly alike. Practically all American and British officers owned pistols made in England. Two principal reasons probably account for this fact: first, America was an English colony, and consequently most of her imports were from the mother country; second, eighteenth-century England enjoyed unparalleled prosperity in most fields, including gunmaking. The supremacy of her sea power, coupled with the decline of commercial powers of other European countries as a result of continual wars, combined to throw the greater part of the world's trade to England. The British gunmakers accepted the challenge to supply arms for a world market, and the combination of mechanical and artistic excellence of their firearms made them among the finest in the world.

The tradesmen involved in the fabrication of pistols consisted of a barrelforger, locksmith, wood stocker or carver, engraver, and metalsmith. Almost all English pistols had the maker's name engraved or stamped across the lockplate, and sometimes on the barrel also. Some of the larger firms made the entire gun in their shops, employing workers from all of the trades mentioned above. Others were simply assemblers of parts which were made to their specifications by the respective specialists, the finished product being assembled by workers in their shops. Gunsmiths engaged in making military arms for the British government followed strict specifications, and supplied either the finished weapon, or else batches of finished parts which were later assembled at the Tower of London or other arsenals. Some made government arms, firearms for military use of special design which were purchased by officers, and sporting arms as well. A few of the leading English gunsmiths immediately prior to and during the Revolutionary period were Bumford, Brazier, Barbar, Freeman, Griffin, Hawkins, Heylin, Jover, Ketland, and Wilson.

Of course there were a number of American-made pistols used in the Revolution, mostly in the form of holster and Kentucky types.

The stocks of these were usually made of native woods such as maple or cherry, although walnut and other woods were sometimes used. For the most part they incorporated a British- or European-made lock, and thus examples which were entirely American-made—lock, stock, and barrel—are very scarce. In contrast to the handsome appearance and expert workmanship of English pistols, most of the American pistols were extremely plain.

The so-called traveling pistol, smaller than the holster pistol, was used for personal protection against highwaymen and footpads by eighteenth-century gentlemen and their servants when traveling along the dark and unsafe roads of the period. Generally speaking, officers came from the aristocracy and, when doing military service, they frequently brought their traveling pistols with them. No doubt many English officers brought these pistols with them to America.

The British flintlock military pistol was not standardized until the reign of William III (1688–1702). At this time, the normal barrel length was about 14 inches, with a caliber of approximately .65 inch, or carbine bore. By the period of George I (1714–1727) the barrel length and caliber were reduced to 12 inches and .56 inch, or pistol bore, respectively, although some pistols continued to be made in carbine bore. In 1756, the barrel was further shortened to 9 inches, but the caliber was restored to .65 inch. The general reduction in barrel length resulted from the development of faster burning gunpowder. Too, the shorter barrel was less cumbersome to handle. The coarse powder of the seventeenth century burned much more slowly than eighteenth-century gunpowder and, because of this, seventeenth-century pistols had longer barrels so that the burning powder could develop its full force before the ball left the barrel.

The number of French pistols used during the Revolutionary War ranked second only to the British. Prior to the War, there were few French pistols in America. Those that were here came from the French colonies, or were acquired from French soldiers serving in the colonial wars. At the outbreak of the American Revolution, however, some French pistols were imported to arm American troops. The 1733 pattern had pin-fastened 12-inch barrels. In 1763 this earlier pattern was superseded by a much improved pattern that used bands to secure the 9-inch .67 caliber barrel. This model was made in two versions: iron mountings for cavalry, and brass mountings for navy. In 1776 another model was adopted, although it was not manufactured until 1777. The caliber remained the same, but the barrel was reduced to 7½ inches. The design of this pistol was different from any produced to that time (see photograph P-74), and it served as the model for the first pistol, the model 1799 North and Cheney, made under contract to the new United States government at the end of the Revolution.

In addition to British and French pistols, some Dutch ones were also used. Benjamin Franklin purchased muskets from Holland, and Dutch pistols were also acquired, although in much smaller quantities. The latter probably included a number of the extra long holster pistols made earlier in the century.

About the only German pistols used in the Revolution were those brought over by Hessian mercenaries. The officers used their personal sidearms, and the mounted enlisted troops used a large variety of styles, some of which were obsolete. Several features which almost all of them had in common were barrels about 14 inches long with large calibers up to .75, brass mountings, and a long, elliptical brass front sight.

One very popular type of pistol which has not been mentioned is the screw-barrel, or cannon-barrel type. Although not nearly so commonly used as the holster type pistol during the Revolutionary War, they nevertheless are important enough to deserve mention in any discussion of flintlock pistols.

Screw-barrel pistols appear to have been developed in England about 1650. The first ones produced were used in a limited way as cavalry holster pistols, but it was not until the reign of Queen Anne at the beginning of the eighteenth century that they became popular. The Queen Anne style had its lock mechanism forged as an integral part of the breech-chamber. Because of the martial motifs used in the decoration of the silver or brass furniture of these pistols, it is likely that some of them were used by officers. They were carried in the belt and used for in-fighting on foot by infantry or light infantry officers.

In their earliest form, these pistols resembled the contemporary holster type, except that their barrels were cannon-shaped and screwed into a breech-chamber that extended a little forward of the lock plate. The wood forestock was eliminated so that the barrel could be unscrewed from the breech section in loading. With the barrel off, the pistol was loaded by placing gunpowder and lead ball in the breech cavity. This system of breech-loading was considerably slower than loading from the muzzle by means of a ramrod, but it had the advantage of making the pistol shoot with greater force and accuracy. In the muzzle loader the ball was slightly smaller than the bore so that it could be easily rammed home. This fact weakened the exploding charge, since some of the gas escaped through the space between the ball and the wall of the barrel—a condition known as windage. Furthermore, the loose-fitting ball wobbled slightly during its journey through the barrel, with resultant loss in accuracy.

In screw-barrel pistols, on the other hand, the ball was slightly larger than the barrel bore and so encountered resistance in entering the barrel from the breech-chamber. This resistance momentarily checked the forward motion of the ball, and during the fraction-of-a-second delay the powder charge became almost fully ignited. The brief confinement of gas generated by the powder explosion caused the ball to be ejected from the barrel with much greater velocity than would have been possible with a muzzle loader. In addition, the tightly fitting ball eliminated windage and wobble and thus made for a stronger and truer shot. In spite of these advantages, however, its slow loading characteristic coupled with the possibility of losing the barrel while loading in the heat of battle prevented the screw-barrel pistol from being adopted as a military arm. Also, the more expensive construction of the screw-type barrel was, no doubt, an important factor against its being accepted for military service.

The screw-barrel pistols previously discussed have side locks, which means that the cock, powder pan, and frizzen are located on the right side of the barrel. About 1750 another variety known as a boxlock was introduced, having its cock, powder pan, and frizzen centered along the top of the barrel.

It is, of course, too late to change history; but, in evaluating the advantages and disadvantages of screw-barrel pistols, one might question why the breech-loading pistol was not selected for military service instead of the muzzle loader.

So far, only pistols used by officers and privates have been mentioned. Besides these, there was another class frequently carried by sergeants which were known as Sergeant's Grade pistols. They were not as ornate as the officer's pistols, yet were somewhat fancier than those of the privates.

Pistols used by naval officers and men followed the same basic pattern as their military counterparts. Quite a few had brass barrels and mountings because of the resistance of this metal to the corrosive action of salt water. Many sailors wore their pistols suspended from a belt or sash by means of a belt hook attached to the weapon.

Horse soldiers carried pistols, in addition to their sword and carbine or musket. In this book, *The Discipline of the Light Horse* of 1778, Captain Hinde gives an interesting bit of advice on how to train horses to the weapons which were to be fired from their backs, as follows:

To use an horse to fire arms, first put a pistol or carbine in the manger with his feed, then use him to the sound of the lock and pan; after which, when you are upon him shew it to him, presenting it forwards, sometimes on one side, sometimes on the other; when he is reconciled to that, proceed to flash in the pan; after which, put a small charge into the piece, and so continue augmenting it by degrees to what is commonly used; if he seems uneasy, walk him forwards a few steps slowly, and then stop, back, and caress him.

Relatively few officer's pistols were marked with the date they were made. It is possible, though, to determine from hallmarks (also referred to as touch marks) the year of manufacture of English arms mounted in sterling silver. Through 1783, London silversmiths marked their pieces with hallmarks consisting of four characters. Beginning in 1784, five characters were used. In both systems, one character was known as the date mark—one of twenty letters of the alphabet (J, V, W, X, Y, and Z were always omitted). When twenty years had elapsed, the letters were repeated in a different form, enclosed in a heraldic shield distinctive to the period. By matching the letter on a gun with an identical mark in one of the many books on English hallmarks, one can establish the date of fabrication. A similar system of hallmarks was used to stamp silver in other English towns.

Although there is no positive way to pinpoint the exact year in which steel- or brass-mounted firearms were made, one can make a reasonable estimate by looking up the period during which the gunmaker in question worked. In instances where the gunmaker's working activities covered a long span of years, the date many times can be narrowed down further by comparing the overall style and other decorative components with those of pistols with definitely established dates of manufacture.

Another means of identifying British firearms is by examining the proof marks stamped on the barrels. No exact date can be given for the time this practice began, but in 1637 the Gunmakers' Company of London was authorized to test firearms for proving, and in 1672 the sale of unproved gun barrels was made illegal throughout England.

Since guns were the product of many different makers, and often were imported from the Continent, there had been no standards set up and enforced to insure that the weapons were safe. As a result, the accident rate was extremely high, with many guns blowing up in the hands and faces of the shooters. Concern for the number of injuries thus inflicted prompted legislation to exercise control over the gun industry and "prove" the safety of the weapons before they could be sold to either military or private buyers.

Specific places were set up for testing gun barrels under the charter of the Gunmakers' Company. This was done by loading each one with a double charge of powder and ball. A number of barrels, often as many as a hundred, were then lined up on racks, aimed at sandbags, and fired by means of a trail of powder running beneath the vents. This process was done twice. The first test was run when the barrels were roughly bored, and if they passed this test, they were stamped with a "V," for view. Following the second, or fine, boring they were again fired and, if passed, were stamped "G.P." meaning Gunmakers' Proof, and over both of these proof marks was stamped a crown. These weapons were then certified as safe and allowed to be sold. Some gunmakers were not members of the Gunmakers' Company, and in 1741 it was ordered that when barrels by these makers were proved, an "F" should be stamped between the "V" and the "G.P." The letter "F" was probably used because makers who were not members of the Gunmakers' Company were known as "foreigners."

In contrast to the uniformity of proof marks on British guns, the barrel markings on American, French, and German pieces present a much more complex picture.

As for American-made guns, the only ones stamped with a barrel proof mark were some made under contract for Committees of Safety in the various states. In fact, the absence of barrel marks is usually one indication that the barrel was made in America.

Although records in the French archives state that French military gun barrels were proved at St. Etienne with a triple powder charge, nothing is mentioned concerning a description of the mark or stamp itself. Later records have been preserved dated 1728 and 1729 which refer to the procedure for proving military weapons, but the only reference to marking is that each inspector was to mark the barrels accepted with a stamp. Unfortunately, nothing was disclosed about the stamp, but it might be reasonable to assume that it consisted of the inspector's initials, since these were used later as the accepted proof mark until 1782. Occasionally the last two digits of the year were also used in conjunction with the initials.

German weapons are even more confusing, since they were made in many different principalities. Some had barrel proof marks, some were stamped with inspection or control marks of the craft or guild, while others had town marks or maker's marks, which had nothing to do with the fact that the barrel had been proved. Consequently, the matter of running down a barrel mark on a German gun often involves the tedious task of searching through books containing the many gunsmith marks.

The close of the Revolutionary War for the most part seemed to mark the end of the handsome and graceful flintlock pistol. Almost immediately the general decoration of pistols, and shoulder arms and edged weapons as well, seemed to take a decided turn toward less artistic design. The mask butt-caps were generally eliminated, and plain or checkered grips came into vogue. The elaborate side-plates and escutcheons either disappeared altogether or were replaced by extremely plain substitutes. The emphasis seemed to be directed solely toward more functional design and workmanship, and the mechanical perfection of the lock mechanism. By the end of the first quarter of the nineteenth century, the flintlock pistol had reached its zenith of mechanical perfection. Although it was extremely well made, it unfortunately did not possess the graceful lines and beauty of its predecessors made up until the beginning of the Revolution.

Following are photographs of the different types of pistols just described, with particular emphasis on the officer weapons.

P-1

P-2

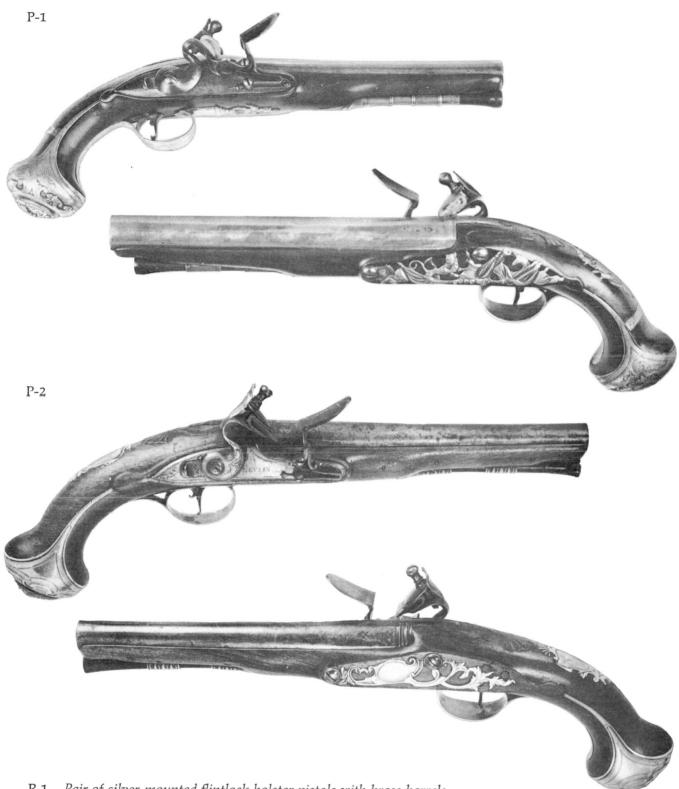

P-1   *Pair of silver-mounted flintlock holster pistols with brass barrels,*
which were owned by George Washington. These were made in London by
Hawkins and are hallmarked with the date letter for 1748. The silver band across
the handle is inscribed "Genl. G. Washington." Length: 13¾ inches.

P-2   *Pair of sterling silver-mounted flintlock officer's holster pistols made by*
Joseph Heylin in the Cornhill section of London. These pistols are
hallmarked for the year 1763. Length: 14¼ inches.

P-3   *Pair of silver-mounted flintlock officer's holster pistols with brass barrels made in London about 1770 by Richard Wilson. The sideplates are the panoply of arms style that was popular on such weapons. Length: 14 inches.*

P-4   *Pair of flintlock officer's holster pistols with sterling silver mountings and brass barrels, made in London by Daniel Moore and hallmarked with the date letter for 1774. Length: 14¾ inches.*

P-3

P-4

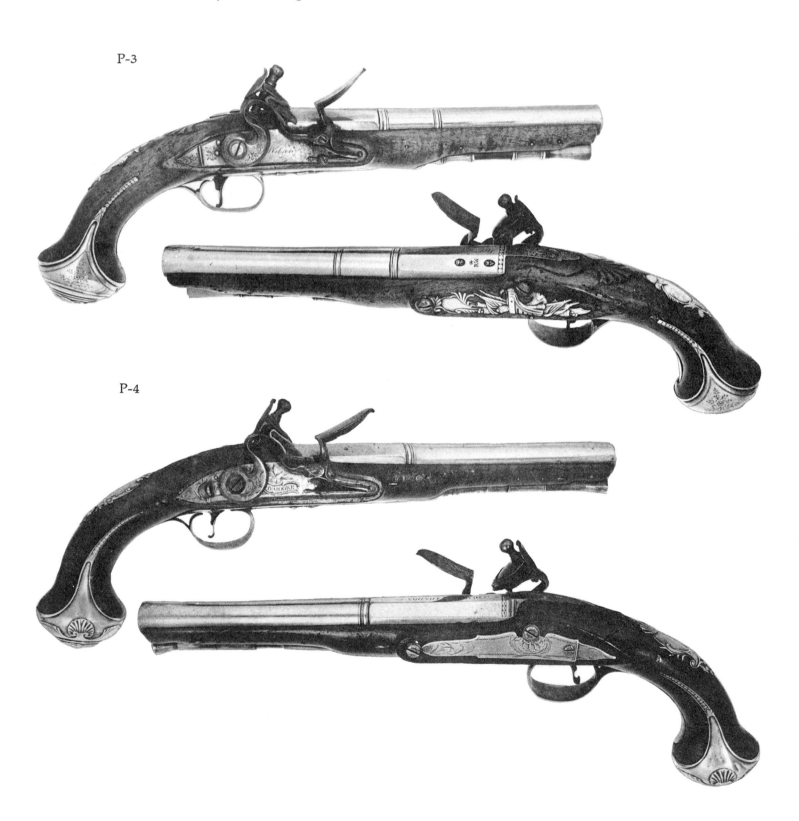

P-5

P-6

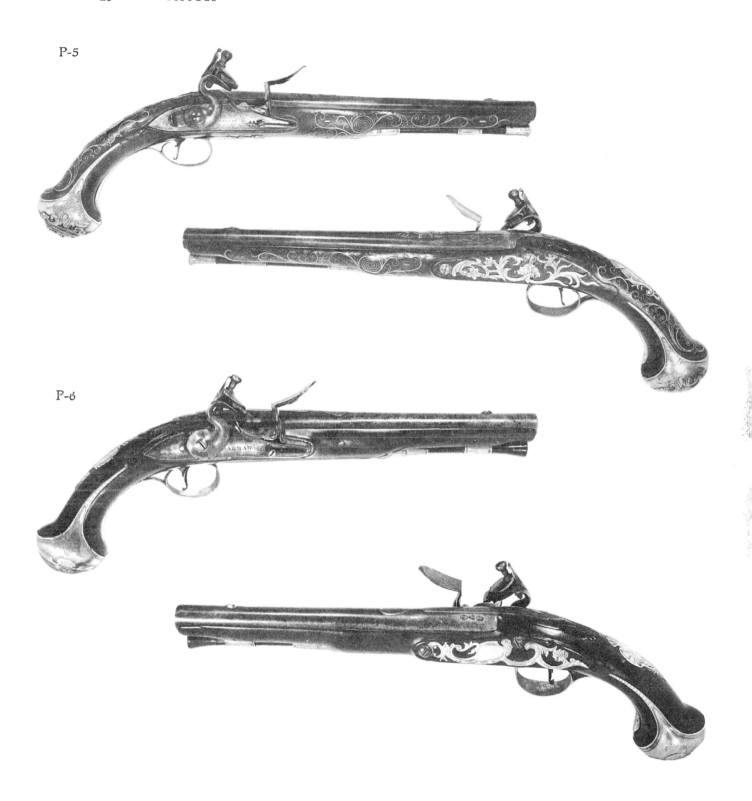

P-5   *Pair of silver-mounted flintlock officer's holster pistols made by*
      Louis Barbar in London and hallmarked 1758. These pistols have unusually long,
      11-inch barrels, and the stocks are profusely inlaid with silver wire.
      Length: 17½ inches.

P-6   *Pair of silver-mounted flintlock officer's holster pistols made*
      by Louis Barbar in London and hallmarked 1766. These pistols have grotesque
      mask butt caps and acanthus, or foliage, sideplates. Length: 15 inches.

P-7 *Pair of flintlock brass-barrel blunderbuss pistols with brass lockplates and furniture by Joseph Heylin, circa 1765. This prolific maker supplied many officers with pairs of pistols during this period. Length: 13 inches.*

P-8 *Pair of silver-mounted flintlock naval officer's boarding blunderbuss pistols with brass barrels and spring bayonets, made by E. F. Taylor in London between 1775 and 1780. Length: 12¾ inches.*

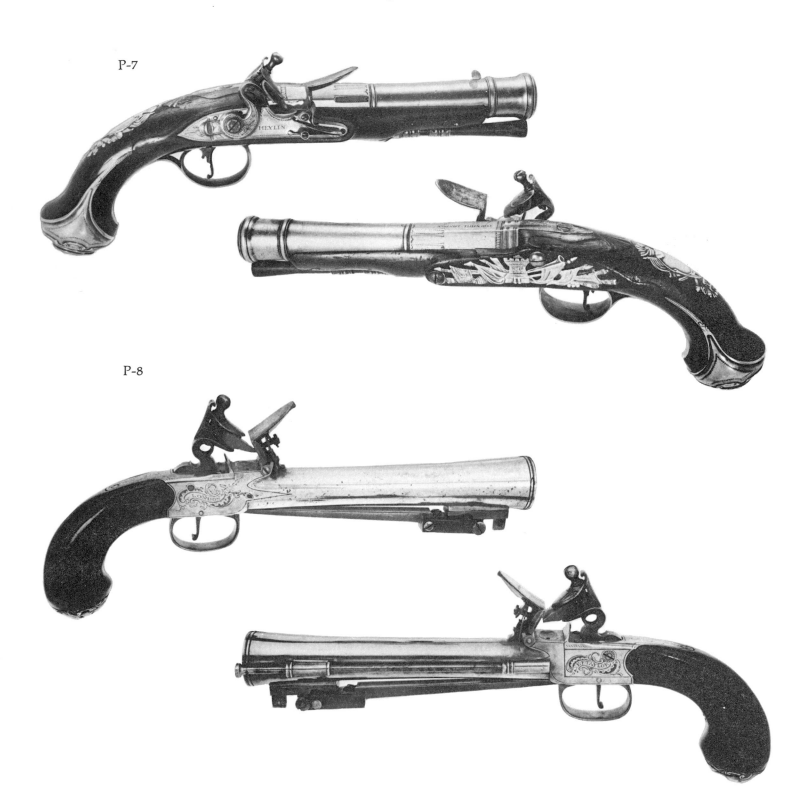

P-7

P-8

P-9

P-10

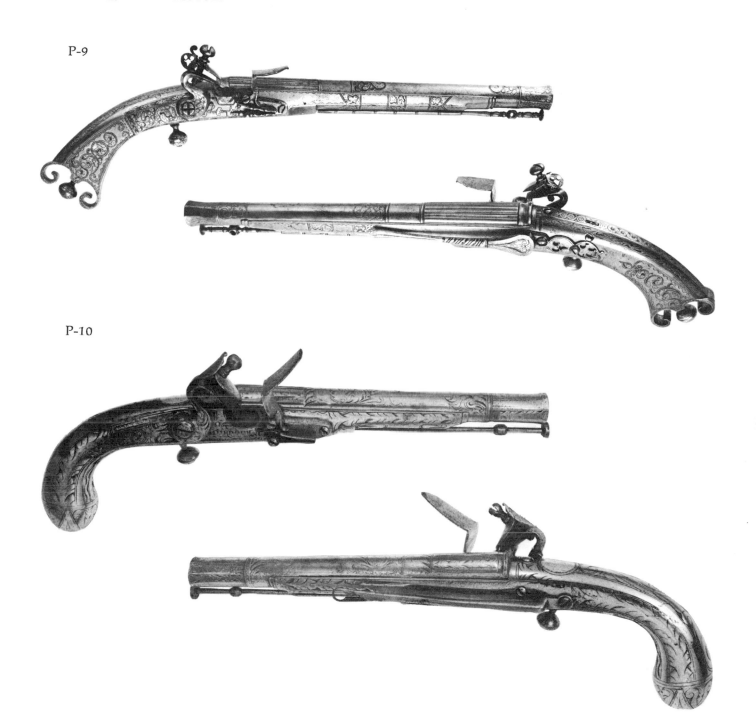

P-9   *Pair of Scottish flintlock pistols by John Campbell, circa 1740.*
      These are typical of the arms carried by officers of the Highland Regiment
      during the French and Indian War and the Revolution. Such a pair of pistols
      was carried by Major Pitcairn during the Battle of Lexington and captured.
      Note the belt hook, which shows that they were carried by an officer of a
      Highland foot regiment. Length: 16½ inches.

P-10 *Pair of Scottish all-metal flintlock pistols made in Leith, Scotland,*
      by T. Murdoch, circa 1770. These pistols have lobe-shaped butts
      and are equipped with belt hooks. Length: 12½ inches.

P-11   *Pair of flintlock center-hammer officer's pistols with sterling silver
mountings and unscrew cannon-shaped barrels. Made in Warsop, England
by I. Kirke, circa 1770. The steel breech is engraved with martial
decorations. Length: 12¼ inches.*

P-12   *Pair of English flintlock pistols by James Freeman, circa 1710.
These pistols differ from the normal Queen Anne screw-barrel type in that the
barrel is fixed to the frame and a ramrod is carried underneath.
These pistols fired a charge of buckshot instead of the ball used in the more
common screw-barrel type. They were known as night pistols because of the
fact that it was easier to hit an adversary at night with a charge of
buckshot than with a single ball. Length: 13 inches.*

P-11

P-12

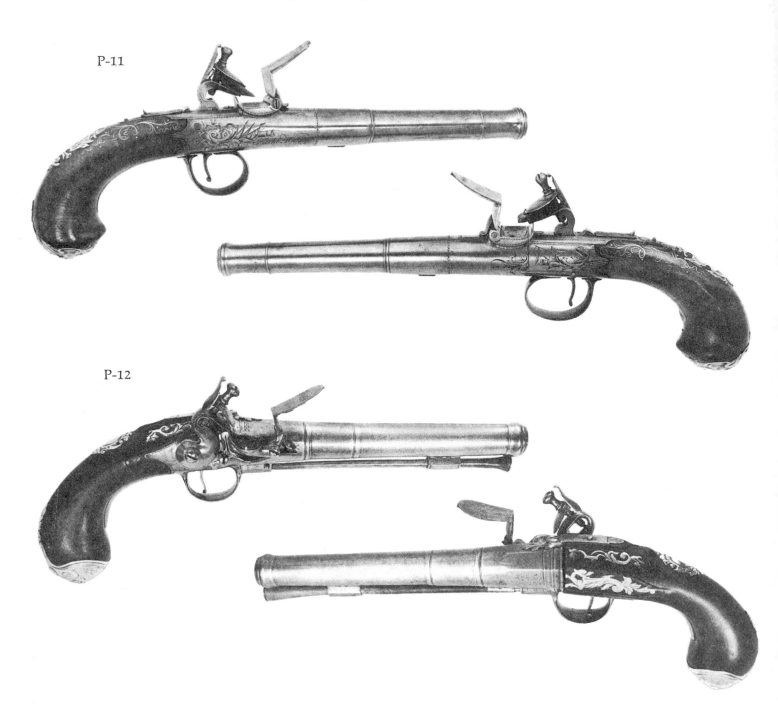

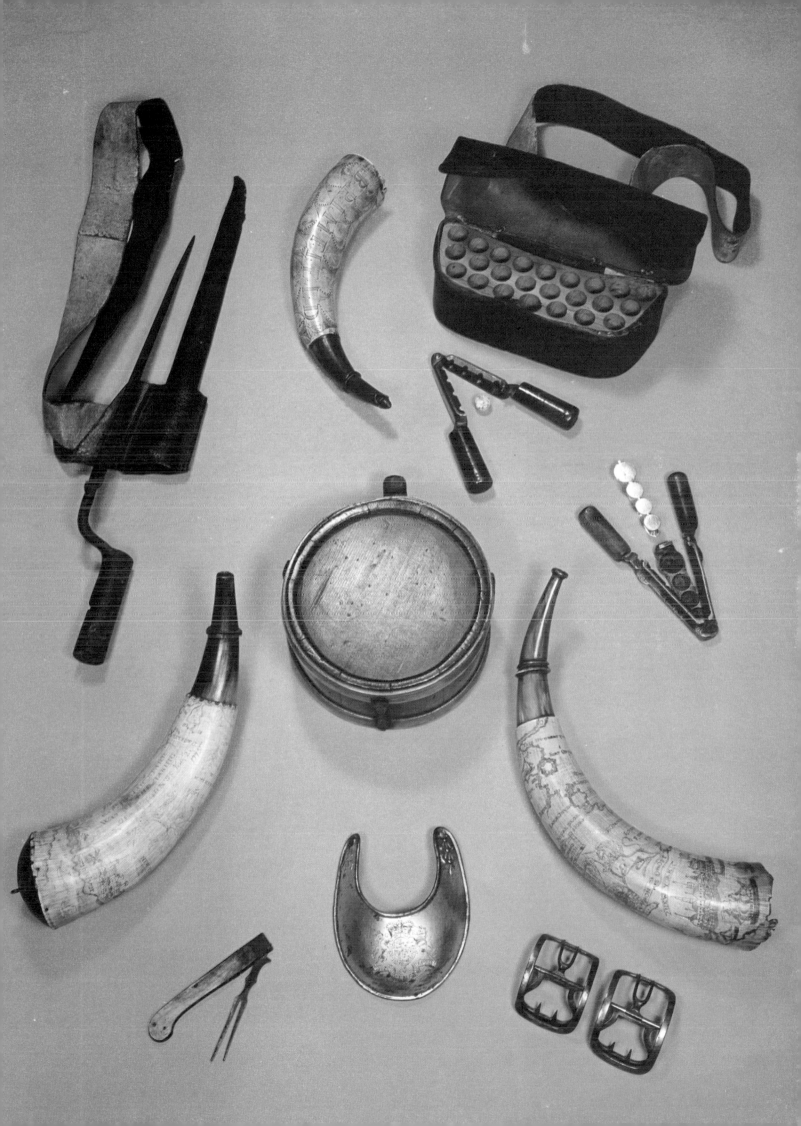

Edged weapons grouped around a sword knot

◄ An assortment of military accoutrements of
the Revolutionary War period

Pistols and a rifle, all American-made—lock, stock, and barrel

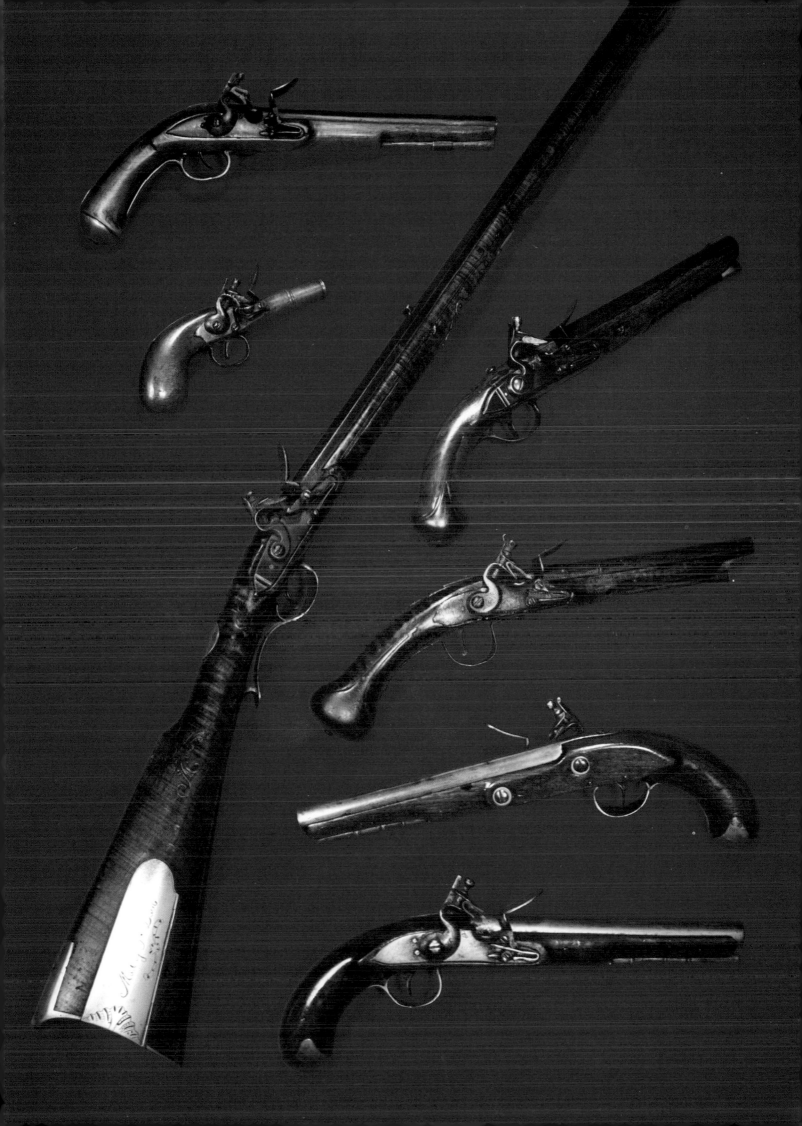

A pair of silver-mounted officer's pistols
with a pair of saddle holsters
of the type in which they were carried.
Below, a pair of boarding-type brass-barreled
blunderbuss pistols with spring bayonets,
hallmarked 1780

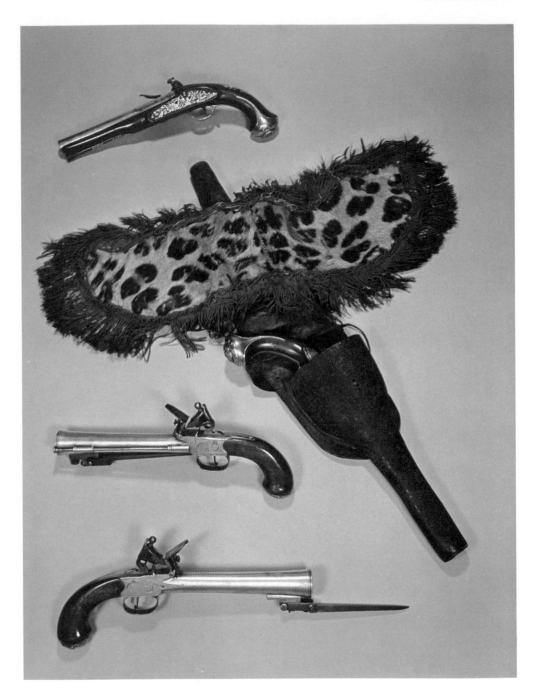

A grouping of Revolutionary War items
photographed in the Old Stone House, built
in Ramsey, New Jersey, in 1740 and maintained
by the Ramsey Historical Association

A dragoon of Colonel E. M. Moylan's
4th Continental Regiment of Light Dragoons, 1779–1781.
Note the leather carbine bucket, saddle bags and
saddle holsters mounted on the horse.
The items surrounding the picture are
the actual pieces which the artist used
as models for this drawing.

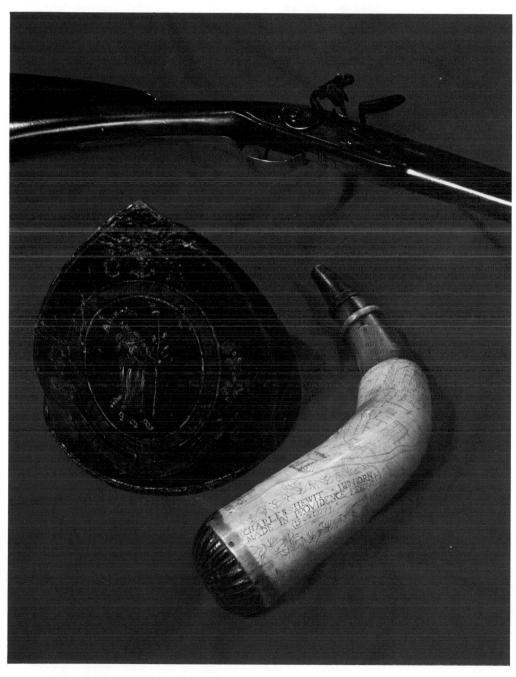

Rhode Island Revolutionary items
—a leather hat of the Newport Light Infantry,
a flintlock fowling piece, and a powder horn
engraved with a map of Providence

AMERICAN
Sergeant,
2nd Maryland Regiment,
Continental Line,
1778–1779.

BRITISH
Private,
Light Infantry Company,
38th Regiment of Foot,
1775–1783.

FRENCH
Chasseur Corporal of
the Soissonnais Infantry,
1780–1783.

HESSIAN
Fusilier,
Regiment Knyphausen,
1776.

P-13

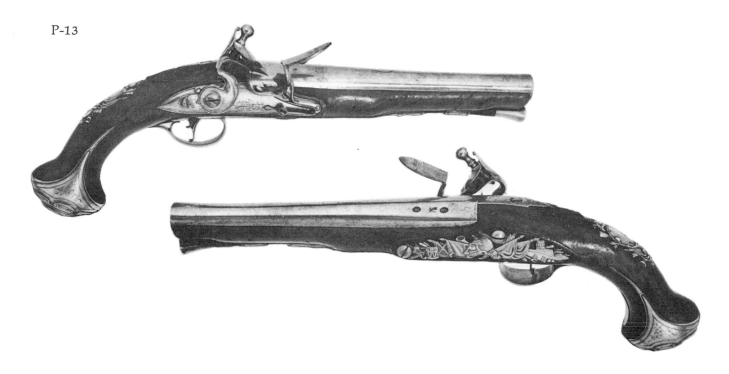

P-14

P-13   *Pair of flintlock officer's holster pistols with sterling silver mountings, made by I. Bumford in London and hallmarked 1761. These pistols are almost identical to George Washington's pair of pistols, except that the barrels are steel rather than brass. Length: 14 inches.*

P-14   *Pair of silver-mounted flintlock officer's pistols made in London by Joseph Griffin about 1760. These pistols could be classified as semiholster, since they could be used for civilian protection or by a military officer. They have been preserved in their original wooden case with green baize lining. Length: 13 inches.*

P-15 *Silver-mounted flintlock pistol made by Godsall in Gloucester, England, circa 1760. This pistol is the true box-lock type with center hammer. The numeral 1 is stamped on the bottom of both barrel and barrel breech. When made in pairs, screw-barrel pistols were commonly stamped with corresponding numerals to insure that the right barrel was matched to the correct pistol when loading or cleaning. Length: 12½ inches.*

P-16 *Exceptionally fine pair of Queen Anne officer's belt pistols made by James Freeman, circa 1725. These pistols have left- and right-hand locks. The silver butt caps have the owner's portrait engraved on the sides, and the terminals have a relief-engraved portrait of George I. Length: 12½ inches.*

P-15

P-16

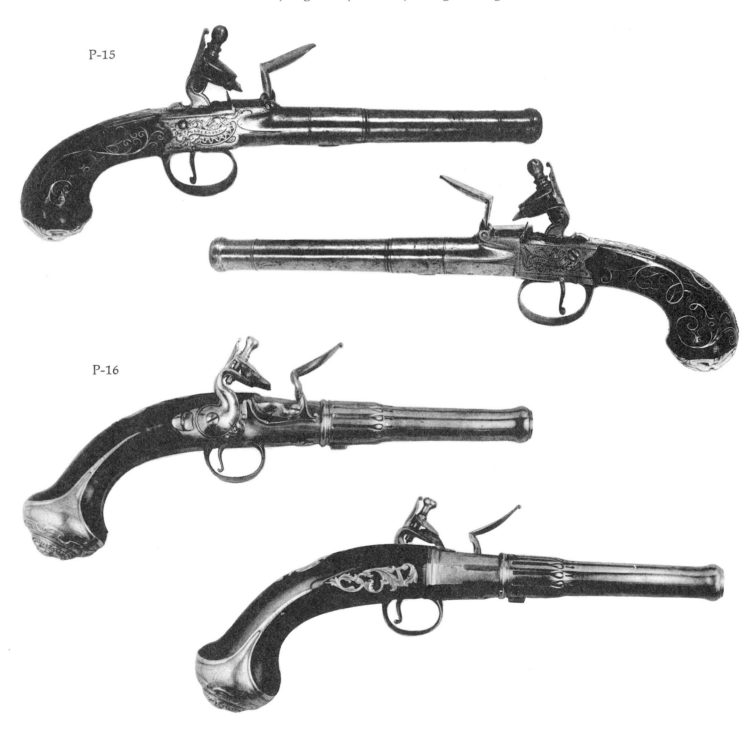

P-17

P-18

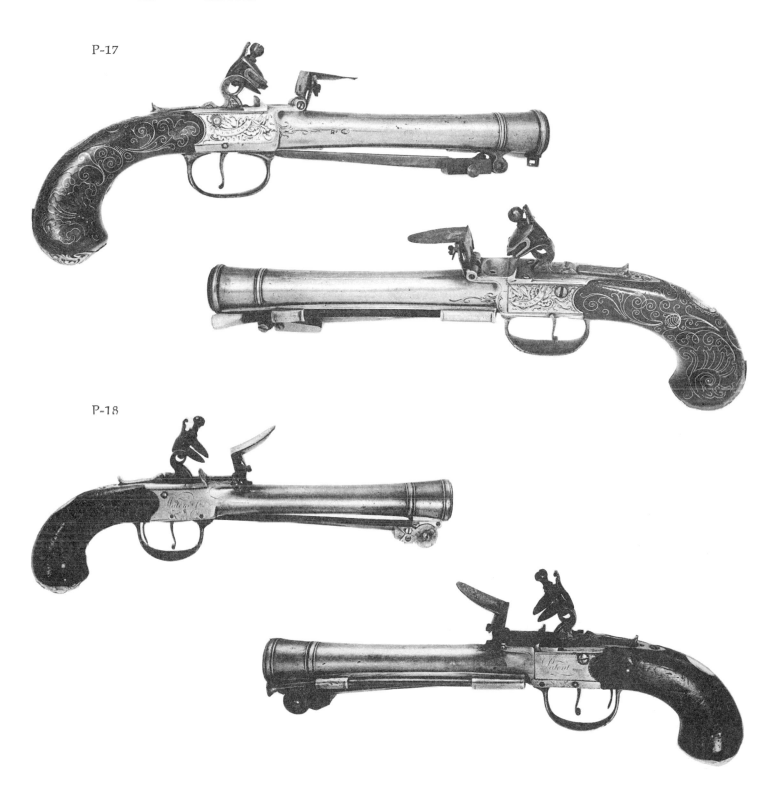

P-17   Naval officer's silver-mounted flintlock boarding pistol with spring bayonet
       and brass barrel, made by William Perry in Birmingham, England,
       and hallmarked 1780. The stock is profusely inlaid with silver wire.
       Length: 13 inches. With bayonet extended: 18 inches.
P-18   Pair of flintlock officer's pistols by Waters with brass blunderbuss barrels
       and folding bayonet, hallmarked 1780. The bayonet, operated by a coiled
       spring, was the earliest form of spring-loaded bayonet. Waters is credited
       with this invention. Length: 13 inches.

P-19   *Pair of English Queen Anne screw-barrel flintlock pistols by Louis Barbar, circa 1705. These pistols have massive breeches that take a heavy charge of powder. They were made during the reign of Queen Anne and are the true ancestors of the many thousands of later, more sophisticated pistols known as Queen Anne pistols which were made in England up to the American Revolution. Length: 11½ inches.*

P-20   *Pair of flintlock Queen Anne pistols by James Freeman, circa 1710. They have all the features typical of screw-barrel pistols made during the reign of Queen Anne. Length: 13 inches.*

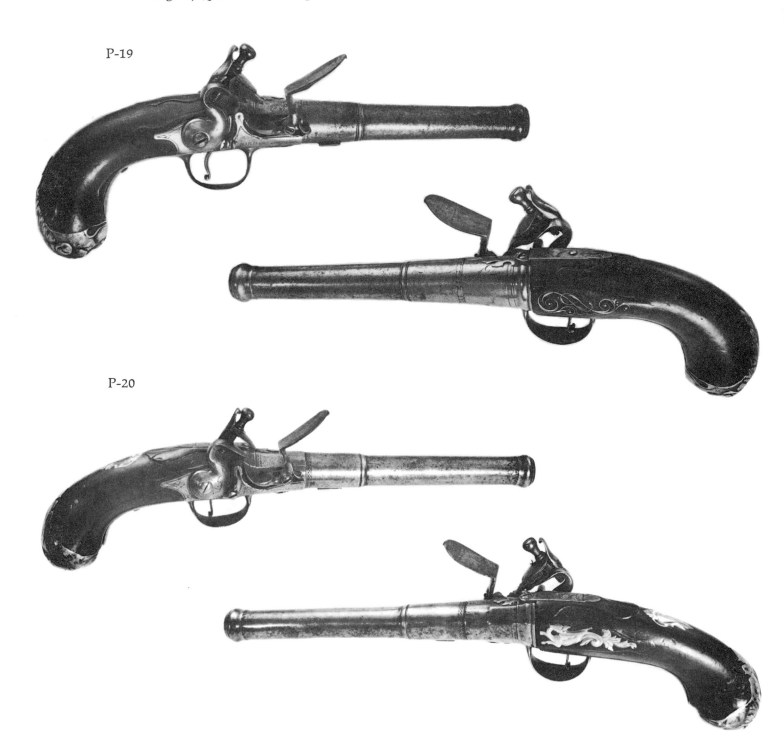

P-19

P-20

P-21

P-22

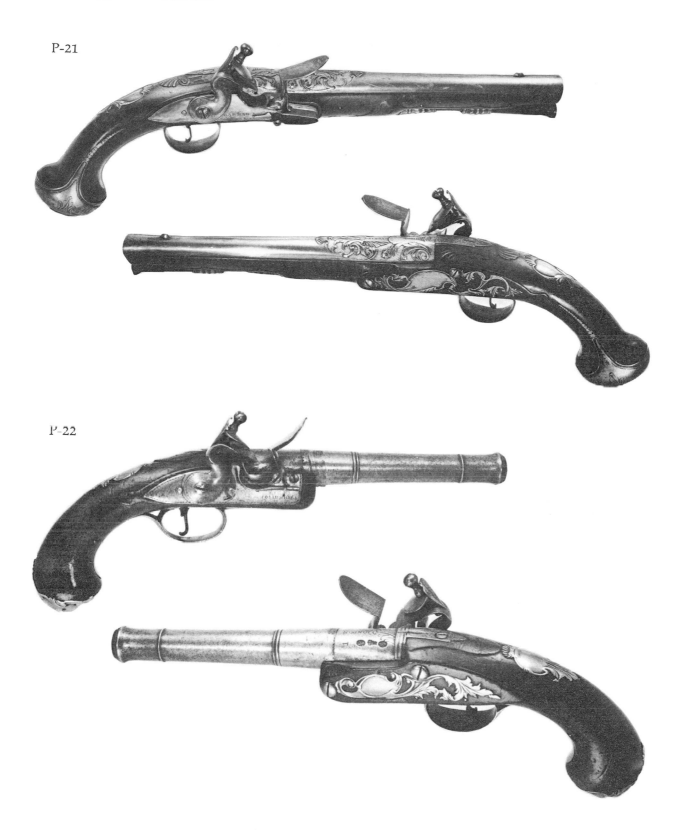

P-21   *Pair of English flintlock officer's holster pistols by Barbar, circa 1755.*
        The exceptionally fine steel furniture and barrels are interesting variations
        of the more common silver-mounted pistols of this period. Length: 16¼ inches.

P-22   *Brass mounted and semimilitary flintlock pistol with unscrew cannon-shaped*
        barrel, made in London by Collumbell about 1740. Length: 12¼ inches.

P-23 *Silver-mounted flintlock pistol made by T. Richards in London about 1760.*
This is the true box-lock type with center hammer. The grip, of an unusual
shape, is heavily inlaid with silver wire in a scroll design.
Length: 11⅝ inches.

P-24 *Pair of European silver-mounted flintlock holster pistols that belonged to the*
American General Charles Lee. They are fitted with Rappahannock Forge locks.
Length: 15 inches.

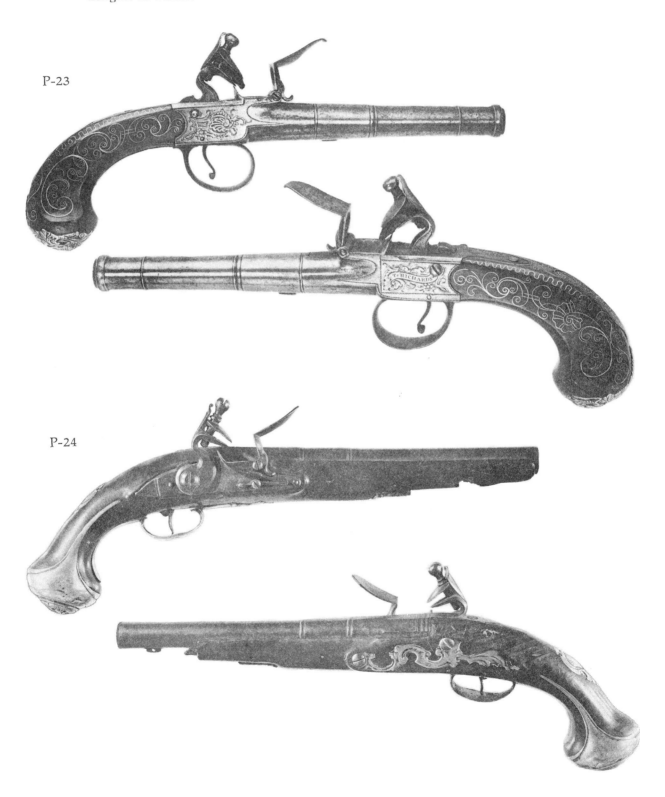

P-25

P-26

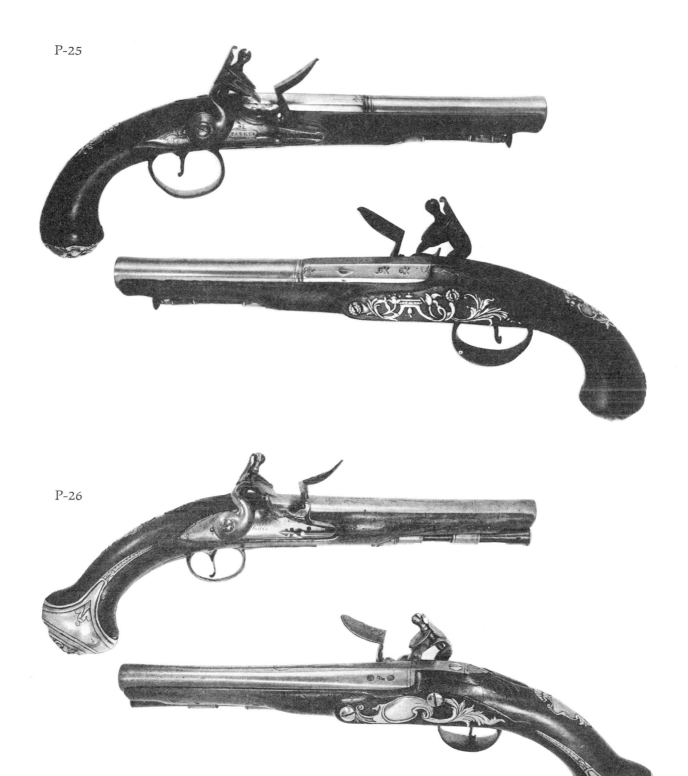

P-25   *Silver-mounted flintlock officer's pistol with brass barrel,*
       made by John Parkes in London about 1770. The stock adjacent to the barrel
       breech is inlaid with silver wire in a military motif. Length: 13¼ inches.

P-26   *Pair of flintlock officer's holster pistols with brass mountings,*
       made by Thomas Jones in London about 1760. Length: 14 inches.

P-27 *Flintlock officer's semiholster pistol with brass barrel and mountings, made by Hadley in London, circa 1760. Length: 14 inches.*

P-28 *Pair of silver-mounted flintlock officer's holster pistols with brass barrels, made by I. B. Brazier and hallmarked 1762. These pistols were restocked about 1780 to incorporate a flintlock mechanism made by H. W. Mortimer, with the early large roller wheel that caused the frizzen to operate with less friction. The massive silver furniture is of the finest quality found on pistols of this period. Length: 14¼ inches.*

P-27

P-28

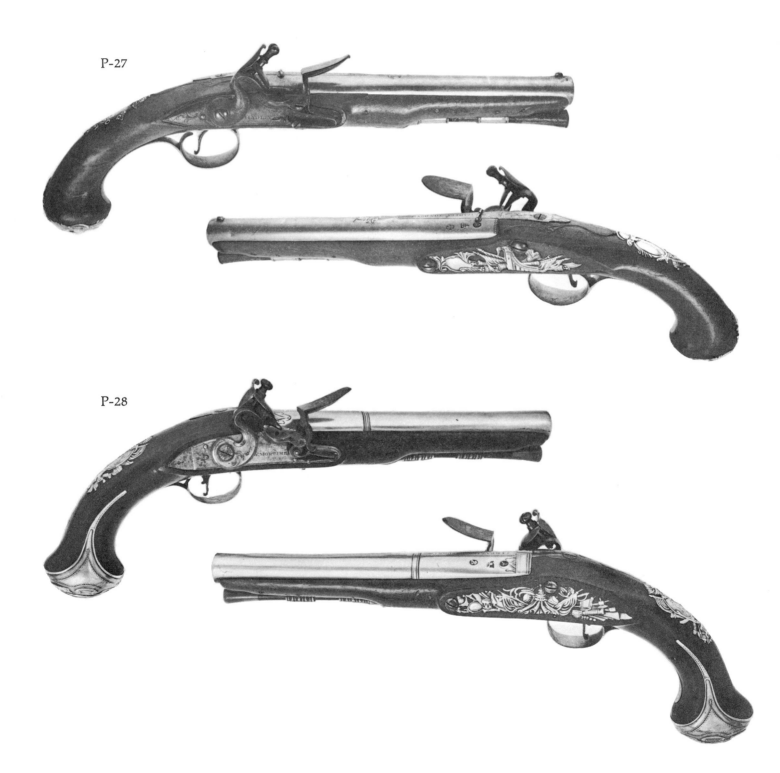

P-29

P-30

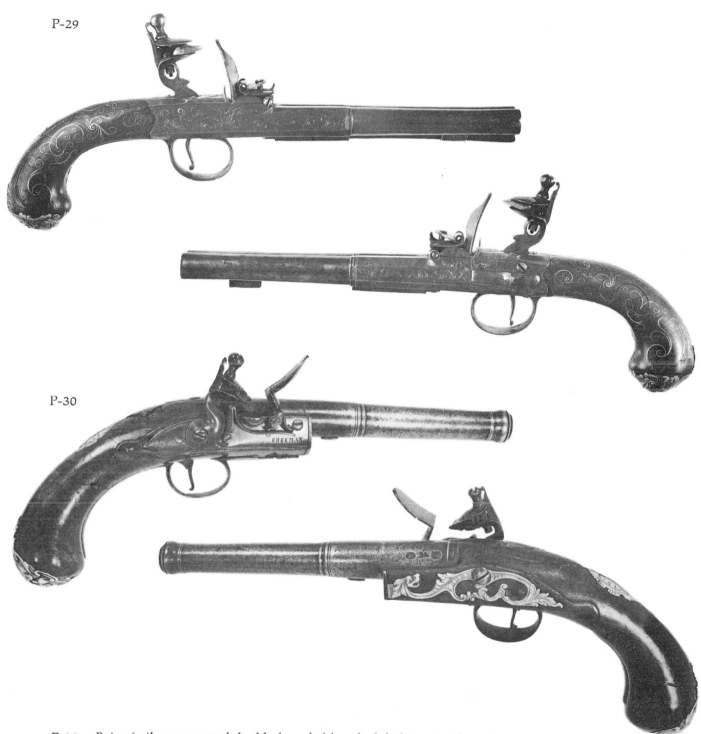

P-29   *Pair of silver-mounted double-barreled box-lock holster pistols made
by Parkes in London around 1770. These pistols belonged to
General Daniel Roberdeau. Length: 14 inches.*

P-30   *Pair of silver-mounted officer's semiholster pistols made by Freeman in
London about 1740. These pistols are unusual in that they have removable
flintlocks instead of locks forged as an integral part of the breech.
However, they utilize the inverted "V"-shaped frizzen spring found on screw-
barrel pistols rather than the typical frizzen spring found on pistols with
removable locks. The forestock ends rather abruptly and is finished off with
a steel plate. Length: 12½ inches.*

P-31   *Pair of flintlock Queen Anne pistols by Griffin and Tow, circa 1775.*
These pistols have unusually rare and beautiful silver furniture, and
represent the end of the Queen Anne pistol. Length: 12 inches.

P-32   *Plain flintlock military pistol with brass mountings, made in London*
by Pickfatt around 1740. Length: 12¾ inches.

P-31

P-32

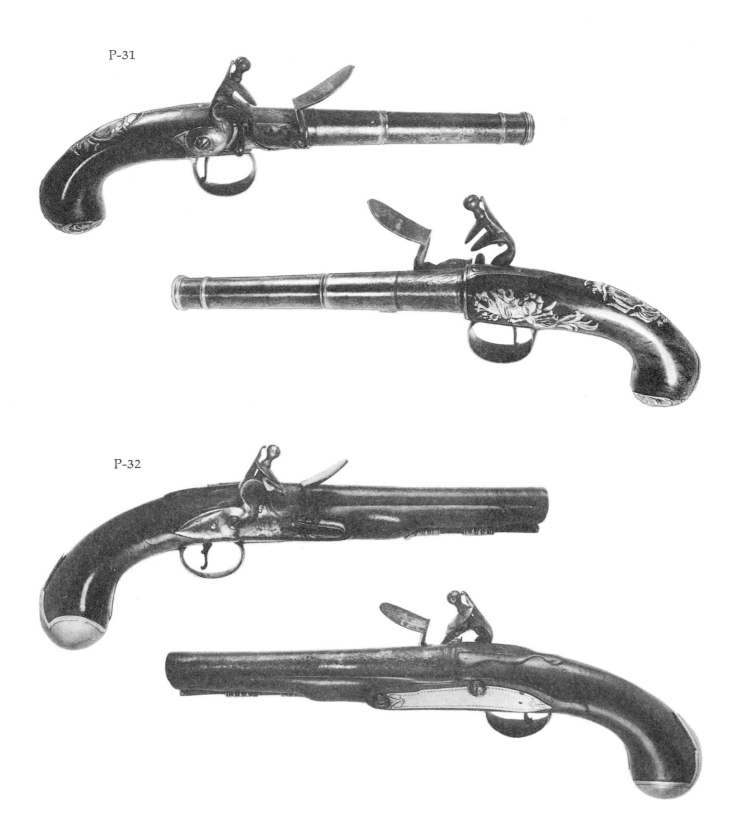

P-33

P-34

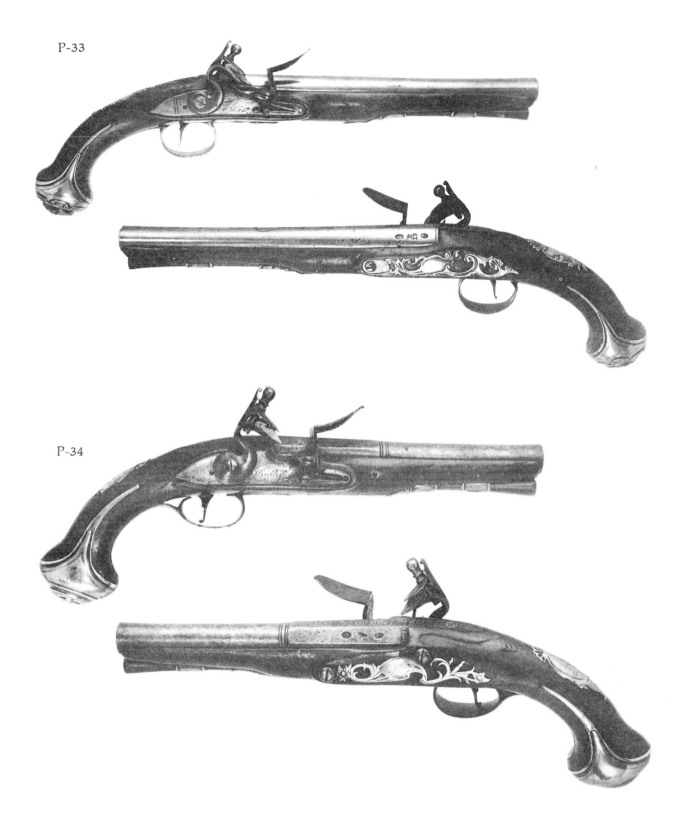

P-33   *Flintlock officer's holster pistol with brass barrel and furniture,*
made by John Rea in London about 1775. Length: 16½ inches.

P-34   *Flintlock officer's holster pistol with brass furniture made by Henry Hadley*
in London about 1770. Length: 12½ inches.

P-35   *Pair of silver-mounted officer's greatcoat screw-barrel pistols
made by F. Galton in England about 1770. These are the box-lock type,
and were usually carried in the large pockets of the greatcoats worn
by officers. Length: 10 inches.*

P-36   *Pair of flintlock officer's holster pistols with brass furniture,
made by T. Hutchinson in London, circa 1760. Length: 13½ inches.*

P-35

P-36

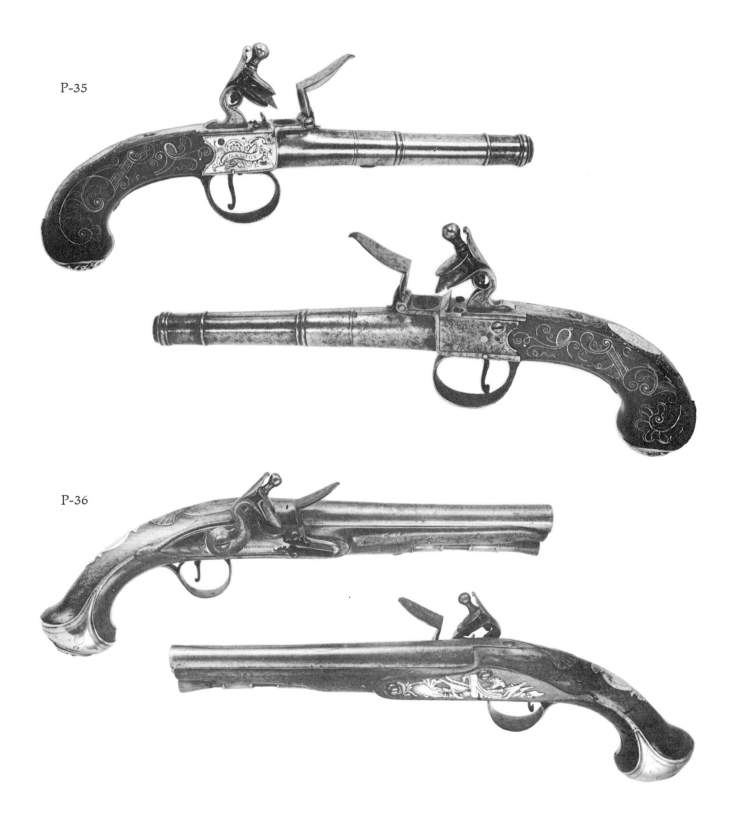

75-6361

P-37

P-38

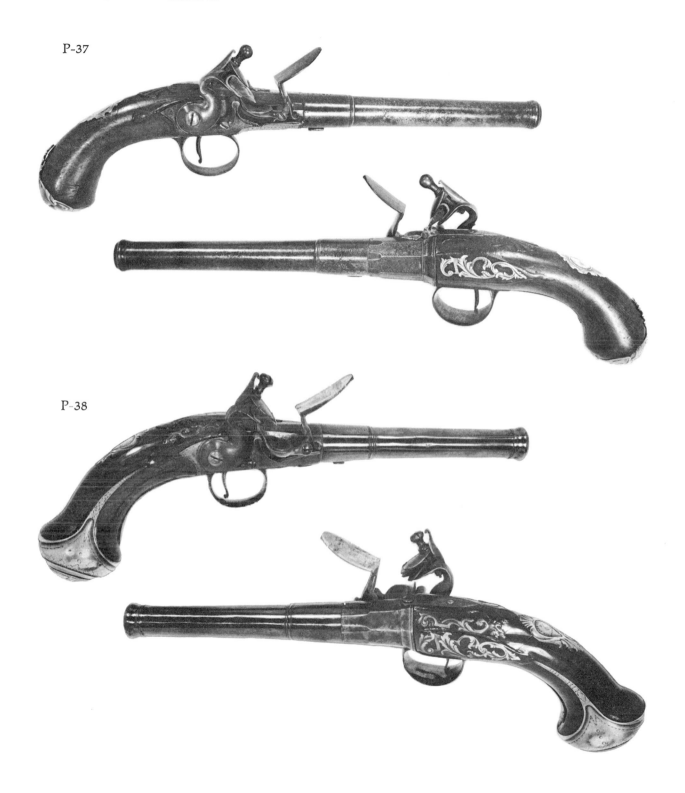

P-37   *Pair of silver-mounted Queen Anne style screw-barrel, or cannon-barrel,*
pistols made by T. Hughes in Cork, Ireland, about 1730.
Length: 13¾ inches.

P-38   *Pair of silver-mounted flintlock screw-barrel officer's pistols*
made by James Freeman in London, circa 1725. They have been preserved in
almost new condition. These fishtail-shaped grips are seldom found on
screw-barrel pistols. Length: 12 inches.

P-39   *Pair of flintlock officer's holster pistols with brass furniture,
made by Joseph Heylin in the Cornhill section of London around 1760.
Since they are an inch or two shorter than the average holster pistols of
this period, they were probably packed in with the officer's personal gear
rather than carried in saddle holsters. Length: 12¾ inches.*

P-40   *Pair of flintlock Queen Anne pistols by Thomas Green, circa 1710.
These pistols combine the fishtail form of butt with the screw-barrel,
a combination seldom found. Length: 12 inches.*

P-39

P-40

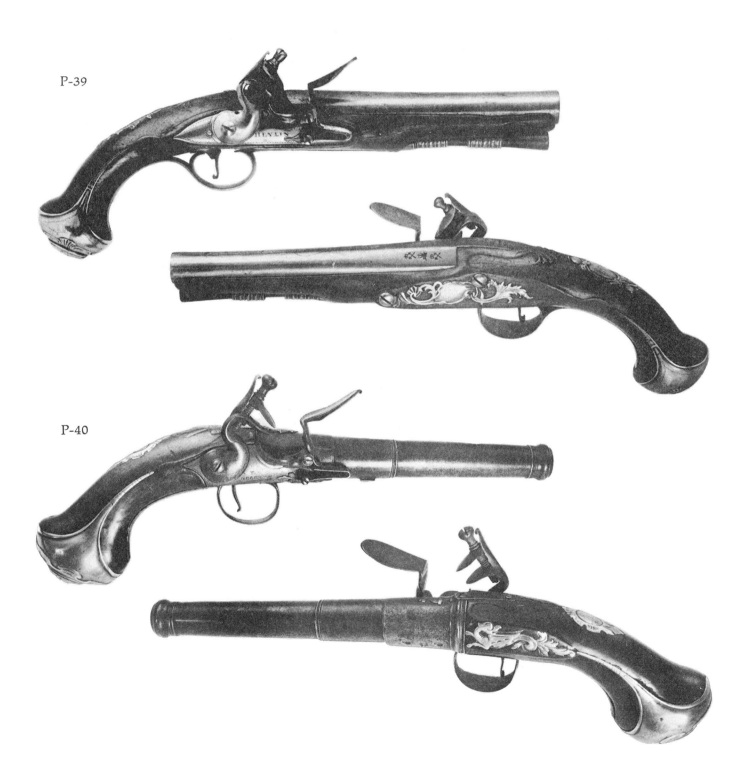

P-41

P-42

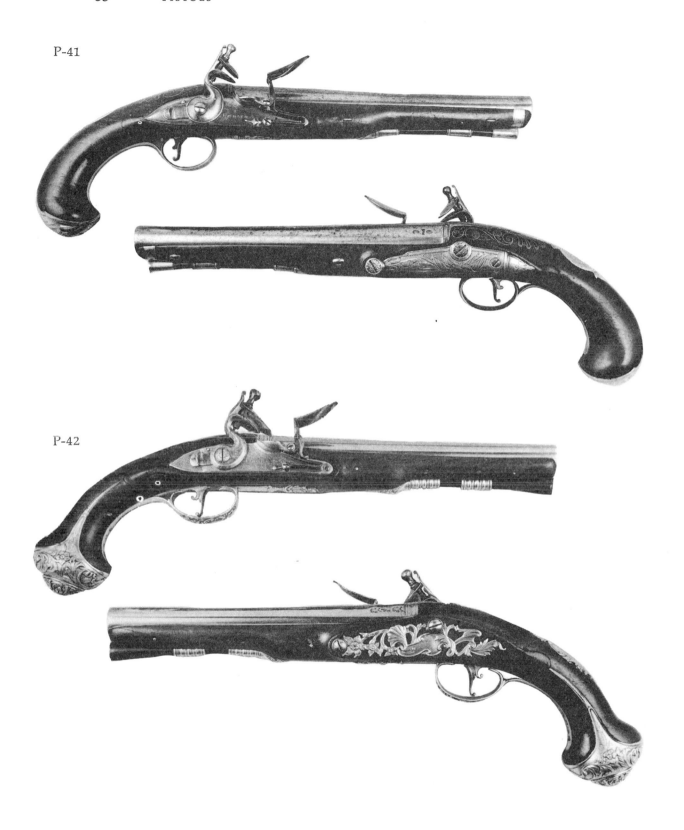

P-41   *Pair of flintlock officer's holster pistols made by T. Richards in London,*
circa 1760. Silver furniture is engraved with martial decorations.
Length: 15¾ inches.

P-42   *Pair of flintlock officer's holster pistols made by Joseph Heylin*
in London about 1765. These pistols have unusually fine silver mountings and
brass lockplates and barrels. Length: 14 inches.

P-43   *Early eighteenth-century flintlock holster pistol with steel mountings,*
made by James Barbar in London. This pistol has the early lock that has no
bridle connecting the frizzen to the powder pan. Length: 15 inches.

P-44   *A cased pair of silver-mounted officer's pistols by Griffin and Tow,*
hallmarked 1771. Rarely are such pistols found in their original cases.
This brass-studded leather case protected the pistols over long journeys.
The pistols, of exceptionally fine quality, have gold-lined flashpans and
touch holes. Few pistols of this length were made at such a late date.
Length: 17½ inches.

P-43

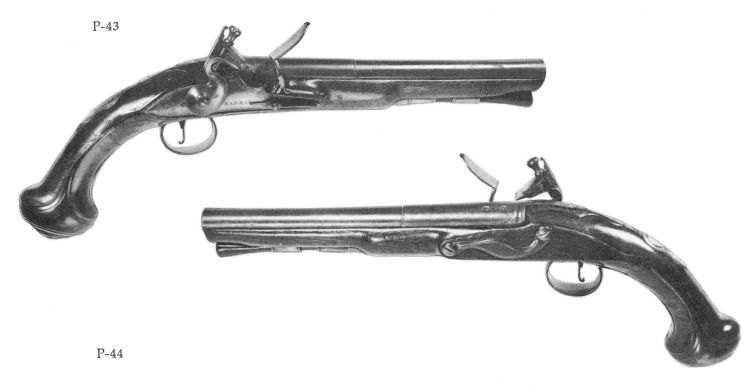

P-44

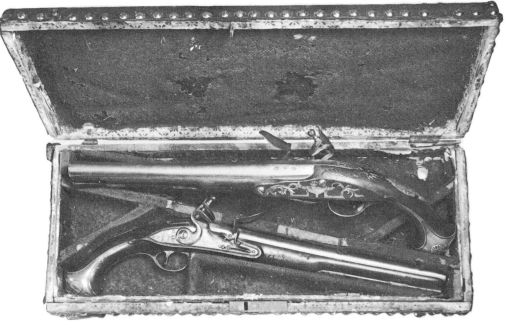

P-45

P-46

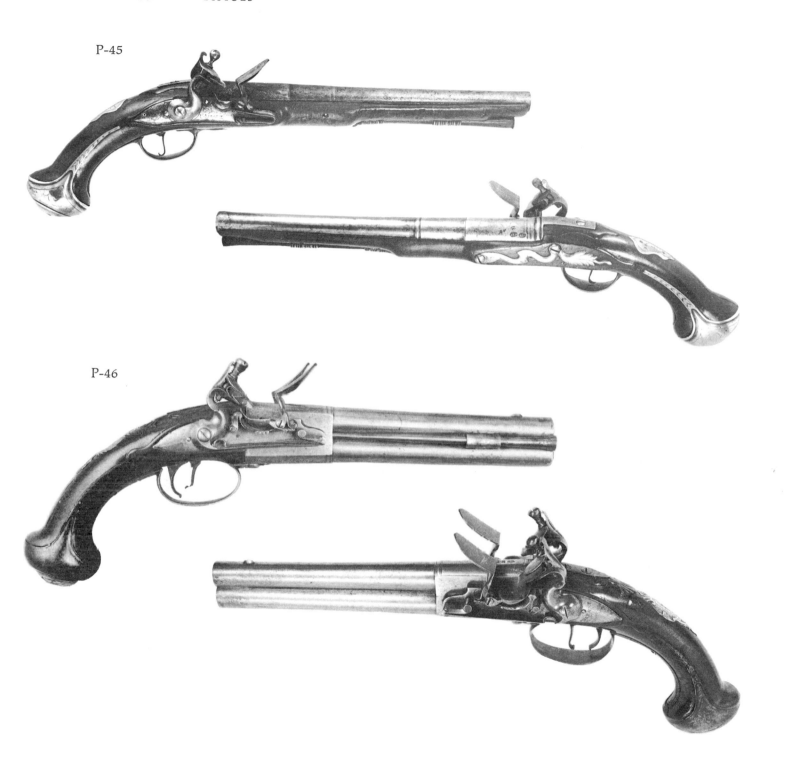

P-45   *Pair of early eighteenth-century flintlock officer's holster pistols with*
       12-inch barrels and brass furniture, made by Francis Smart in London.
       These are fine examples of horse pistols. The "H C 4" engraved on
       the escutcheons probably stands for heavy cavalry. Length: 19 inches.

P-46   *Pair of double-barreled flintlock holster pistols by James Barbar*
       made about 1750. An interesting feature of these pistols is the placing of
       the main locksprings on the outside of the lock. These are typical
       high-grade officer's holster pistols having steel furniture and silver mask
       butt terminals. Length: 15 inches.

P-47   *Pair of sergeant's-grade flintlock holster pistols with plain brass mountings made by Joseph Griffin in London about 1760. Length: 13⅝ inches.*

P-48   *Pair of brass-mounted sergeant's- or trooper's-grade flintlock holster pistols made by A. M. Love in London about 1730. Length: 18½ inches.*

P-47

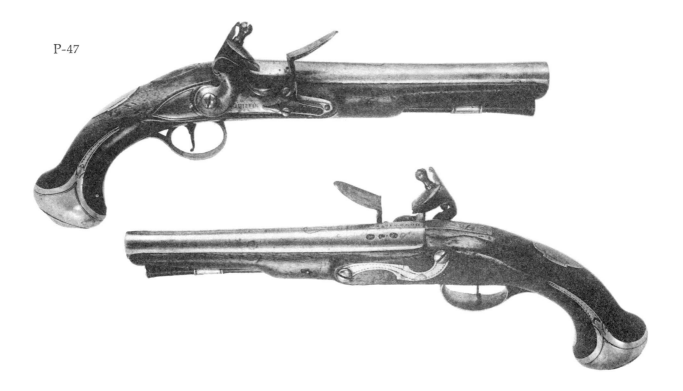

P-48

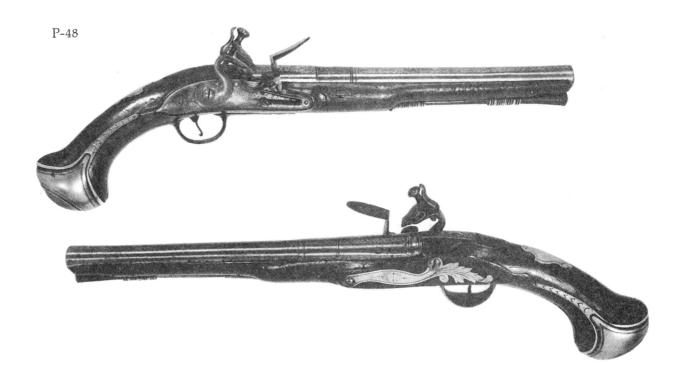

P-49

P-50

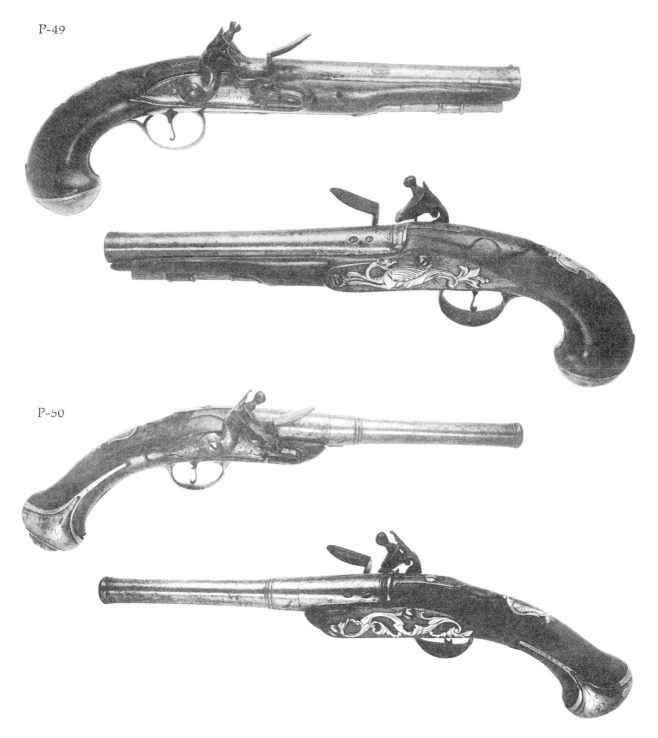

P-49   Late seventeenth-century flintlock officer's pistol with brass furniture
        made in London by T. Blockley. The dragon sideplate was popular during
        this period. Length: 13 inches.

P-50   Late seventeenth-century screw-barrel flintlock officer's holster pistol
        with brass mountings, made by L. Annely. This is the early form of
        the unscrew-barrel cavalry holster pistol with the conventional flintlock
        mechanism of this period. A few years later, the Queen Anne type screw-barrel
        pistol was developed, with its lock mechanism forged as an integral part
        of the breech chamber and utilizing a "V"-shaped frizzen spring.
        Length: 14¾ inches.

P-51   *Pair of brass-barreled flintlock blunderbuss pistols with brass mountings made by Barbar in London about 1770. Length: 14 inches.*

P-52   *Pair of early eighteenth-century flintlock officer's holster pistols with brass mountings, made in London by Samuel Love. Length: 13 inches.*

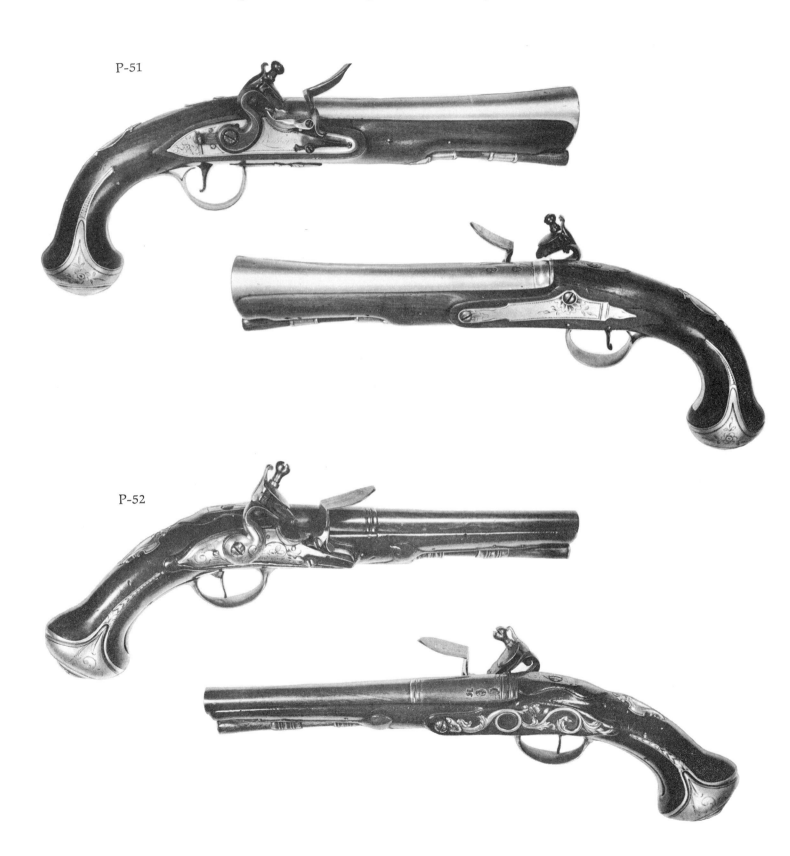

P-51

P-52

P-53

P-54

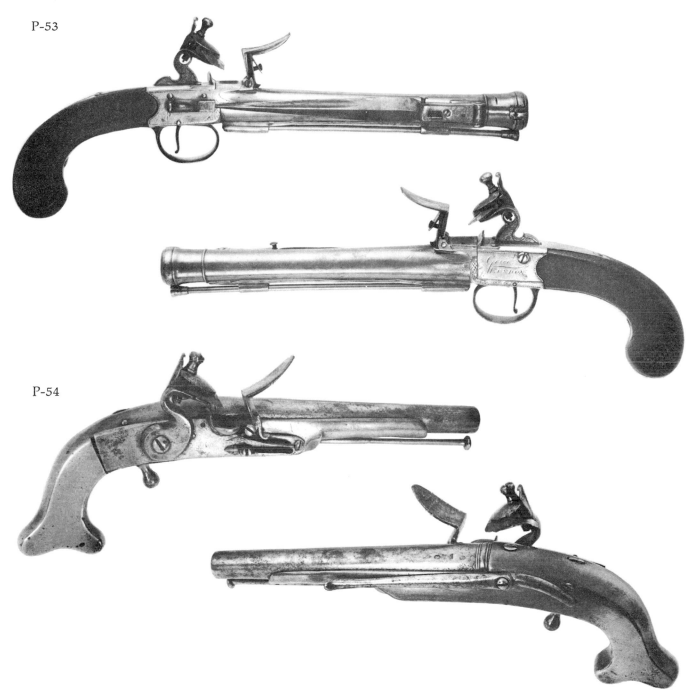

P-53 Naval officer's boarding flintlock pistol with brass cannon-shaped barrel
and frame and box-lock action. It was made by Grice, and although marked
London, it was probably produced in Birmingham between 1775 and 1780.
The spring bayonet is the early type with trowel-shaped blade,
which is released by pulling back the thumb latch directly above the
trigger guard. Length: 14¾ inches.

P-54 Black Watch all-metal flintlock military pistol, with the usual bronze stock.
The mark on the barrel shows it was made by Waters in Birmingham, England,
circa 1765. This type of pistol was carried by both officers and
enlisted men of the Scottish Highland Regiments in America during the
Revolution. The pistol is fitted with a belt hook that attaches to a
shoulder strap. Length: 12 inches.

P-55   *British light dragoon pistol with .65 caliber carbine bore and 9-inch barrel. The lock is marked with the name of the contractor, Vernon, and dated 1760. This model was carried by the British cavalry during the American Revolution. Length: 15½ inches.*

P-56   *British light dragoon pistol with .65 caliber carbine bore and 10-inch barrel. The lock is marked "Tower" and dated 1760. This is the first model of the light dragoon pistol. Length: 16½ inches.*

P-55

P-56

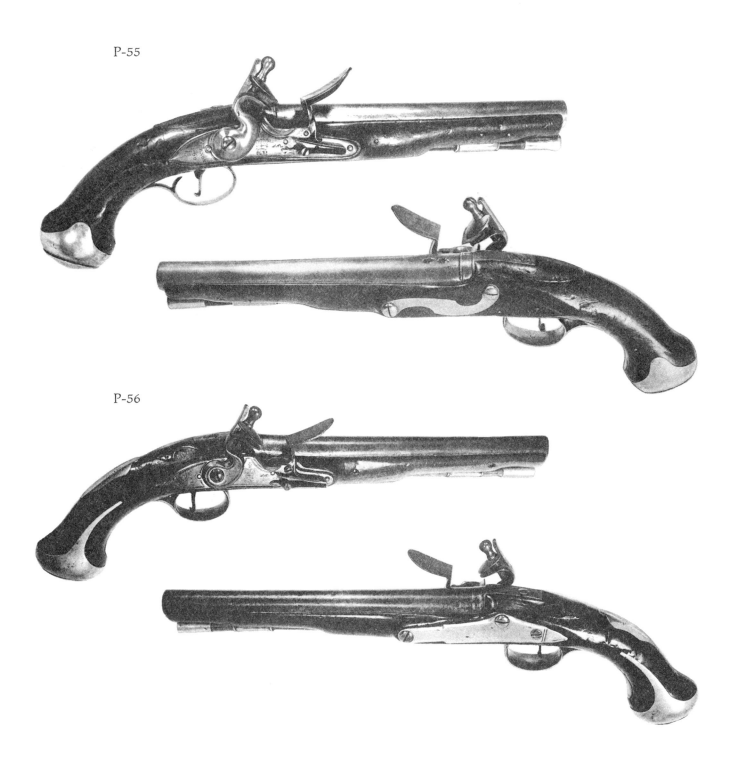

P-57

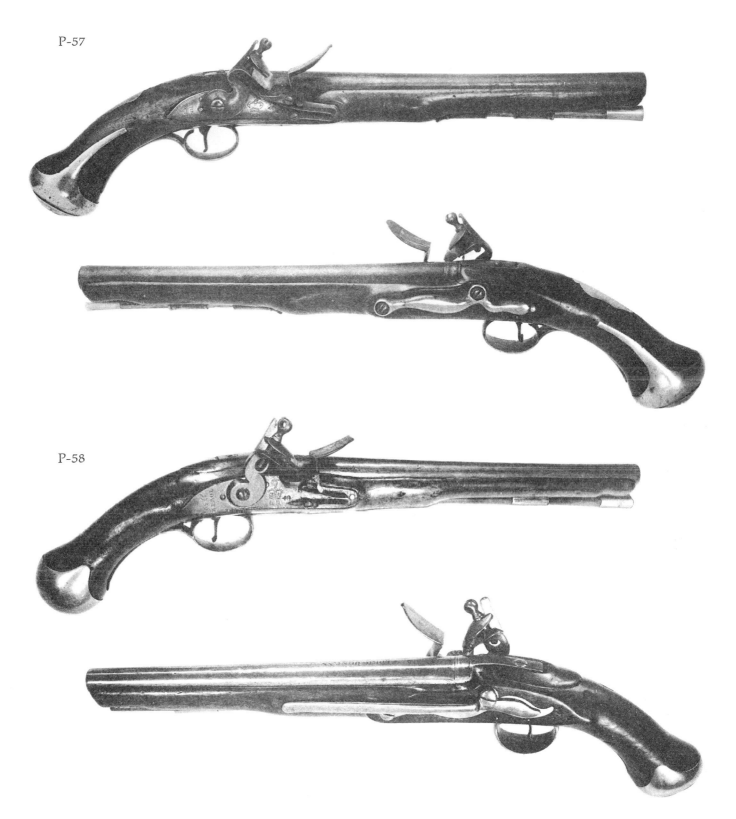

P-58

P-57   *British military heavy dragoon flintlock pistol with 12-inch barrel
and brass furniture. The lockplate is inscribed "Grice 1759," and the barrel
is marked "Royal Dragoons." Length: 19¼ inches.*

P-58   *British Sea Service flintlock pistol with brass furniture and regulation
12-inch barrel. The lock is marked "Tower" and dated 1736.
Length: 18½ inches.*

P-59   *Pair of flintlock officer's holster pistols stocked in cherrywood.*
These pistols, dating about 1770, are American-made, lock, stock, and barrel.
They are said to have been carried by an officer who lived in what is now
Rockland County, New York, and were found in their original black leather
saddle holsters with leopard-skin flaps or covers. Length: 13½ inches.

P-60   *Extremely rare flintlock military pistol, American-made, lock, stock,*
and barrel, circa 1770. This pistol is in almost perfect condition,
with very plain brass furniture and maple stock. The barrel tang is secured
by a screw passing up through the wood stock just forward of the trigger.
The pistol has a steel belt hook, which could signify service during
the Revolution, either aboard an American privateer or suspended from
the belt of an officer. In a drawing by H. Charles McBarron, Jr.,
an officer of Glover's Marblehead or Marine Infantry is shown with an almost
identical pistol suspended from his belt. Length: 15 inches.

P-59

P-60

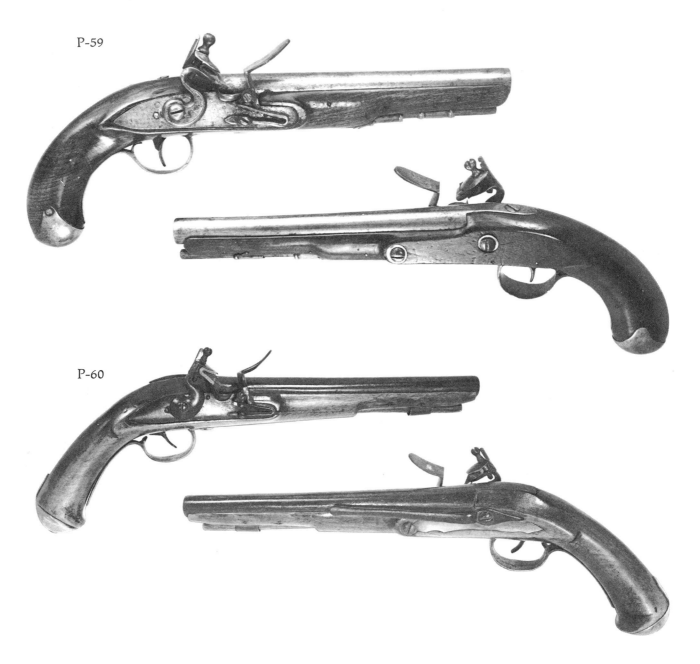

P-61

P-62

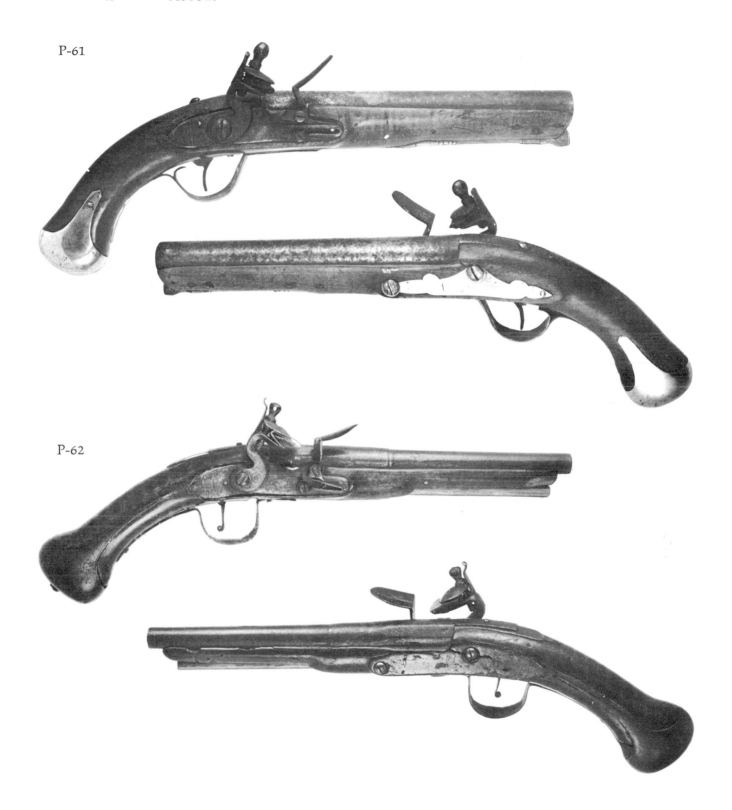

P-61   *All-American-made flintlock officer's holster pistol with clear maple stock
and very plain, crude brass furniture nailed to the stock. This is a fine example
of an American military pistol made just prior to the Revolutionary War.
Length: 14 inches.*

P-62   *American flintlock pistol with steel furniture and curly-maple stock,
made about 1740. This pistol incorporates a French flintlock mechanism.
Length: 15¼ inches.*

P-63 *American Kentucky flintlock pistol with a grip of unusual shape, circa 1775. This pistol incorporates an early British lock made by Thomas Ketland in Birmingham. Length: 18¼ inches.*

P-64 *Pair of all-American-made flintlock Kentucky pistols with curly-maple stocks and hand-forged lock mechanisms, dating about the period of the Revolutionary War. Length: 16¼ inches.*

P-63

P-64

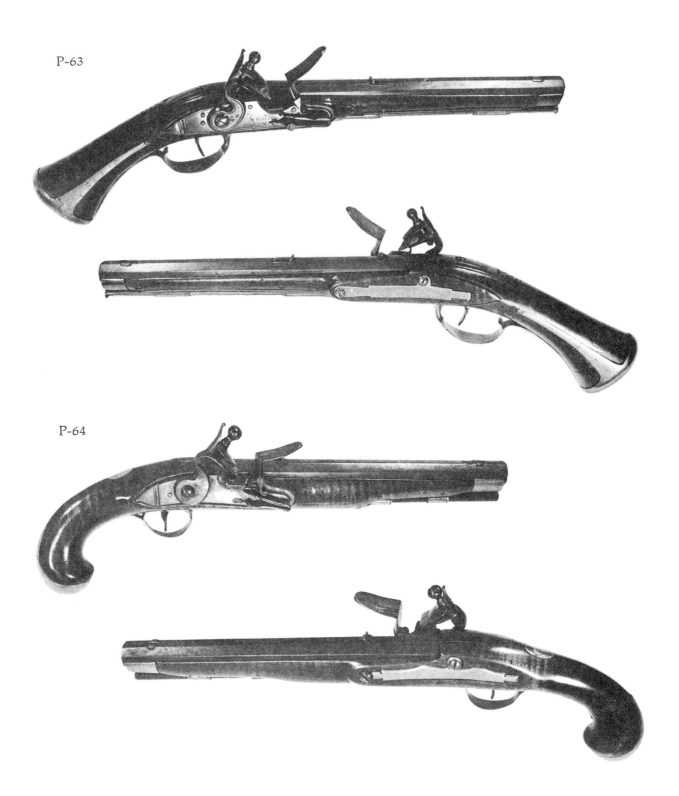

P-65

P-66

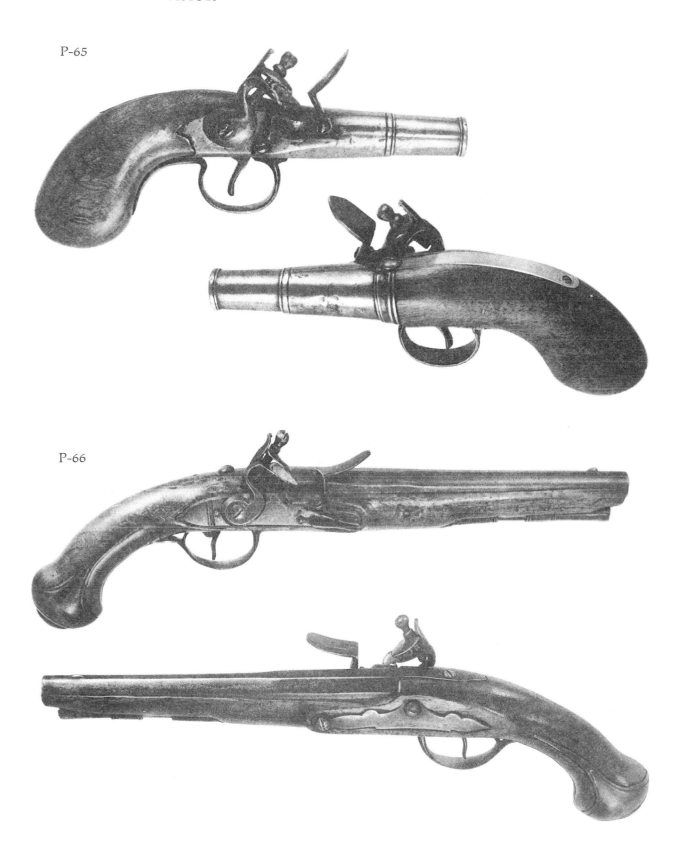

P-65   *Completely American-made pocket pistol with cherry stock and brass barrel,
made around 1770. Length: 7½ inches.*

P-66   *Pair of American or French steel-mounted flintlock holster pistols,
circa 1770. Length: 15¾ inches.*

P-67   *American cherry-stocked flintlock pistol with brass furniture, made with the barrel and lock from a European weapon, circa 1750. Length: 13 inches.*

P-68   *American maple-stocked flintlock pistol with 10-inch barrel, signed with the maker's name, Mathew Sadd, circa 1750. This pistol has brass furniture and a hand-forged lock. Length: 16½ inches.*

P-67

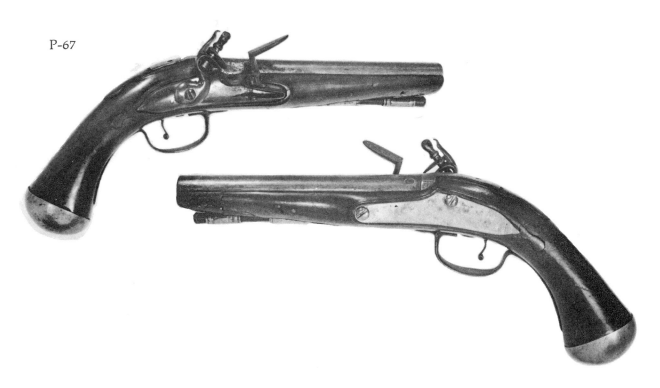

P-68

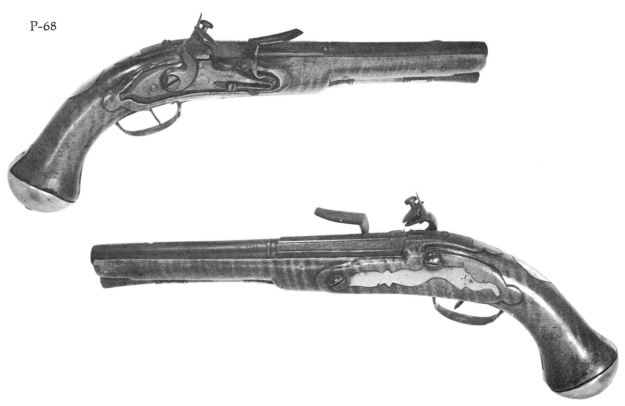

P-69

P-70

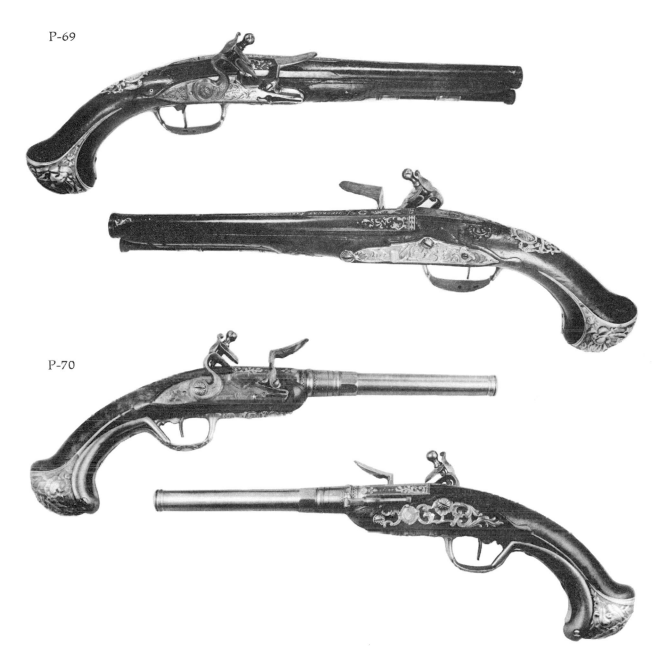

P-69 *Exceptionally fine pair of French silver-mounted flintlock officer's holster
pistols made by Puiforeat in Paris, with the hallmarks for 1748 on
the inside of the trigger guard. This pair is unusual in that it is
hallmarked and has military decorations, not too often found on French pistols
of this period. Portions of the silver furniture have a light gold wash
applied to highlight the deeply embossed designs. Length: 15 inches.*

P-70 *Pair of flintlock officer's belt pistols made by Frappier in Paris, circa 1740.
These pistols are of exceptional quality, having fine silver furniture and
gold-decorated barrels. The screw-off barrels are held by links fixed to
the stocks so as to prevent their loss during reloading. The sash hooks
attached to the handles were opened and a sash attached to the user's belt
was passed through. The hook was then clipped back into position,
and the pistol could not be lost in the heat of battle on foot or when
the user required his sword. Length: 14 inches.*

P-71   *Pair of French flintlock officer's pistols by Le Loraine à Valence,*
       circa 1745. French pistols of such superb quality and with the French imperial
       eagle motif were evidently carried by very high-ranking officers.
       This maker produced considerable numbers of fine pistols for French officers.
       Length: 14½ inches.

P-72   *French model 1733 dragoon pistol made at St. Etienne, with 12-inch barrel*
       and brass furniture. Note resemblance to British pistol of the same period.
       Length: 19 inches.

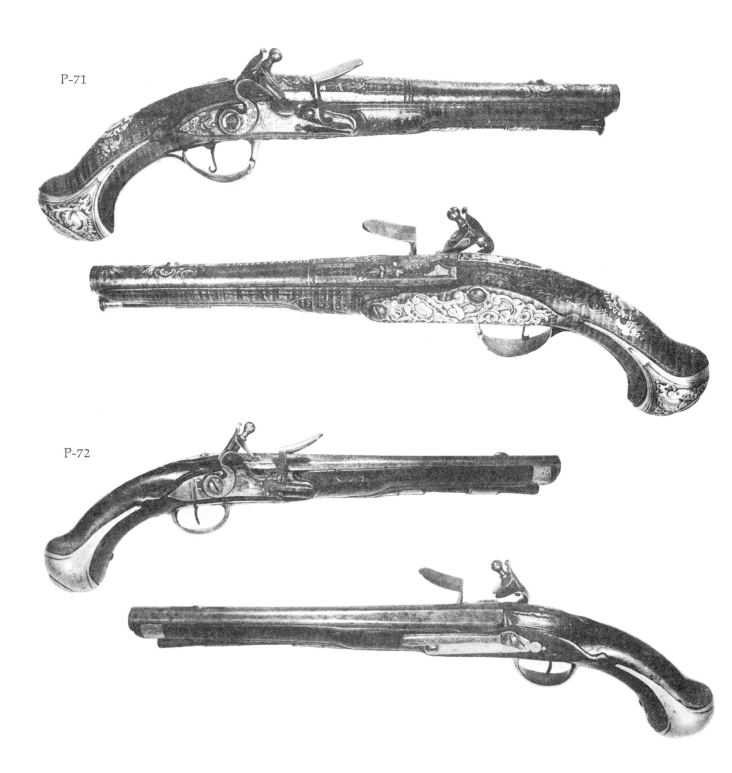

P-71

P-72

P-73

P-74

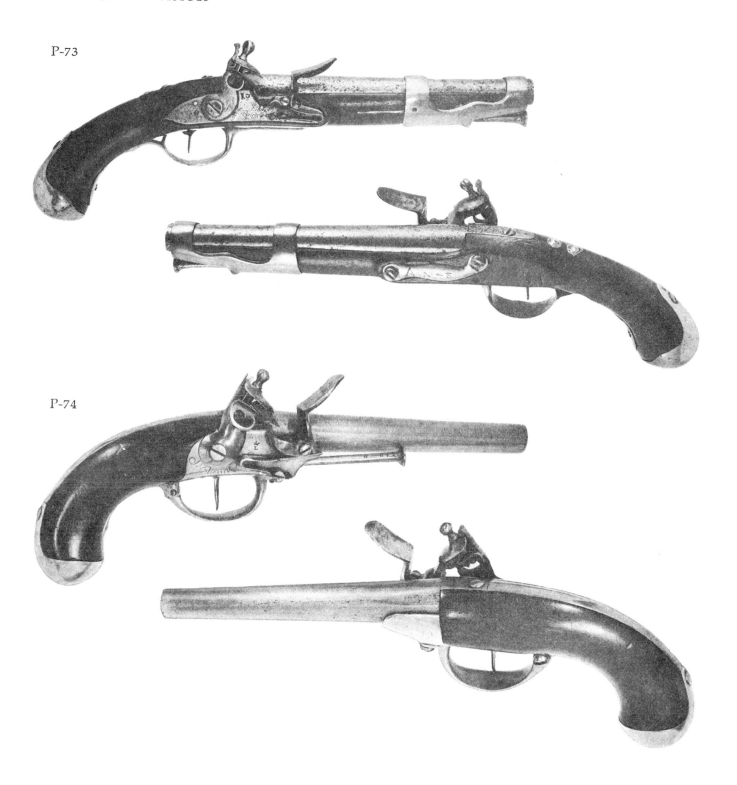

P-73   *French Charleville pistol, model 1763, with brass mountings.*
        The French Royal Manufactorie, "Charleville," is engraved on the lockplate.
        Length: 15¾ inches.

P-74   *French enlisted man's military pistol model 1777 with brass furniture*
        and marked "St. Etienne," which denotes the French arsenal where it was made.
        It was the model for the first martial pistols made under contract for the
        United States government after the Revolutionary War. Length: 13¼ inches.

P-75   *Pair of silver-mounted German flintlock officer's holster pistols,*
circa 1750, decorated with martial motif. The unusually fine workmanship and
ornate decoration indicate that they were probably owned by
a high-ranking officer. These pistols are unusual in that the frizzen springs
are concealed rather than located on the exterior of the lockplates.
Length: 17 inches.

P-76   *Pair of flintlock holster pistols by Sleur of Amsterdam, circa 1745.*
Long Dutch holster pistols of this type were almost certainly among the arms
ordered from Holland by Benjamin Franklin. The great length of these pistols
was more typical of the holster pistol used during the early 1600s and 1700s.
Length: 19½ inches.

P-75

P-76

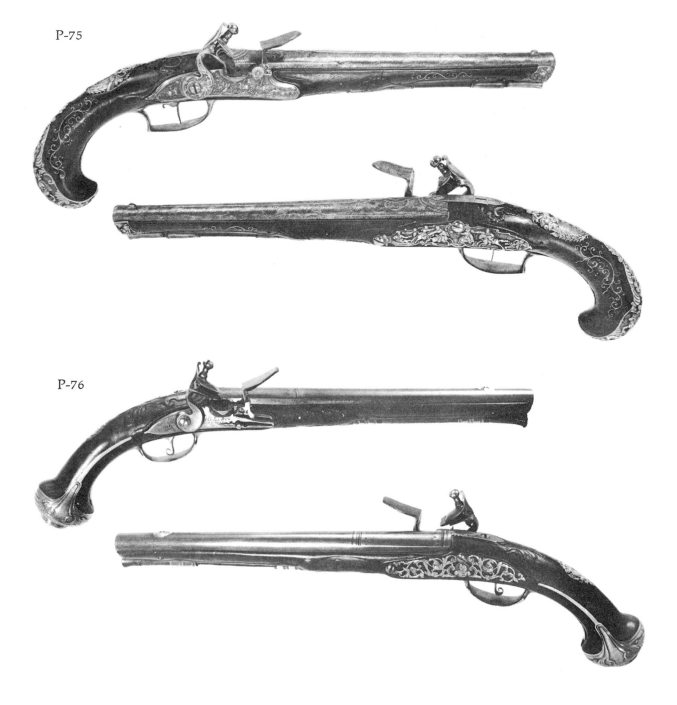

P-77

P-78

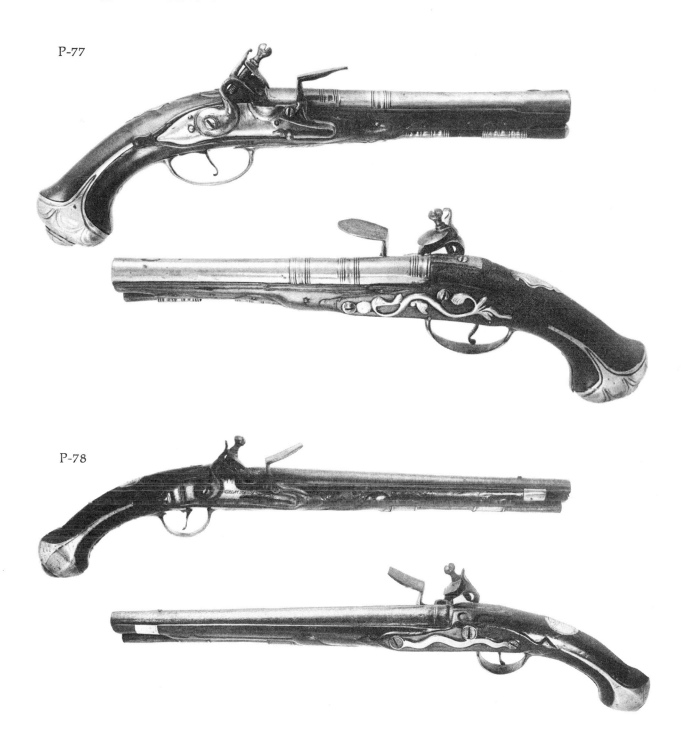

P-77   *Pair of Dutch or Belgian brass-barrel flintlock officer's holster pistols*
with brass furniture, circa 1740. The lockplates are brass and are
inscribed "Da Low," which is probably the maker's name. The escutcheons
are also engraved with the Latin "ex pugnant." Length: 15 inches.

P-78   *Extra-long flintlock Prussian horse pistol with brass furniture, circa 1725.*
The escutcheon is engraved with the cipher "FR," for Frederick the Great.
The brass furniture, flintlock mechanism, and curving on the wood stock are
almost identical to those features on the Prussian musket shown in the section
on shoulder arms. The lockplate is marked "Potsdam." Length: 22¼ inches.

P-79   *Brass-mounted Belgian or Dutch flintlock horse or holster pistol,
circa 1740, with the early banana-shaped lockplate and curled trigger.
Length: 21½ inches.*

P-80   *Steel-mounted German flintlock pistol with barrel partly round and
partly octagonal, circa 1740. An unusual feature is the belt hook,
seldom found on pistols this long. Length: 22 inches.*

P-79

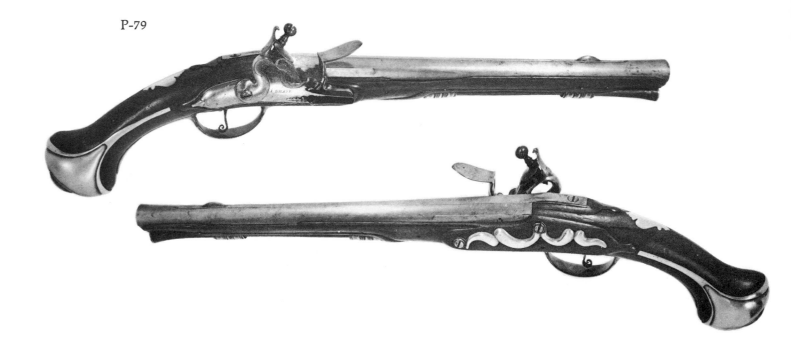

P-80

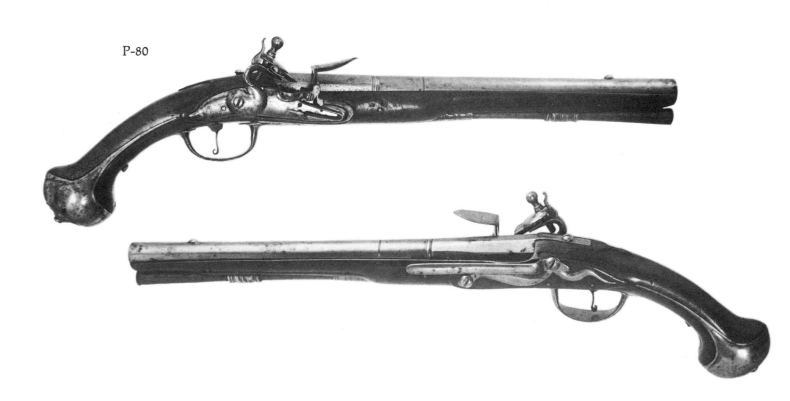

P-81

P-82

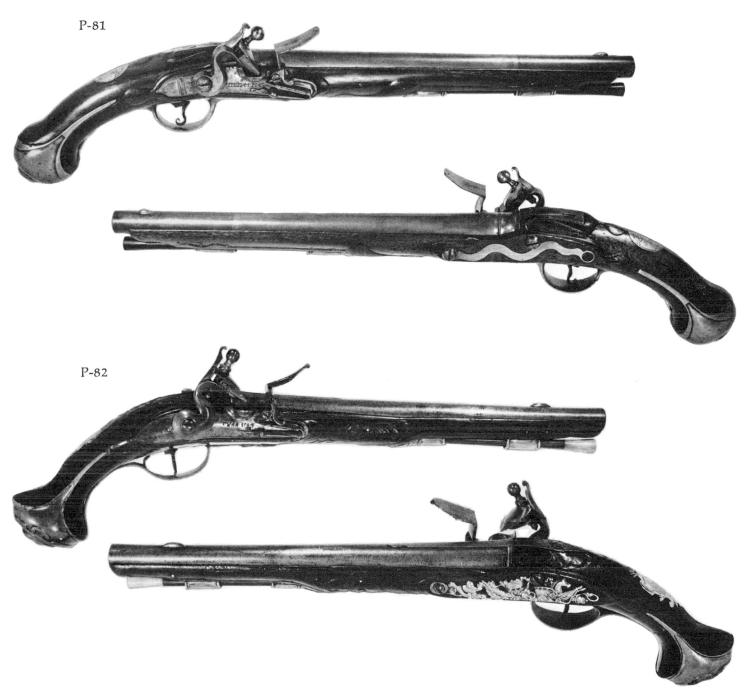

P-81　*Early eighteenth-century German flintlock holster pistol with brass
mountings and the early banana-shaped lock with beveled edge. The lockplate
is engraved "POTZDAM MAGAZ SET D." The large oval escutcheon is marked
with the crowned "FR" monogram, which stands for Frederick Rex.
Length: 22 inches.*

P-82　*Pair of Russian flintlock officer's holster pistols with brass furniture and
the inscription "Tula 1744" engraved on the lockplates. Russia hired British
and French gunsmiths to assist in setting up gunmaking facilities at the Tula
arsenal, located south of Moscow. Although it is very unlikely that
such pistols ever saw service in America during the Revolution,
they are illustrated here to show their striking similarity to British
and French models. Length: 17½ inches.*

SHOULDER
ARMS

NOMENCLATURE OF SHOULDER ARMS

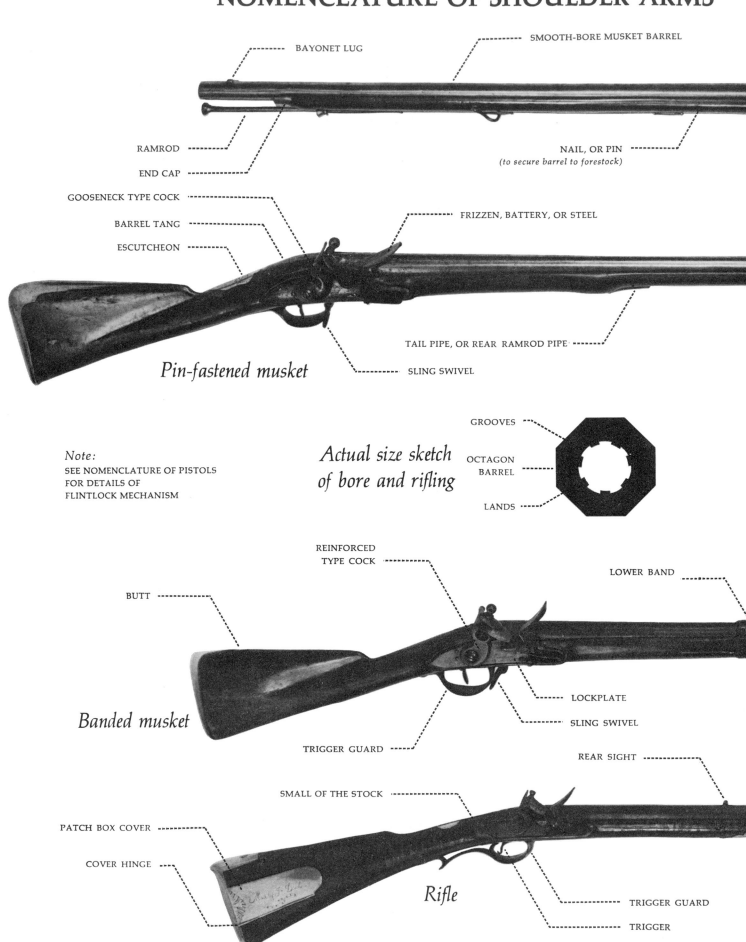

BAYONET LUG

SMOOTH-BORE MUSKET BARREL

RAMROD

END CAP

NAIL, OR PIN
(to secure barrel to forestock)

GOOSENECK TYPE COCK

BARREL TANG

ESCUTCHEON

FRIZZEN, BATTERY, OR STEEL

TAIL PIPE, OR REAR RAMROD PIPE

SLING SWIVEL

Pin-fastened musket

Note:
SEE NOMENCLATURE OF PISTOLS
FOR DETAILS OF
FLINTLOCK MECHANISM

*Actual size sketch
of bore and rifling*

GROOVES

OCTAGON
BARREL

LANDS

REINFORCED
TYPE COCK

LOWER BAND

BUTT

LOCKPLATE

SLING SWIVEL

Banded musket

TRIGGER GUARD

REAR SIGHT

SMALL OF THE STOCK

PATCH BOX COVER

COVER HINGE

Rifle

TRIGGER GUARD

TRIGGER

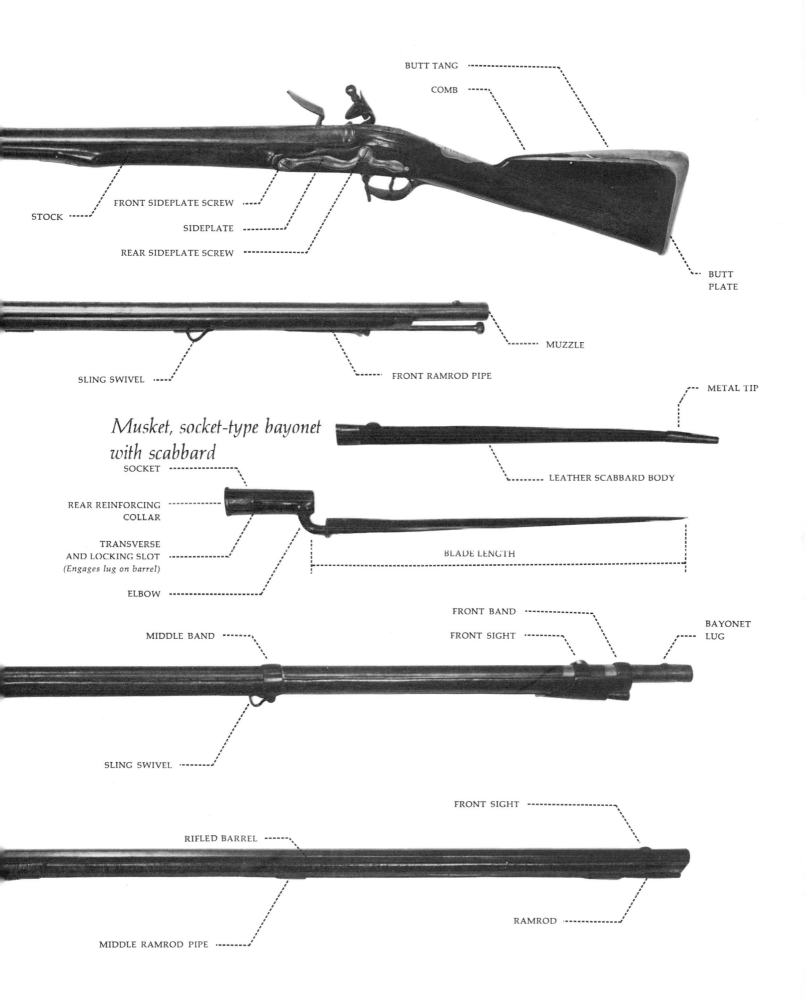

BUTT TANG

COMB

STOCK

FRONT SIDEPLATE SCREW

SIDEPLATE

REAR SIDEPLATE SCREW

BUTT PLATE

MUZZLE

SLING SWIVEL

FRONT RAMROD PIPE

METAL TIP

Musket, socket-type bayonet with scabbard

SOCKET

LEATHER SCABBARD BODY

REAR REINFORCING COLLAR

TRANSVERSE AND LOCKING SLOT
(Engages lug on barrel)

BLADE LENGTH

ELBOW

FRONT BAND

MIDDLE BAND

FRONT SIGHT

BAYONET LUG

SLING SWIVEL

FRONT SIGHT

RIFLED BARREL

RAMROD

MIDDLE RAMROD PIPE

The principal shoulder weapon of the Revolutionary War was the smooth bore flintlock musket. Most of the battles were fought by two or three lines of men armed with this musket, and standing shoulder to shoulder. The men could load and fire three or four times a minute, and could hope to hit the enemy with accuracy up to about fifty feet. In a typical engagement, each side exchanged two, or at most three, volleys before deciding the issue in hand-to-hand bayonet fighting. In this type of warfare, speed of firing was more important then aiming for accuracy, and the musket filled the bill.

As far as the use of the rifle is concerned, there are many who feel that it, rather than the musket, was responsible for America gaining her independence. A study of the battles indicates that all but a few engagements were fought in the accepted European fashion, with the men standing in close ranks and firing volleys. In the early part of the war several American companies were formed entirely of riflemen. These outfits enjoyed initial success because of their marksmanship, but this ended abruptly when the British began charging them with bayonets fixed. The riflemen were equipped with a belt ax to compensate for the lack of a bayonet, but a belt ax was no match for a bayonet affixed to the end of a musket, and the Americans were forced to scatter in hasty retreat. The American commanders realized the weakness of the rifle when used in this manner, and in subsequent encounters the rifleman served as a flanker, or sharpshooter, in order to take as heavy a toll as possible of the advancing British troops before withdrawing. The supporting musket troops then fired a volley at the enemy before joining in bayonet fighting. The rifle used with the support of muskets was a very deadly and formidable weapon and, although it lacked the bayonet and was slow to load, it made possible many American military victories.

AMERICAN WEAPONS

Many types of American-made shoulder arms were used. The colonist usually had only one gun which he used for hunting, protection, and militia duty. When the war began, there was an extreme scarcity of military guns, and the men were urged to bring along for service any shoulder arms they owned. As a result many were armed with hunting pieces, such as the Hudson Valley and New England fowlers. Many other such guns were used, and relatively few were equipped with bayonets. By early summer of 1775, gunsmiths throughout the

59

country were under contract to local Committees and Councils of Safety to produce muskets patterned closely after the British Brown Bess. Each colony issued its own specifications for these Committee of Safety muskets, which were produced just prior to and during the early months of the war. While all of the specifications differed somewhat, the muskets were basically similar. The barrel length ranged from 42 to 46 inches, the caliber was about .75, and metal ramrods were always specified. Most of the colonies required markings on these guns. In a strict sense, a gun had to be made under a specific contract for one of the Committees of Safety to qualify as a Committee of Safety musket, and unfortunately few specimens have survived. This is probably due in part to the fact that these pieces were made in the early stages of the war, and consequently saw a great deal of hard use. Also, the extreme scarcity of gun parts both before and during the Revolution resulted in components of these muskets being used in later guns.

In addition to smooth bore muskets and fowlers the Americans used an arm with a rifled barrel. This was the American rifle, more familiarly known today as the Kentucky or Pennsylvania rifle. It was developed by German gunsmiths who settled in Pennsylvania about 1710. Its ancestor was the German jaeger rifle, and through the years the curly-maple stocked Americanized version evolved with a much longer barrel and smaller bore. It is difficult to say with certainty just when it first appeared, with its graceful lines and distinctive style of decoration. No doubt the first rifles that German gunmakers produced in this country were similar to the ones they had been making in Europe; however, a debut date as early as 1740 would seem to be a reasonable estimate. The rifling usually consisted of seven spiral grooves which gave the ball a twist, or rotation, of about three-quarters of a turn before it left the barrel. The high and low points of the rifling are known as lands and grooves respectively. When a lead ball was loaded, it only made contact with the land portion of the rifling, and consequently a greased piece of cloth known as a patch was wrapped around the ball in order to seal the gaps between the ball and the low point of the rifling. An expert rifleman could hit an enemy soldier at a range of around 300 yards, although a very windy day would reduce this distance. This is about four or five times the effective range of a musket ball.

An interesting contemporary account of the accuracy of the American rifle is given by a British major, George Hanger, who fought with Burgoyne and was taken prisoner after the Battle of Saratoga. In his book *To All Sportsmen* published in London in 1814 he made the following comments:

Colonel, now General Tarleton, and myself, were standing a few yards out of a wood, observing the situation of a part of the enemy which we intended to attack. There was a rivulet in the enemy's front, and a mill on it, to which we stood directly with our horses' heads fronting, observing their motions. It was absolutely a plain field between us and the mill; not so much as a single bush on it. Our orderly-bugler stood behind us about three yards, but with his horse's side to our horses' tails. A rifleman passed over the mill-dam, evidently observing two officers, and laid himself down on his belly; for in such positions, they always lie, to take a good shot at a long distance. He took a deliberate and cool shot at my friend, at me, and at the bugle-horn man. Now observe how well this fellow shot. It was in the month of August, and not a breath of wind was stirring. Colonel Tarleton's horse and mine, I am certain, were not anything like two feet apart; for we were in close consultation, how we should attack with our troops which laid 300 yards in the wood, and could not be perceived by the enemy. A rifle-ball passed between him and me; looking directly to the mill I evidently observed the flash of the powder. I directly said to my friend, "I think we had better move, or we shall have two or three of these gentlemen shortly amusing themselves at our expense." The words were hardly out of my mouth when the bugle-horn man behind me, and directly central, jumped off his horse and said, "Sir, my horse is shot." The horse staggered, fell down, and died.... Now speaking of this rifleman's shooting, nothing could be better.... I have passed several times over this ground and ever observed it with the greatest attention; and I can positively assert that the distance he fired from at us was full 400 yards.

BRITISH WEAPONS

The chief shoulder arm of the British forces in the American Revolution was the musket commonly called the "Brown Bess." According to the British arms expert Howard L. Blackmore, the earliest printed reference to the term Brown Bess appeared in 1785. However, this name is now commonly used to describe the flintlock muskets of the British army from the 1720s to the 1830s. The original designation for the 46-inch barrel gun was Long Land Musket, while the 42-inch barrel was known as the Short Land Musket. As far as the origin of the term Brown Bess is concerned, nothing can be determined with any certainty. Some feel that "Bess" is a corruption of the German word buchse (gun), while others think it is merely a term of affection. As to the "Brown," it could refer to the color of the stock or the barrel. The earlier weapons had black painted stocks, and the contrast of the Brown Bess' walnut wood stained a reddish-brown color supports the theory of the brown color being associated with the stock. Besides the regulation Brown Bess musket with a 46-inch or 42-inch barrel, there was a light infantry model and a marine or militia model, which also had a 42-inch barrel.

Major Hanger's book also includes his comments on the range and accuracy of the musket:

A soldier's musket, if not exceedingly ill-bored (as many of them are), will strike the figure of a man at eighty yards; it may even at 100; but a soldier must be very unfortunate indeed who shall be wounded by a common musket at 150 yards, provided his antagonist aims at him; and as to firing at a man at 200 yards with a common musket, you may just as well fire at the moon and have the same hopes of hitting your object. I do maintain and will prove, whenever called on, that no man was ever killed at 200 yards, by a common soldier's musket, by the person who aimed at him.

The British also made limited use of a breech-loading rifle developed by Captain Patrick Ferguson of the 70th Regiment. The action had a threaded plug, attached to the trigger guard, that engaged a vertical threaded section in the breech end of the barrel. This idea was not new, but Ferguson greatly improved it by using fast threads so the plug could be dropped with only one clockwise rotation of the trigger guard. Moreover, the plug was never detached from the barrel, and one counterclockwise turn easily returned it to firing position. In loading, the plug was lowered and the barrel tipped slightly downward. The ball was first dropped into the breech cavity where it rolled to a stop after striking the lands in the barrel rifling. The rest of the breech cavity was then filled with powder and the plug closed. Although the Ferguson rifle was an excellent and efficient weapon and superior to the musket, fewer than 200 of them were in use in America. In all probability, they were used as military weapons only in America.

The reasons for the British failure to capitalize on the superiority of the Ferguson rifle remain a puzzle even today. The answer probably lies somewhere between the political incompetency of Lord North's administration and the military incompetency of the War Office. It has been said that a large number of these weapons in the hands of trained men would have won the Revolution for the British in its first few months.

Ferguson attained the rank of colonel, and while serving under Sir Henry Clinton, he was killed on October 7, 1780 in the Battle of King's Mountain in South Carolina.

In addition to barrel proofs, arms of the British government were stamped on the lockplate with a crowned broad arrow mark which signified government ownership. A plain broad arrow mark was sometimes found on the stock as well. The Brown Bess lockplates also bore the Royal Cypher of the three King Georges, consisting of a crown with the initials GR (Georgius Rex) below. Arms proved at the Tower of London before 1764 were inscribed with the word "Tower" and the date of proof, on the section of the lockplate behind the cock. There were also many guns made before this date which bore a maker's name and date. This resulted when traveling viewers visited the gunmaker and proved his weapons right in the shop. In addition to the arms assembled and proved at the Tower of London, others were assembled at Dublin Castle in Ireland, and the lockplates of these weapons were marked "Dublin Castle."

FRENCH WEAPONS

French muskets were second only to British muskets in quantities used during the Revolution. Until then America had always fought with England against France in the numerous wars for control of the North American continent. During this period French muskets were weapons of the enemy. However, after the War for Independence began and France became America's ally, French arms were imported in large numbers. The basic types of French muskets used in this country were the models 1717, 1728, 1746, 1754, 1763, and 1777. Instead of being pin-fastened as were all British arms, the barrels of French shoulder weapons were secured to the stock with metal bands. Toward the end of the war, the colonists began to favor the French Charleville and the 1763 musket, like the French pistol, served as the model for the first musket, the 1795 Springfield, made under contract to the new United States government after the Revolution.

Charleville is a generic term often used to designate eighteenth-century French military muskets and pistols. The use of this term might imply that all government weapons were manufactured at the Royal Manufactorie at Charleville; however, many were also made at other French arsenals, such as St. Etienne and Maubeuge.

GERMAN WEAPONS

A sizeable number of German shoulder weapons were carried by the German, or Hessian, auxiliaries of the British Army. Their muskets were usually obsolete models, and the types represented varied greatly since they came from a number of the individual principalities of Germany. There were some characteristics which almost all had in common, such as heavy stocks with an unusually high comb, brass mountings, and an elliptical brass front sight. The barrel was secured to the stock by either pins or brass bands.

The German musket used least in America was the Prussian model, easily identified by the ten pins that fastened the barrel to the stock.

The scarcity of this musket can be attributed to Frederick the Great's reluctance to send his soldiers to fight in America.

In addition to muskets, some Hessians were armed with the German jaeger rifle, which was about 44 to 46 inches in length. They varied about as much as the muskets, but one distinguishing feature was the patch-box with sliding wooden cover, located in the butt.

The poor showing made by the Hessian mercenaries in the war can be explained by the fact that instead of being genuine jaeger (professional hunters), as were members of the German rifle corps, they were peasants dragged from the field who had no will whatsoever to fight for the cause of their employer, King George III. Moreover, the motley array of weapons with which they were equipped were of such poor quality as to be next to useless.

In August of 1776, fourteen companies of American riflemen, each consisting of 90 men, had been raised in Pennsylvania, Maryland, and Virginia. That fall they arrived in the vicinity of Boston and when they began to take part in battles, they had a devastating effect upon the British regulars. The American riflemen could conceal themselves in the forest, far out of range of the Brown Bess, and pick off the British, who were charging an unseen enemy. When this information was received in London, it was decided to hire soldiers from some of the German princes, who had been selling the services of their subjects to foreign armies for many years.

The British were particularly interested in hiring a number of jaeger, or professional German rifle hunters, to compete with the American riflemen. Some 20,000 regulars with muskets were contracted for first, and then the British sought to hire 4,000 jaeger at double the price for a regular. The Landgrave of Hessen-Kassel provided the 4,000 men requested in February of 1777, but the fact that most of them were not jaeger was left for the British to find out later. Similarly, most of the weapons that the regulars and the jaeger brought with them turned out to be unusable. Although the British contracted for around 37,000 Germans between 1776 and 1781, only some 7,200 of these, including the jaeger, were actually Hessians. This term became generic for all Germans taken into British service because the Landgrave of Hessen-Kassel was the most notorious dealer in human beings among all the German princes.

DUTCH WEAPONS

America also purchased small quanties of muskets from Belgium and Holland. The Belgian pieces were poor in quality, but the Dutch muskets proved to be very serviceable. Many were shorter and lighter than the English and French muskets, and one distinguishable feature was the two large roundhead screws that protruded from the butt plate. Some Hessian troops carried Dutch-made arms.

SPANISH WEAPONS

There have been several references made concerning the use of Spanish muskets by American troops during the Revolution, particularly among the New England soldiers. Some of these were probably guns captured by the Americans from the Spanish in Cuba during the siege of Havana in the summer of 1762. Havana was a Spanish stronghold in the eighteenth century, and when Spain made an alliance with France, England declared war against Spain and sent an expedition against Havana. Among the British troops were 2,300 colonial soldiers under the command of General Phineas Lyman of Connecticut. This engagement, incidentally, was the last in which American colonial forces served overseas under the British flag. During the siege, which lasted forty days, the American troops suffered severe casualties. It is more than likely that the survivors brought home with them captured Spanish weapons which were later used in the Revolution. No doubt other Spanish guns were acquired by the Americans by either sale or trade before the outbreak of the Revolution.

CARBINES

Another category of shoulder weapon is the carbine. These were used by the horse, dragoons, and light dragoons, and also by artillerymen. Barrel lengths usually ranged from about 28 inches to 37 inches, and cavalry models had a saddle ring and bar device. Little is known today of these early short-barreled carbines carried by the horse, or heavy cavalry.

Light dragoon carbines were carried in a bucket that hung just in front of the rider's leg and was further supported by a strap attached to the pommel of the saddle and passed around the wrist of the carbine. Thus, the gun could be left on the horse even when the man dismounted.

In addition to the sword belt slung from his right shoulder, the horse trooper and light dragoon carried a carbine on a belt slung over his left shoulder, to which was attached a swivel, chain, and "T" to spring his carbine. This let the gun hang muzzle-down and made it instantly available. From contemporary illustrations it appears that the carbine was fired while still attached to the swivel, as this ran up and down the sling freely. This probably prevented loss of the gun, and by simply dropping this weapon, his sword or pistols were ready for immediate use. While the carbine was the most popular shoulder weapon for a mounted man, it is doubtful whether it was available in any great quantity to American light dragoons.

In all probability, muskets or even blunderbusses were simply slung over the shoulder. Since the heavy dragoons usually fought dismounted, they had no occasion to use the swivel, chain, and "T" device. Consequently, they carried their muskets, with either a 37-inch or 42-inch barrel, on their backs by means of a sling.

OFFICER SHOULDER WEAPONS

Officer shoulder weapons were of lighter construction, finer quality, and considerably more ornate than the arms of enlisted men. They are generally referred to as fusils, a French word designating a light flintlock musket. The officers purchased their own shoulder arms, just as they bought their pistols, and therefore the degree of ornateness varied according to the taste or pocketbook of the owner. In English guns it is sometimes difficult to distinguish between a sporting or fowling piece and an officer's fusil, since sporting arms were sometimes decorated with military motifs. The appearance of sling swivels, and especially a bayonet lug, however, may be indicative of military use.

MISCELLANEOUS SHOULDER WEAPONS

Besides muskets, rifles, and carbines a few other specialty type firearms were used in the Revolution, such as the blunderbuss, wall piece or rampart gun, and grenade launcher.

Possibly a few blunderbusses were carried by mounted troops, although they were primarily used as a naval weapon for boarding enemy ships. As a rule, blunderbusses made for naval use had brass barrels and mountings as a safeguard against rust.

Grenade launchers were brought to America by the British many years before the Revolutionary War. They were of two distinct types: one was simply a steel launching cup that was fastened to the muzzle of a special musket, similar to the way in which a bayonet was attached; the other had the launching cup built as an integral part of the butt. Both were operated by two men. One man held the launcher, which was loaded with powder only, while the other placed the grenade in the cup and lit the fuse.

It may be stretching a point to categorize the wall, or rampart gun as a shoulder weapon, yet these firearms resembled the musket in every respect except size. Many had a swivel fork on the forestock so the weight of the gun could be supported by placing the fork in a hole in a fortress wall.

On January 30, 1777, the newly formed United States issued an order requiring all arms, tools, and accoutrements that were the property of the federal government to be stamped, or surcharged "United States." This applied to captured as well as American-made items. Marked pieces in existence today bear inscriptions such as "US," "U States," and "United States." Some were stamped on the barrel, lock-plate, and stock, while others were marked in only one or two places. This directive applied only to weapons owned by the

United States, and not to the pieces which were the property of individuals or the separate states.

DEFINITION OF HORSE, HEAVY DRAGOON AND LIGHT DRAGOON

Throughout this text the terms dragoon and horse have been used in reference to the horse soldier. In the British Army the cavalry is designated as horse, heavy dragoons, and light dragoons or light horse. The horse fought their battles on horseback, relying heavily on their initial shock value, while the dragoons were, generally speaking, mounted infantrymen who dismounted to fight and used the horse as a means of getting to and from the fighting area. There were no heavy horse in the American army, all mounted troops being light horse, such as the four regiments of Continental Light Dragoons. As a rule, light dragoons were used for scouting, skirmishing, and as courier duty.

A troop of horse was the cavalry unit corresponding to a company of infantry. Two or more troops constituted a squadron. Two or more squadrons constituted a regiment of cavalry under the command of a colonel. The troop consisted of one Captain, one Lieutenant, one Cornet, one Quartermaster, two Sergeants, three Corporals, two Drummers, sixty Privates, including one Farrier who performed the duties of a blacksmith.

In 1756 several companies of British light dragoons were formed and attached to the horse regiments. They, like the horse troopers, fought from horseback, but their weapons were usually smaller and lighter. At first, a troop of light dragoons was added to each regiment of dragoons in the British cavalry, and they carried pistols with 10-inch barrels. By 1759, when regiments of light dragoons were formed, the barrel length was reduced to 9 inches and had a carbine bore. Their swords usually had a blade about 34 inches long and a plain hilt rather than the heavy basket hilt. They carried carbines with a barrel about 2 feet, 5 inches long. Light dragoons frequently carried stirrup-hilted swords, formed by bending one quillon up to join the pommel. Swords used by the dragoons and light dragoons were a little shorter than those of the horse or heavy cavalry. The dragoons wore their swords when dismounted, while the horse troopers usually left theirs on the horse. The dragoon swords generally had half-basket hilts.

It is of interest to note, from looking at paintings of that period, how the horse trooper fired his pistol. Instead of holding it in the normal position, the pistol was turned vent side up to lessen the possibility of misfiring. This position made it more conducive for the ignited priming powder in the flash pan to fall into the vent opening in the barrel with the help of gravity. This somewhat awkward method of firing would seem to compensate for the disadvantage of getting off a shot while the horse was in motion.

AMERICAN
SHOULDER ARMS

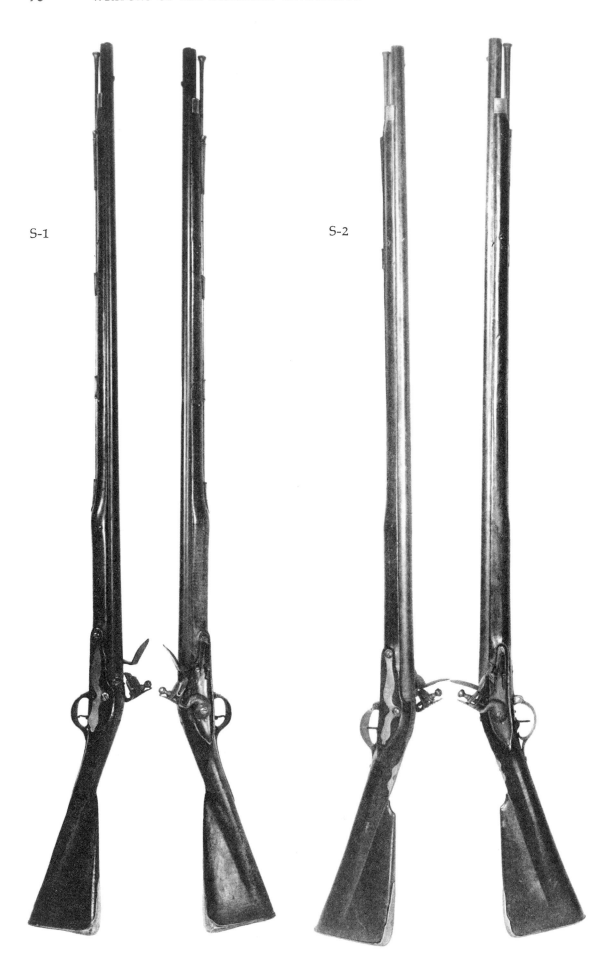

S-1   S-2

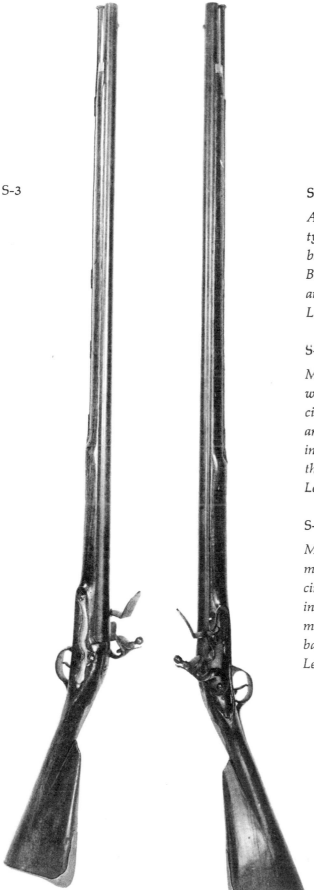

S-3

S-1

American-made Committee of Safety type flintlock musket with 42-inch barrel, patterned after the British Brown Bess. This musket has brass mountings and is stocked in American curly maple. Length: 4 feet 10½ inches.

S-2

Maryland Committee of Safety musket with .80 caliber, 42-inch barrel, circa 1775. The lock, stock and barrel are stamped with the maker's initials, "J.S." This is a copy of the British Second Model Brown Bess. Length: 4 feet 9 inches.

S-3

Massachusetts Committee of Safety musket with .80 caliber, 42-inch barrel, circa 1775. This gun is stocked in chestnut rather than walnut or maple. The number 78 engraved on the barrel is probably a rack number. Length: 4 feet 10 inches.

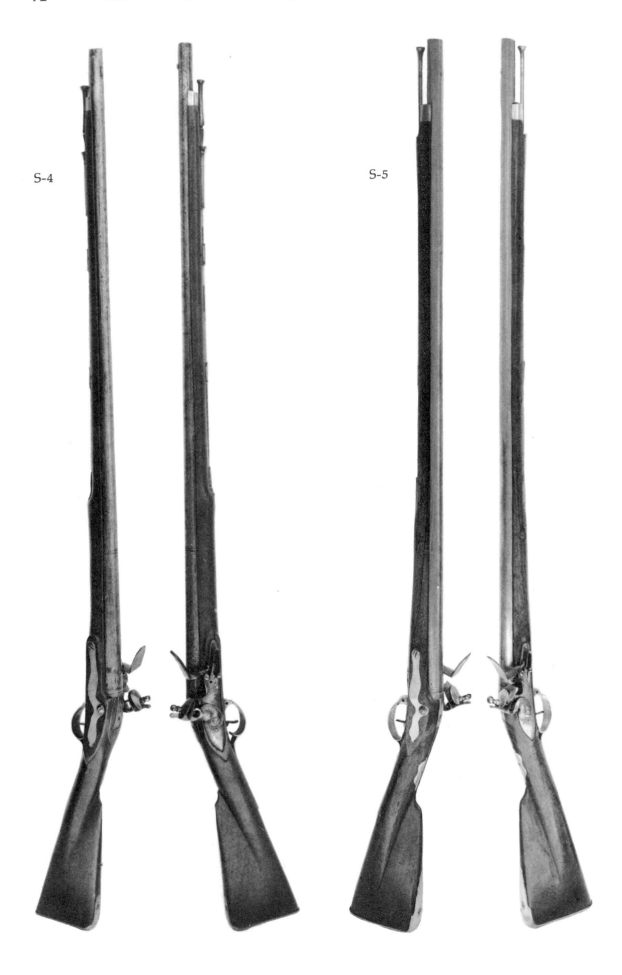

S-4

S-5

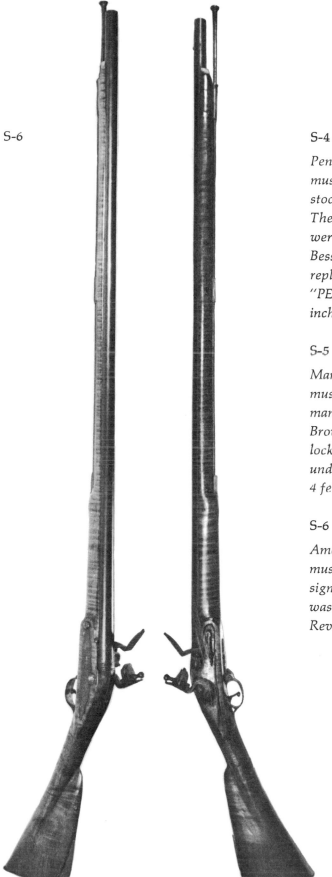

S-6

S-4

Pennsylvania Committee of Safety type musket with American-made barrel, stock, sideplate and trigger guard. The lock, thimbles and butt plate were salvaged from a British Brown Bess musket, and the cock is a later replacement. The barrel is engraved "PENNSYL^AN 298." Length: 4 feet 8½ inches.

S-5

Maryland Committee of Safety musket, entirely of American manufacture and copied from a British Brown Bess. "PS" is stamped on the lock and barrel, and "VII" on the underside of the sideplate. Length: 4 feet 10 inches.

S-6

American curly-maple-stocked flintlock musket with 44-inch .80 caliber barrel, signed "Abaigh Thompson." Thompson was a colonial armorer prior to the Revolution. Length: 4 feet 11½ inches.

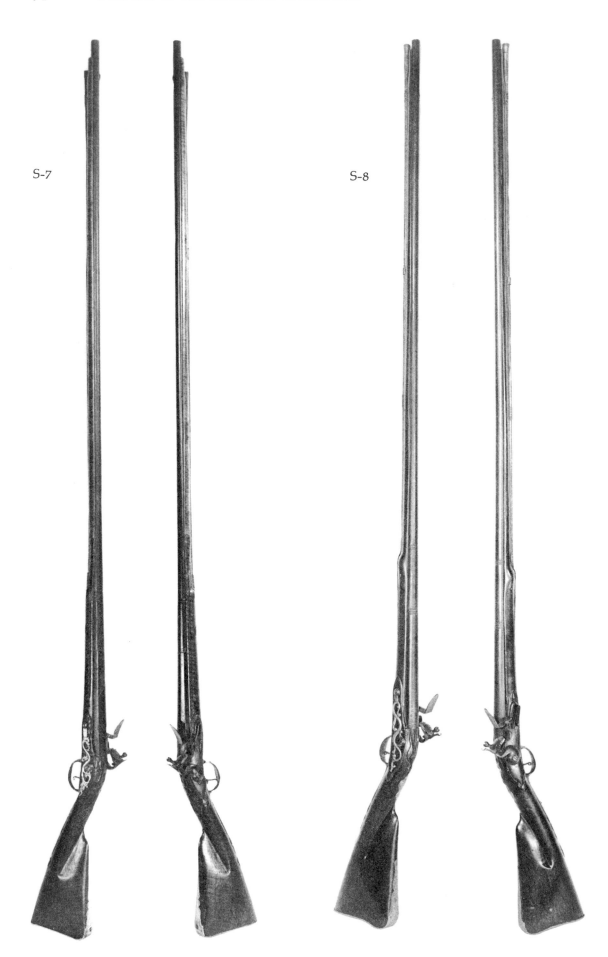

S-7

S-8

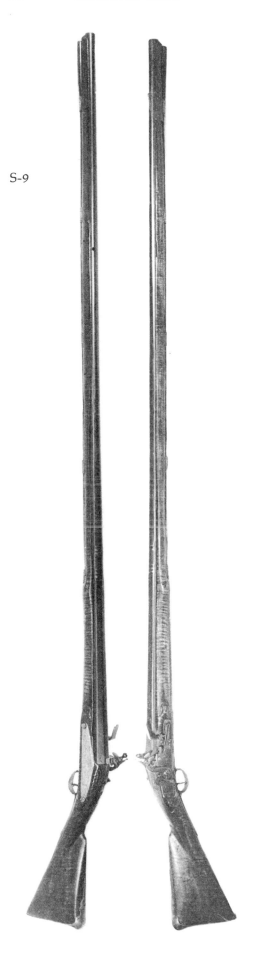

S-9

S-7

American Hudson Valley long fowler with curly-maple stock and brass furniture. It has a British lock marked with the maker's name, Farmer. Length: 6 feet 10 inches.

S-8

Hudson Valley flintlock fowler, full stocked in cherry. The barrel is marked in large letters "Cornelius Wynkoop." Cornelius Wynkoop's will, dated September 1739, bequeaths this same gun to his son, also named Cornelius. Length: 6 feet 3 inches.

S-9

Hudson Valley fowler with curly-maple stock and early doglock, circa 1680. This piece is from the Hasbrouck family, which owned the Washington Headquarters house in Newburgh, N.Y. Its large size indicates that it was probably used as a rampart or fortress defense weapon. Length: 7 feet 3 inches.

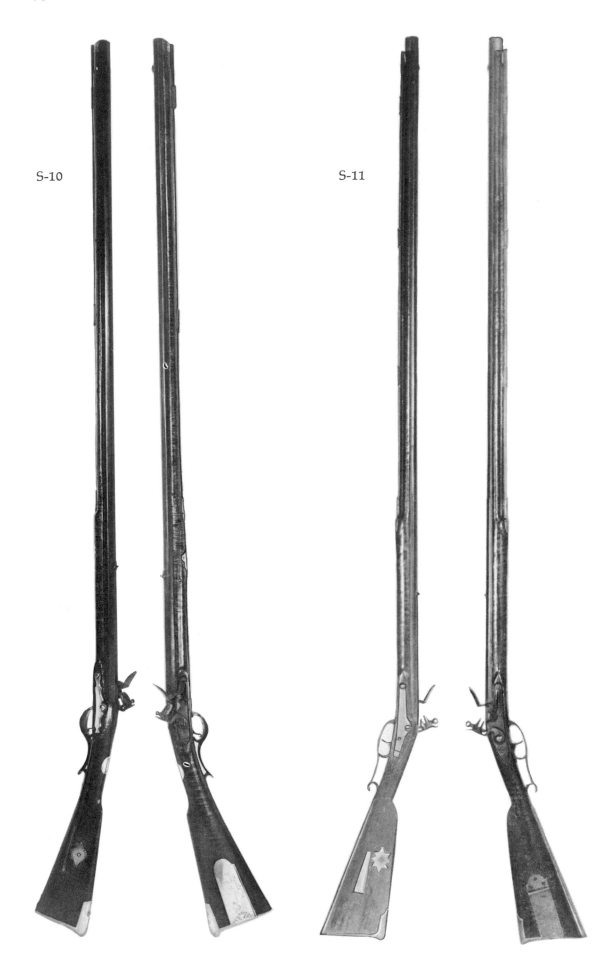

S-10

S-11

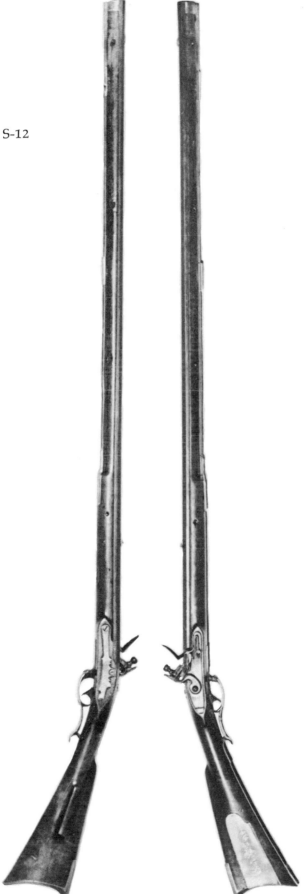

S-12

S-10

Flintlock Kentucky rifle stocked in curly maple, made in Pennsylvania by J. Daub about 1775. The brass patch-box cover is fitted with a hinge running lengthwise and engraved "Mad by J. Daub." Length: 5 feet.

S-11

Flintlock American or Kentucky rifle, with 47 ½-inch barrel, part octagonal and part round. The .62 caliber barrel is smooth bore, but was probably cut from a smaller rifle bore. Curly-maple stock is relief-carved on the butt with a bone cheek-rest and also bone on the underside of the butt. The brass patch-box lid is engraved "John Schneider Mͬ 19, 1776." The lockplate is engraved "J.S."
Length: 5 feet 3 inches.

S-12

Kentucky rifle with curly-maple stock, carried in the Revolutionary War by Nicholas Allen of Virginia, who served under Colonel Daniel Morgan, leader of Morgan's Riflemen. The mountings and side-hinged patch box are brass. The sideplate is engraved with the initials "N A" and the date "1770." This rifle is attributed to Jacobus Scout, a gunsmith working during colonial times at Davisville, Pennsylvania. Length: 4 feet 11 inches.

S-13

S-14

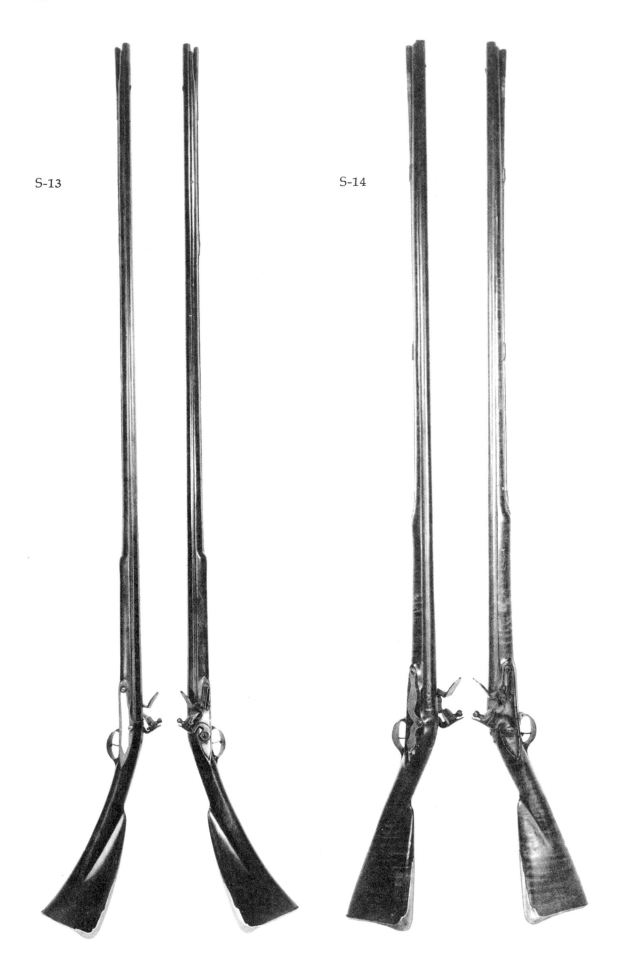

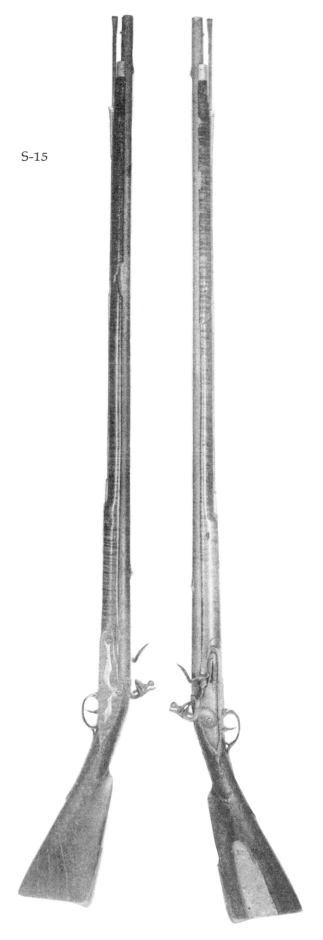

S-15

S-13

Long New England fowling piece stocked in apple or pear wood, with brass mountings. The lock is stamped "Ketland" on the inside. This gun is believed to have been made by Jeremiah Smith of Lime Rock, Rhode Island prior to the Revolution, and is in almost new condition. This is typical of the personal weapons that many New Englanders brought into military service with them at the outbreak of the Revolution.
Length: 6 feet 1½ inches.

S-14

American fowler-musket, circa 1775, with maple stock and imported 52½-inch British barrel. The lock and furniture were salvaged from British muskets. This was a typical militia weapon, and did not take a bayonet.
Length: 5 feet 9½ inches.

S-15

Flintlock small-bore musket showing influence of the Kentucky rifle. This gun was made in Pennsylvania around 1770, and is stocked in curly maple, with some relief carving on the stock. The brass patch-box lid, hinged lengthwise along the bottom, is engraved "Liberty or Death." The 42-inch round barrel, .62 caliber smooth bore is fitted with front and rear sights and a bayonet lug.
Length: 4 feet 9 inches.

**BRITISH
SHOULDER ARMS**

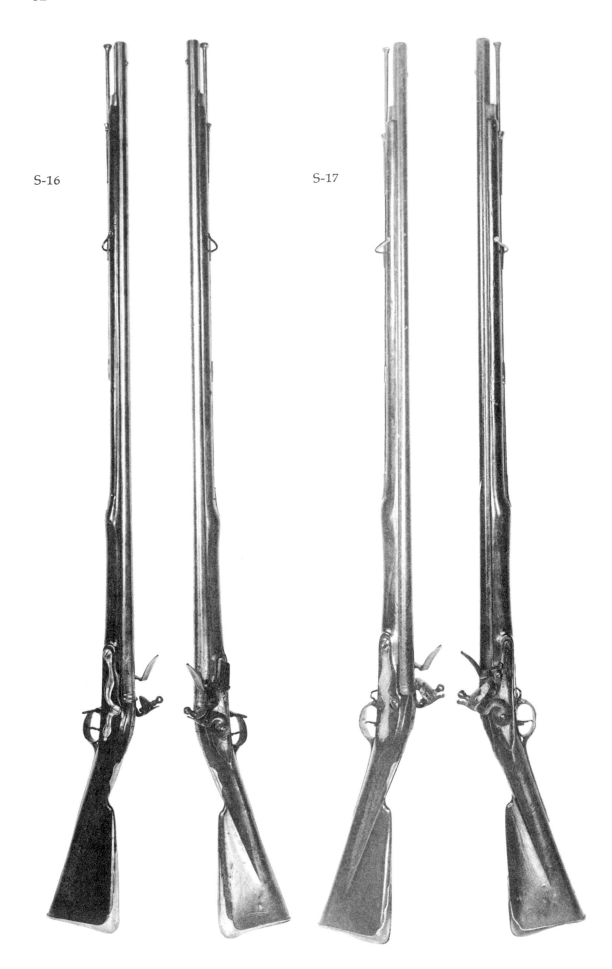

S-16

S-17

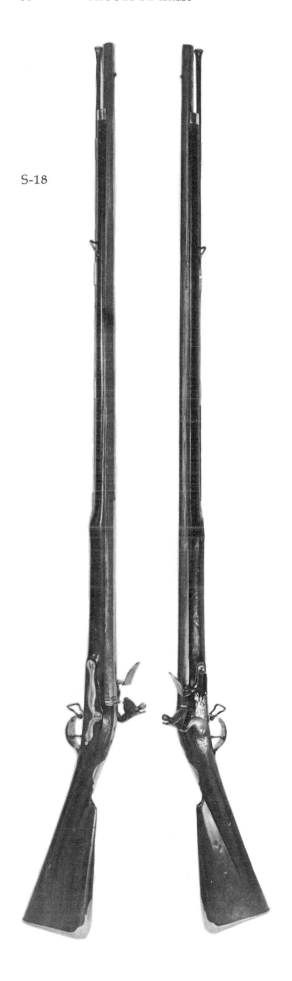

S-18

S-16

British Brown Bess flintlock musket with 46-inch barrel. "Grice 1760" is engraced on the lockplate, together with the Royal Cypher and broad arrow mark, which denotes government ownership. Length: 5 feet 1½ inches.

S-17

Second Model British Brown Bess with 42-inch barrel, circa 1770. The lock is marked "Tower" with crown over "GR," and the barrel is marked "14th Regiment." This was the standard British weapon of the American Revolution. Length: 4 feet 10 inches.

S-18

British Brown Bess light infantry musket with 42-inch barrel. This musket is fitted with First Model Brown Bess furniture, and the maker's name, Grice, and date 1759, are engraved on the lockplate. Length: 4 feet 10 inches.

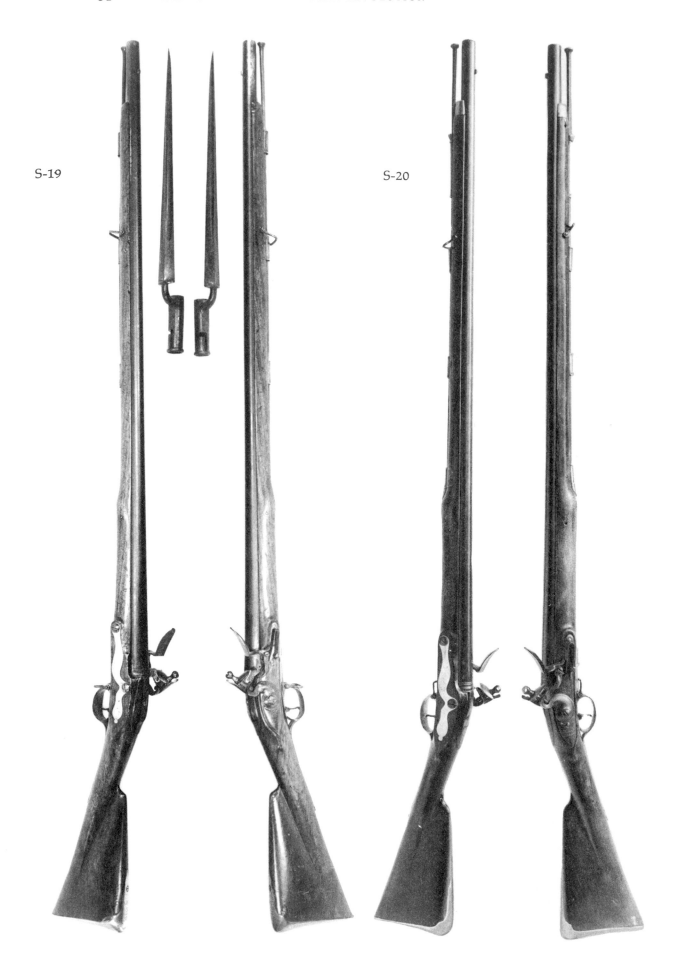

S-19

S-20

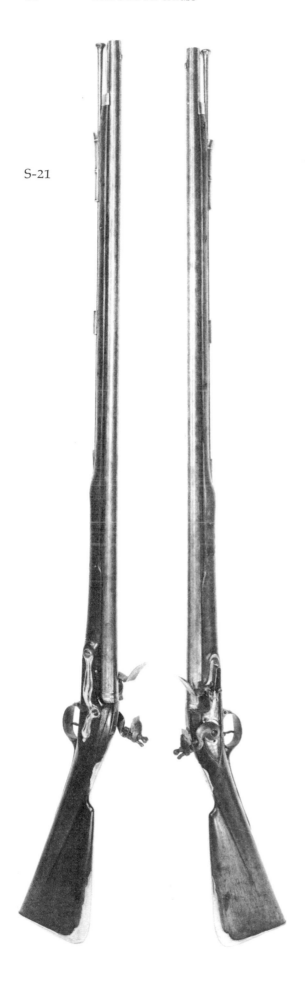

S-21

S-19

*British Brown Bess marine or militia
flintlock musket made by William Grice
in Birmingham, with the name Grice and
the date 1759 inscribed on the
lockplate. This musket, complete with
its original bayonet, bears the
military marking "3/53" to match the
identical marking on the tang of the
brass butt plate.
Length: 4 feet 10 inches.*

S-20

*Second Model British Brown Bess made
at Dublin Castle, circa 1775, with a
42-inch .80 caliber barrel marked "55th
Regiment." Dublin Castle muskets are
somewhat rarer than the ones made at
the Tower. Length: 4 feet 9 inches.*

S-21

*British artillery carbine with First
Model Brown Bess brass furniture and
36-inch barrel. The lockplate bears
the contractor's name, Wilets, and the
date 1762. The escutcheon is engraved
with the number 56.
Length: 4 feet 3½ inches.*

S-22

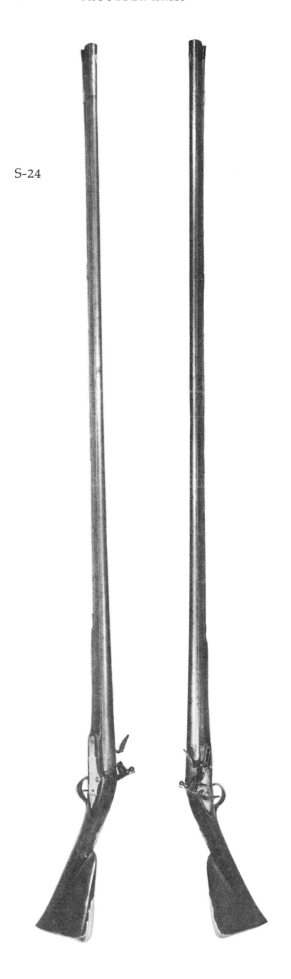

S-24

S-22

Officer's breech-loading Ferguson rifle, shown with its 25½-inch long bayonet with wide flat blade. This rifle was presented by Ferguson to Captain Frederick De Peyster, who was Ferguson's second in command in the southern campaign. The obverse side of the butt is fitted with a metal plate bearing an inscription concerning the presentation. Length: 4 feet 1½ inches.

S-23

British enlisted man's breech-loading Ferguson rifle. Length: 4 feet 1 inch.

S-24

Extremely long English fowler with brass mountings, made by Thomas Ketland in Birmingham, circa 1770. Many guns of this type were exported to colonial America. The sight at the end of the 60½-inch barrel is made of silver in the form of a grotesque mask. Length: 7 feet 6 inches.

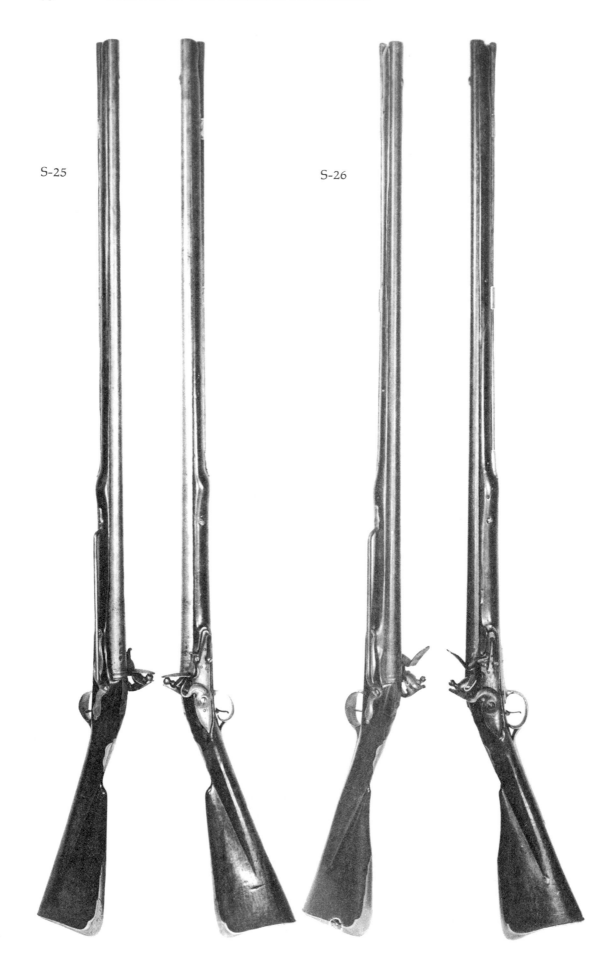

S-25

S-26

S-27

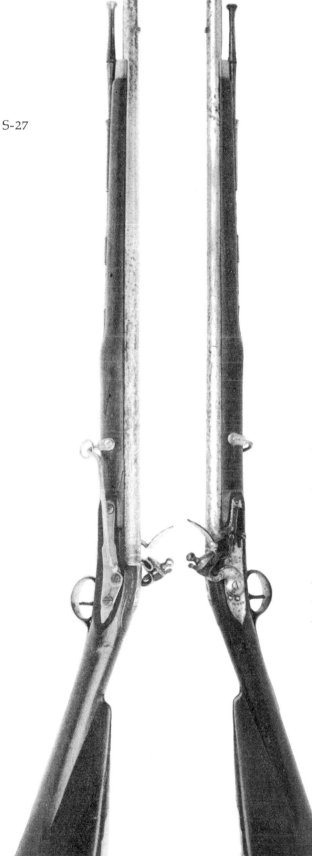

S-25

Officer's cavalry carbine of the type carried in the light dragoons, with 37-inch barrel. The lock is signed by Buckmaster, a private maker, circa 1760. Length: 4 feet 5 inches.

S-26

British light dragoon carbine with .65 caliber, 37-inch long barrel. The lock is marked with the maker's name, Edge, and dated 1762.
Length: 4 feet 4½ inches.

S-27

British Elliott cavalry carbine with 28-inch barrel, circa 1780. Note the saddle ring and bar fitting. The ring snapped into a sliding swivel clip on the trooper's shoulder belt. There is some question as to whether carbines of this type were used in America during the Revolution. Nevertheless, the one above is being presented as an example of a carbine with 28-inch barrel. Length: 3 feet 8 inches.

S-28   S-29

S-30

S-28

British flintlock blunderbuss with brass barrel, made in London around 1770 by William Walsingham. The decorative brass furniture and fine quality indicate that it was probably carried by an officer. The sling swivels denote military use. Length: 2 feet 8 inches.

S-29

British military flintlock blunderbuss with steel barrel and sling swivels, made by R. Watkin around 1740. The brass furniture is the same as that used on the First Model British Brown Bess musket. Length: 3 feet 4 inches.

S-30

British Sea Service flintlock blunderbuss with 16-inch brass barrel, circa 1760. The lock is signed by the maker, Bumford. Length: 2 feet 7 inches.

FRENCH
SHOULDER ARMS

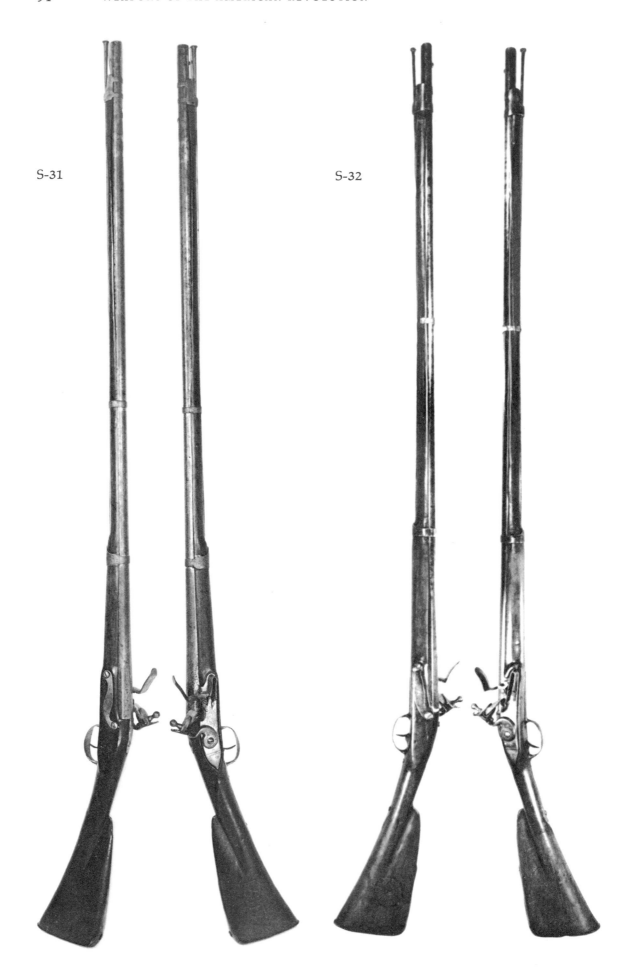

S-31

S-32

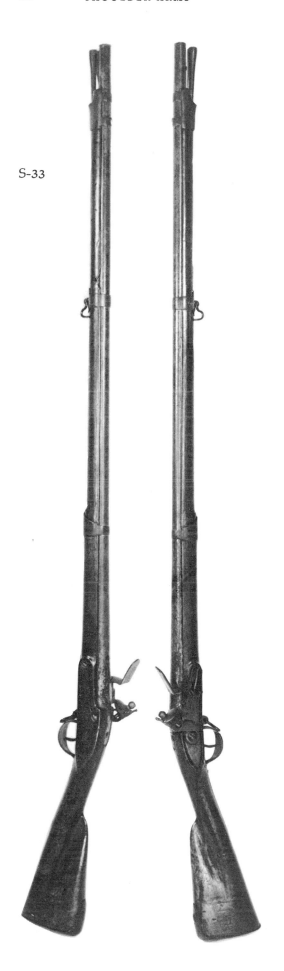

S-33

S-31

*French model 1728 flintlock musket with
iron furniture, made at St. Etienne,
with .75 caliber, 47-inch barrel.
This was the first model to be banded.
Length: 5 feet 2 inches.*

S-32

*French model 1746 flintlock musket
with iron furniture and 46½-inch barrel.
The side sling swivels, originally
located behind the side plate and on
the center band, are missing.
Length: 5 feet 2 inches.*

S-33

*French model 1763 infantry musket with
.75 caliber, 44½-inch barrel, made at
St. Etienne. The lock is 6¼ inches long.
This was the most widely used French
weapon of the Revolution.
Length: 5 feet.*

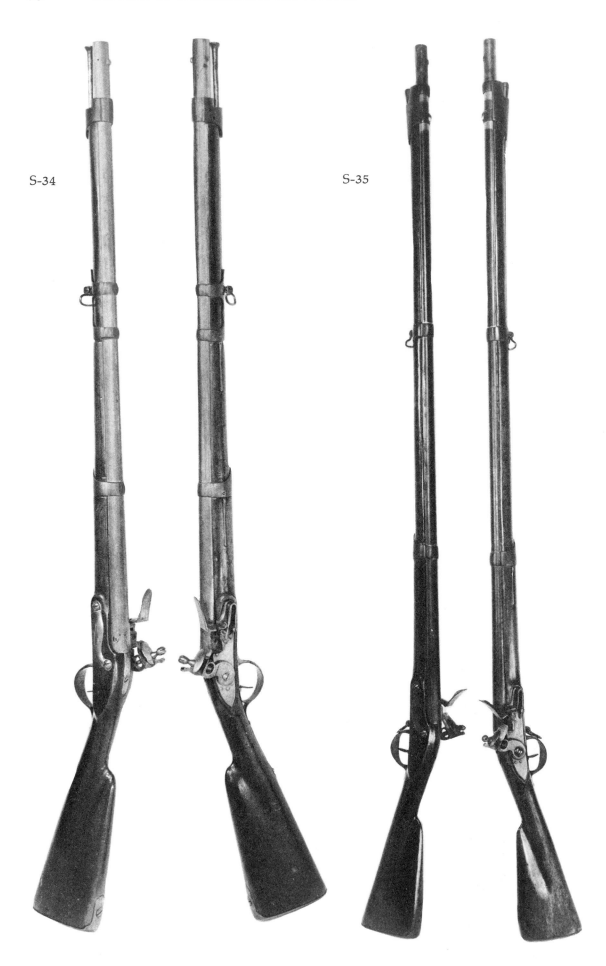

S-34

S-35

S-36

S-34

French model 1763 flintlock musketoon with steel furniture. This type of weapon was probably carried by grenadiers or possibly cavalrymen. The front band is an improper replacement. Length: 3 feet 8½ inches.

S-35

French model 1766 infantry musket with .75 caliber, 44½-inch barrel and 6¼-inch long lockplate engraved "Charleville." Charleville muskets of this style served as the pattern for the first official United States government muskets made after the Revolutionary War. Length: 5 feet.

S-36

French flintlock artillery carbine, model 1766, with "US" surcharged, or stamped, at the rear of the lockplate. Length: 4 feet 6 inches.

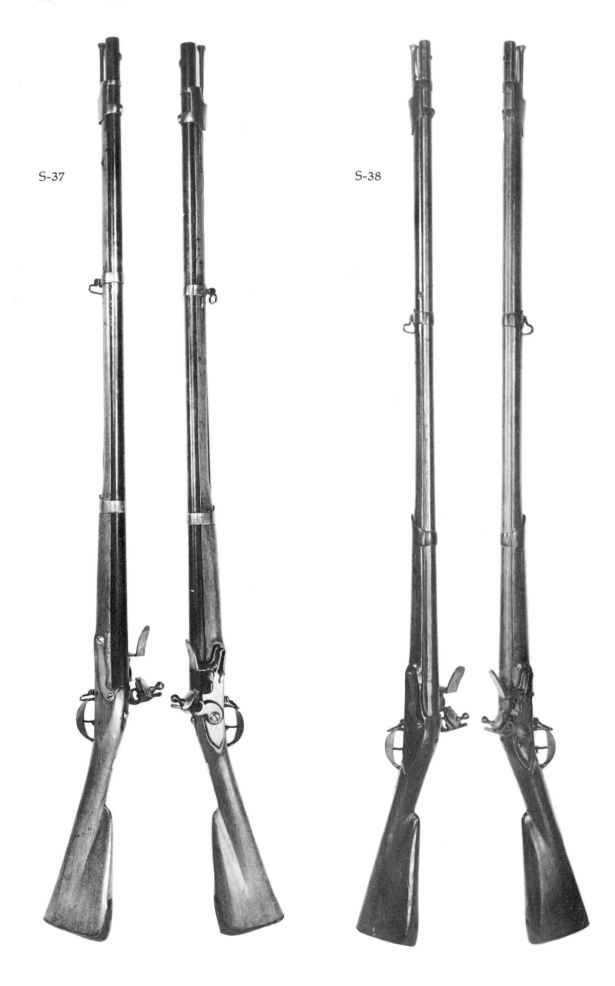

S-37

S-38

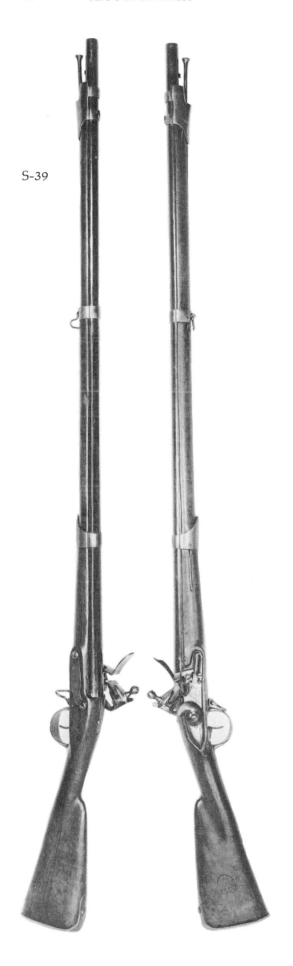

S-39

S-37

*French officer's or sergeant's
flintlock musket with 38-inch barrel.
It is unusual in that the steel barrel
bands, sideplate, lockplate, and part
of the trigger guard are covered with a
sort of brass veneer. This is
basically the model 1763 type, with
minor variations.
Length: 4 feet 6 inches.*

S-38

*French model 1774 flintlock musket
made at Charleville with .75 caliber,
44½-inch barrel and 6¼-inch long lock.
The stock is stamped "United States"
to denote American government
ownership. Length: 5 feet.*

S-39

*French flintlock Charleville musket,
model 1774. Length: 4 feet 11 inches.*

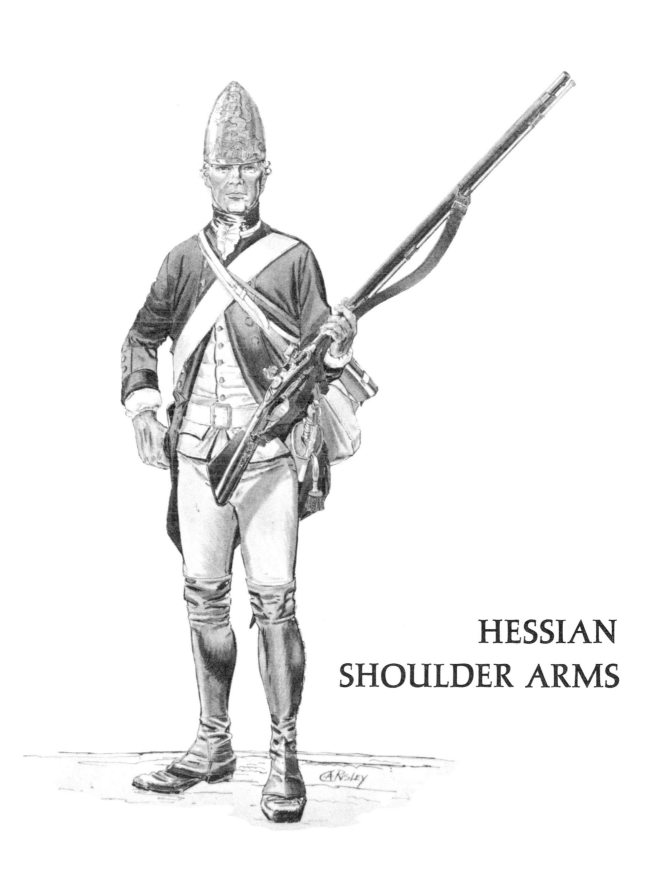

HESSIAN
SHOULDER ARMS

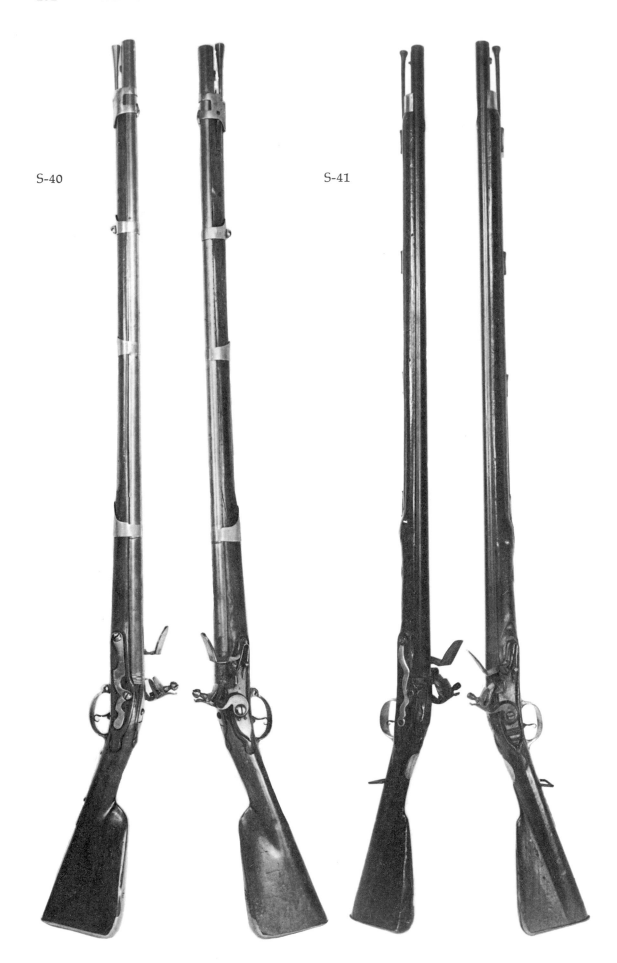

S-40

S-41

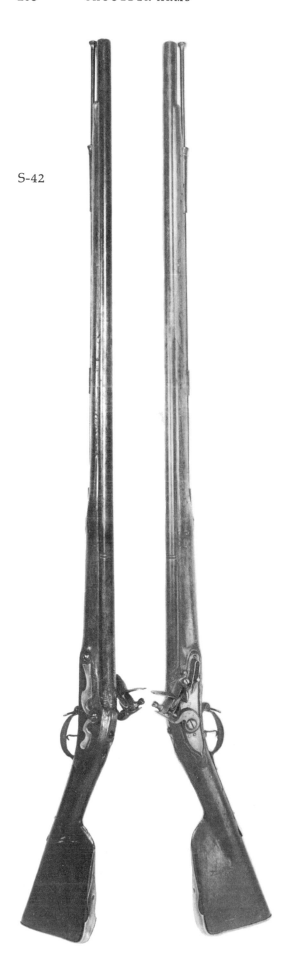

S-42

S-40

Mid-eighteenth-century banded German flintlock musket with brass mountings, in unusually fine condition.
Length: 4 feet 8 inches.

S-41

Rare Prussian flintlock musket with brass mountings and ten pins securing barrel to wood forestock. Prussian muskets had lighter lines than the typical German musket.
Length: 4 feet 8½ inches.

S-42

Pin-fastened German, or Hessian, flintlock musket with brass mountings, circa 1760. The barrel appears at one time to have been fastened to the wood stock by brass bands.
Length: 4 feet 8 inches.

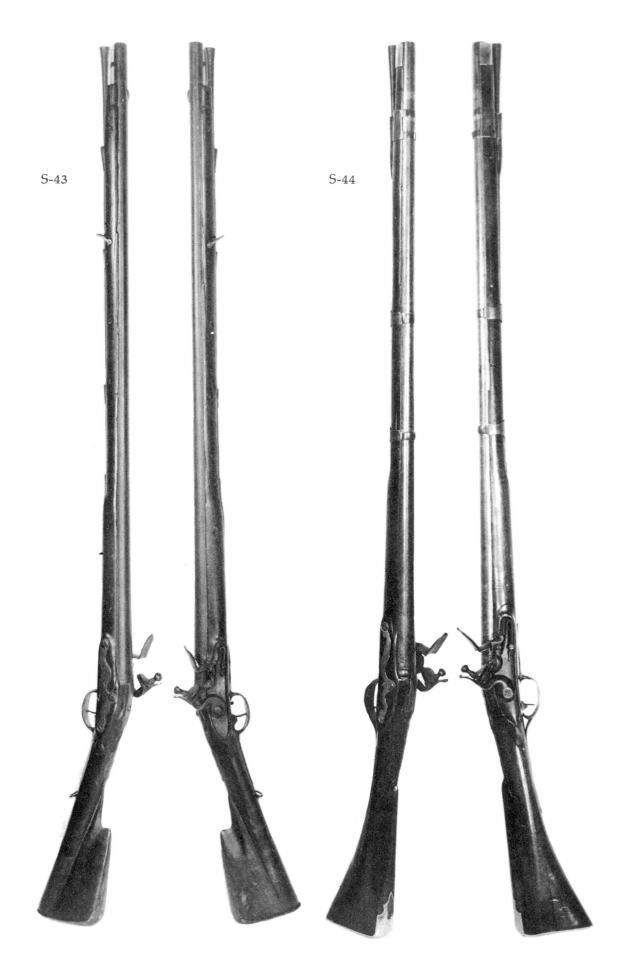

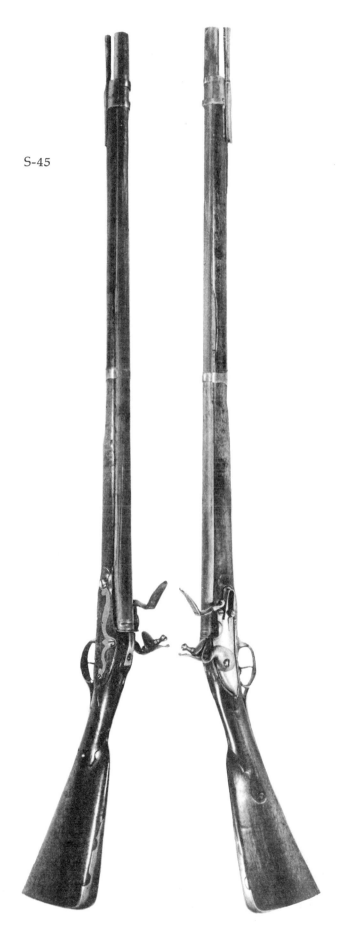

S-45

S-43

*German pin-fastened musket with
.80 caliber, 43-inch barrel,
circa 1750. The high comb is typical
of the period. Many of these arms
were captured in the Revolution.
Length: 4 feet 10 inches.*

S-44

*German rifled carbine, made in Suhl,
with .75 caliber, 36-inch barrel,
circa 1770. This type was carried by
some of the mounted Hessians during
the Revolutionary War.
Length: 4 feet 3 inches.*

S-45

*German rifled flintlock carbine
with brass mountings, circa 1770.
Length: 4 feet 3 inches.*

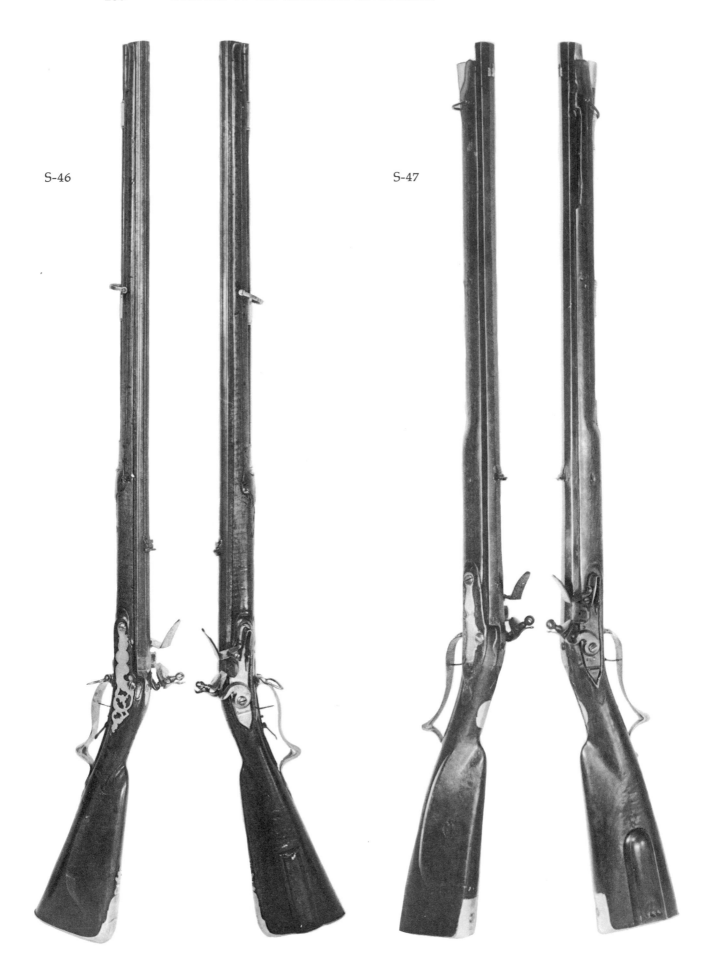

S-46

S-47

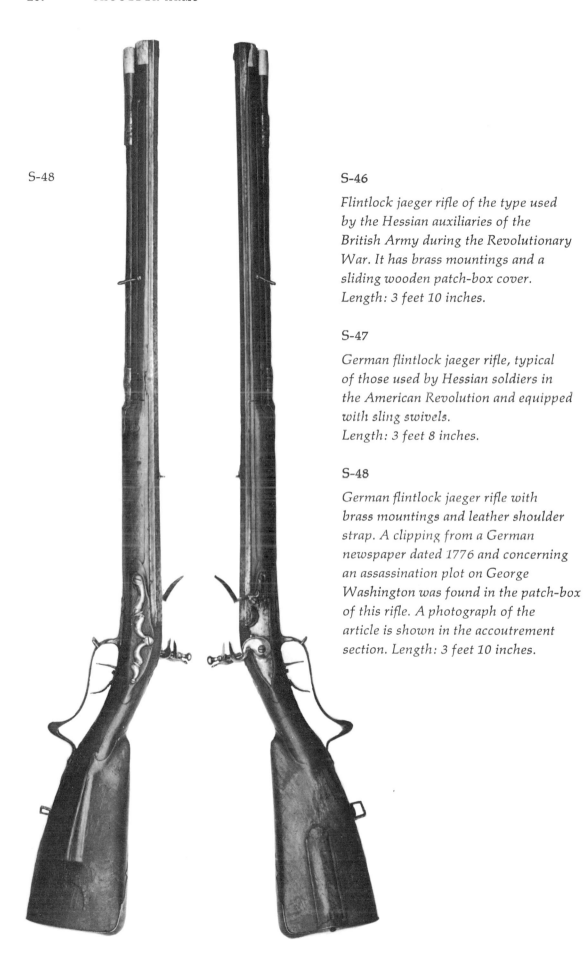

S-48

S-46

Flintlock jaeger rifle of the type used by the Hessian auxiliaries of the British Army during the Revolutionary War. It has brass mountings and a sliding wooden patch-box cover. Length: 3 feet 10 inches.

S-47

German flintlock jaeger rifle, typical of those used by Hessian soldiers in the American Revolution and equipped with sling swivels. Length: 3 feet 8 inches.

S-48

German flintlock jaeger rifle with brass mountings and leather shoulder strap. A clipping from a German newspaper dated 1776 and concerning an assassination plot on George Washington was found in the patch-box of this rifle. A photograph of the article is shown in the accoutrement section. Length: 3 feet 10 inches.

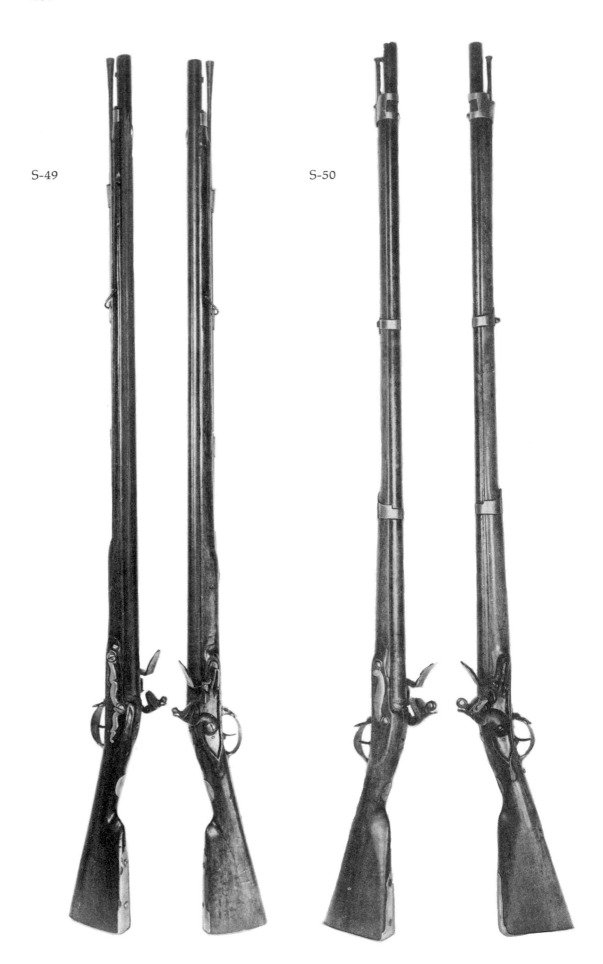

S-49

S-50

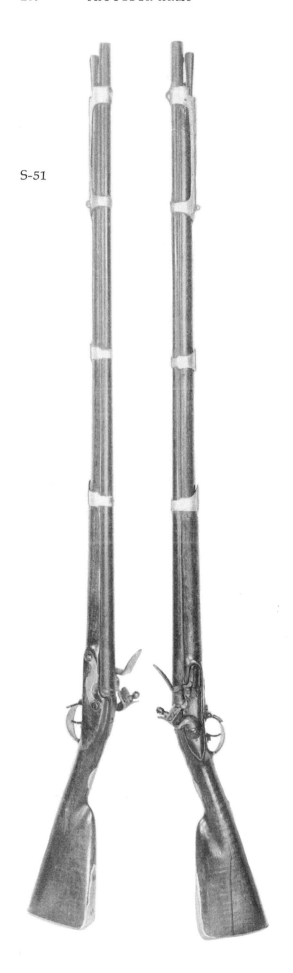

S-51

S-49

Dutch flintlock musket with brass mountings, of the type purchased from Holland by Benjamin Franklin for use by the American colonial troops in the Revolutionary War.
Length: 4 feet 6 inches.

S-50

Revolutionary War Dutch flintlock musket. The bottom of the butt plate is engraved "John Douglas, 3rd Regt., Alby Coty, N. Y. Mila. 1780."
Length: 4 feet 11 inches.

S-51

Dutch fusil with 41-inch barrel, circa 1775. The lock is marked "Thone, Amsterdam." It is typical of the arms bought in Holland by Benjamin Franklin. Length: 4 feet 7 inches.

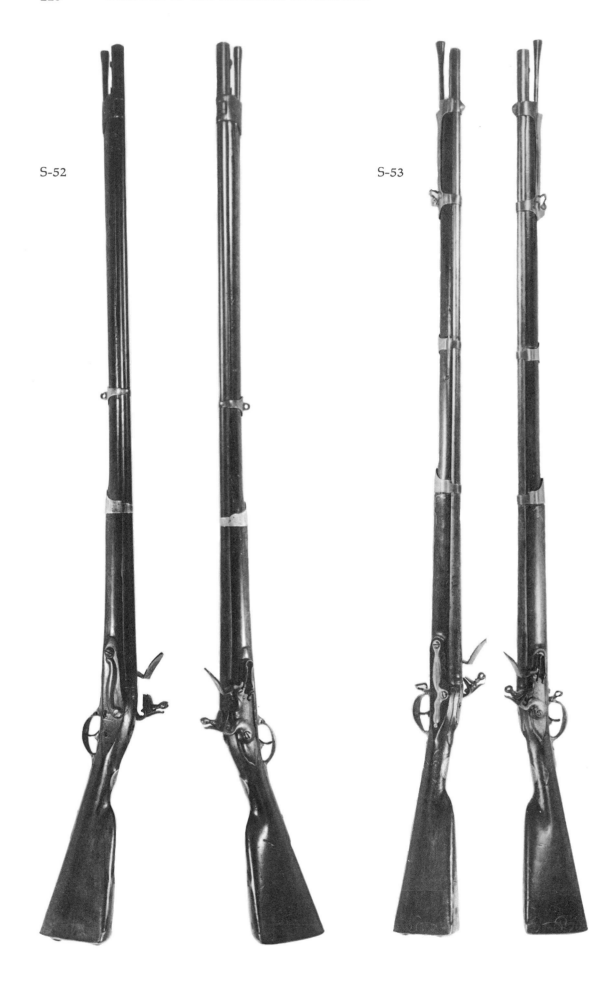

S-52

S-53

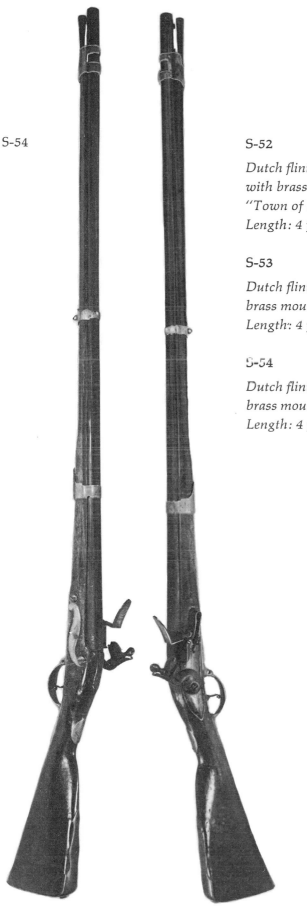

S-54

S-52

Dutch flintlock musket, circa 1770,
with brass mountings.
"Town of Boston" is carved on the butt.
Length: 4 feet 6 inches.

S-53

Dutch flintlock officer's fusil with
brass mountings, circa 1775.
Length: 4 feet 7 inches.

S-54

Dutch flintlock musket with
brass mountings, circa 1770.
Length: 4 feet 6 inches.

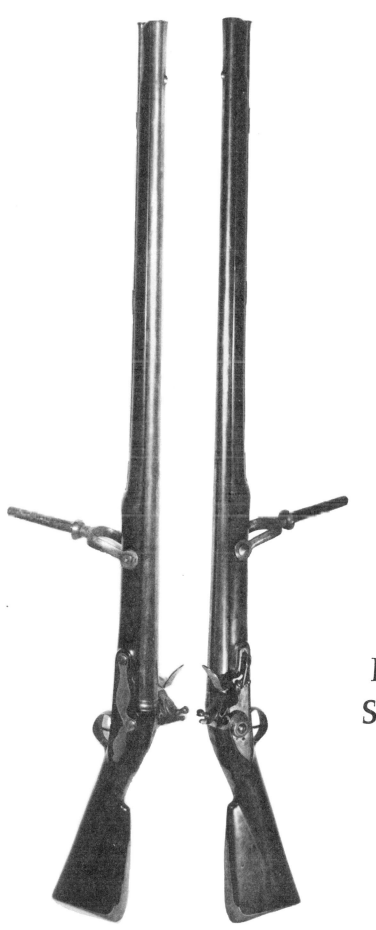

British flintlock naval or rampart gun with brass mountings and a swivel bar, circa 1770. The 54-inch-long barrel has a caliber of 15/16 inches. Except for the large size, this piece is almost identical in design to the second model Brown Bess musket. The lockplate is marked "Tower" with the broad arrow, and the maker's initials "H. N." on the lock interior probably stand for Henry Nock. Guns of this type were generally used on small boats, or for defense of hastily erected forts. Length: 6 feet ¾ inch.

MISCELLANEOUS SHOULDER ARMS

S-55

S-56

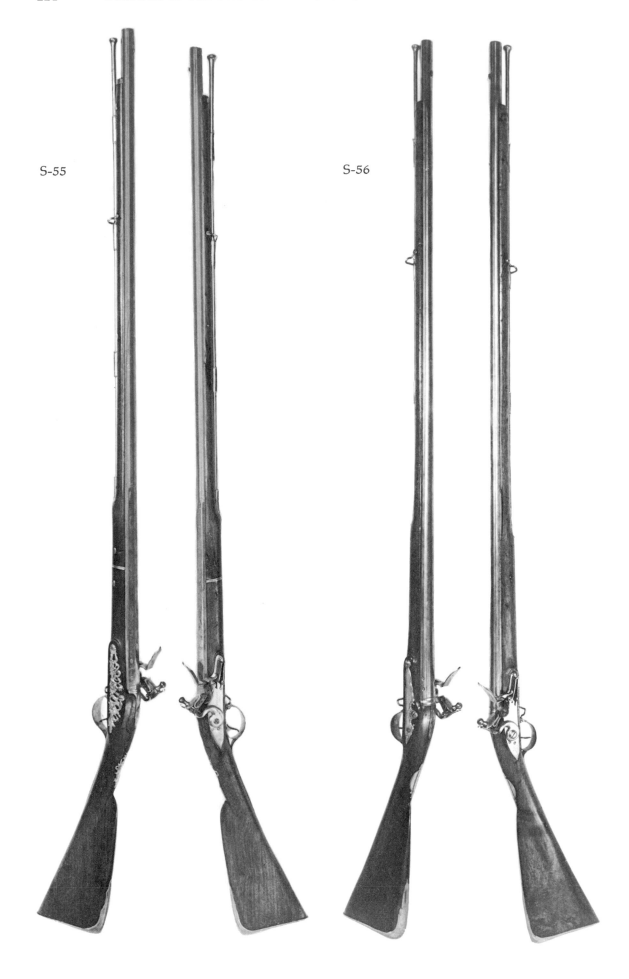

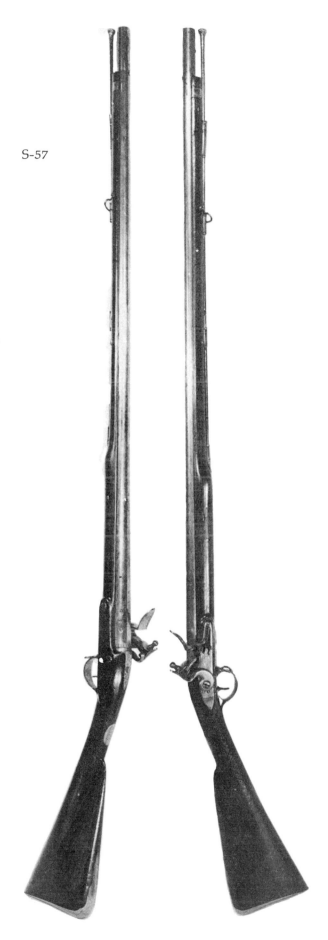

S-57

S-55

Flintlock takedown type officer's fusil made by Thomas Ketland in England about 1775. It has an unusually fine brass sideplate and escutcheon decorated in a military motif. The frizzen spring is fitted with the early large roller-wheel feature. Length: 4 feet 6 inches.

S-56

Flintlock officer's fusil with brass mountings, made by Jover in England about 1770. The butt-plate tang is engraved with a bow and arrow, which may indicate use in colonial America. Length: 4 feet 10 inches.

S-57

Flintlock officer's fusil with steel mountings made by Jover in England around 1780. This fusil has the early-type checkering on the wood stock. It also has sling swivels and bayonet lug on the underside of the barrel. Length: 4 feet 5 inches.

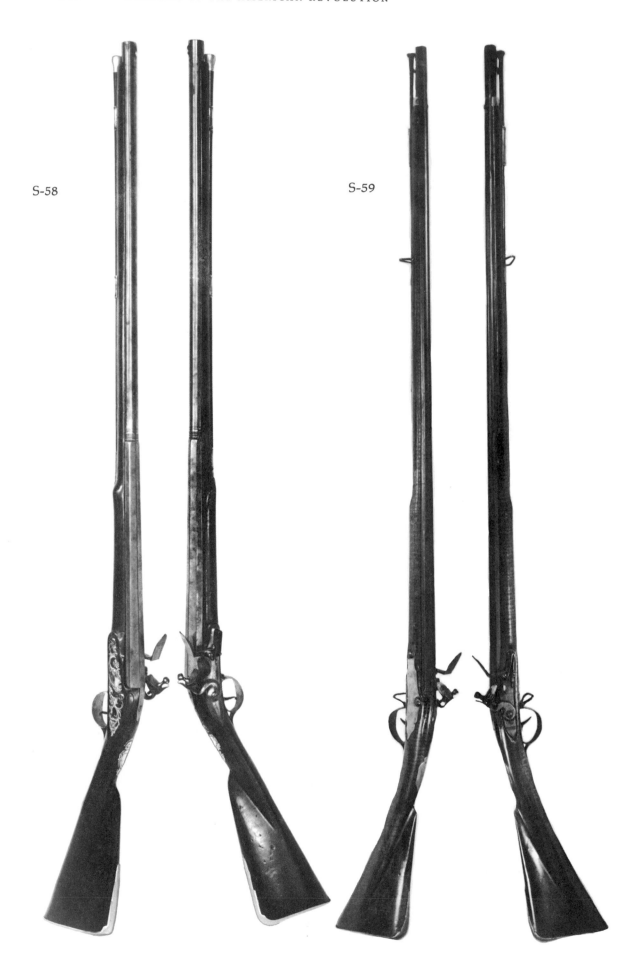

S-58

S-59

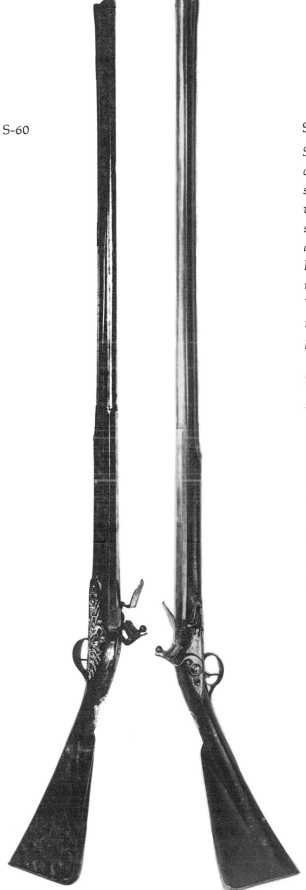

S-60

S-58

Silver-mounted officer's fusil with canted stock. The cant enabled the shooter to sight with his left eye while holding the gun to his right shoulder. This gun was made in England, although it is fitted with a German lock and barrel, probably at the request of the original owner. The silver furniture is almost identical to that found on contemporary pistols. Length: 4 feet 2 inches.

S-59

American flintlock officer's fusil with curly-maple stock and brass mountings, circa 1775. The bayonet lug is located on the underside of the barrel. Length: 4 feet 9 inches.

S-60

British silver-mounted flintlock fowling piece. The military decoration of the sideplate and escutcheon could indicate an officer's weapon. Made by J. King in London about 1770. Length: 4 feet 5 inches.

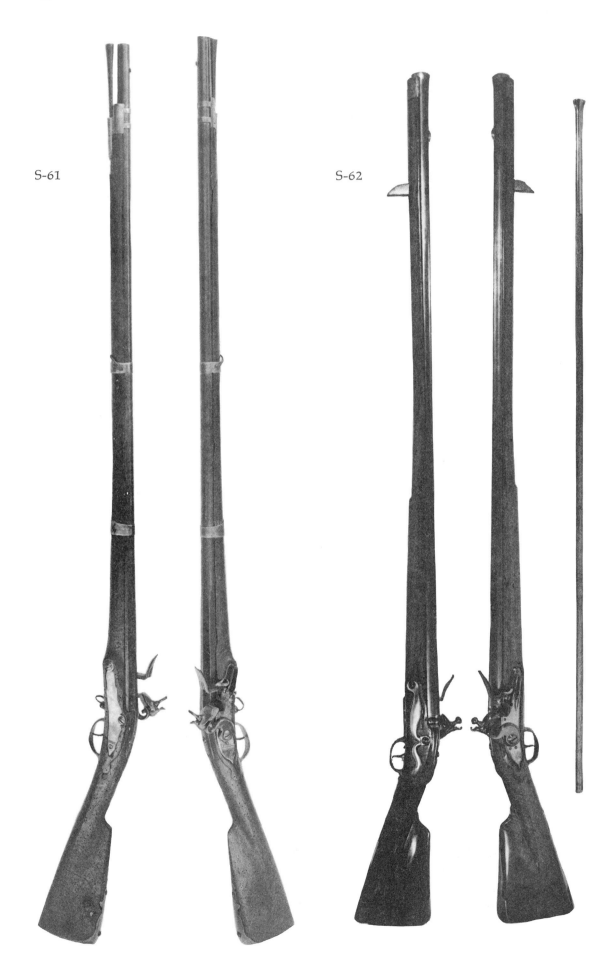

S-61

S-62

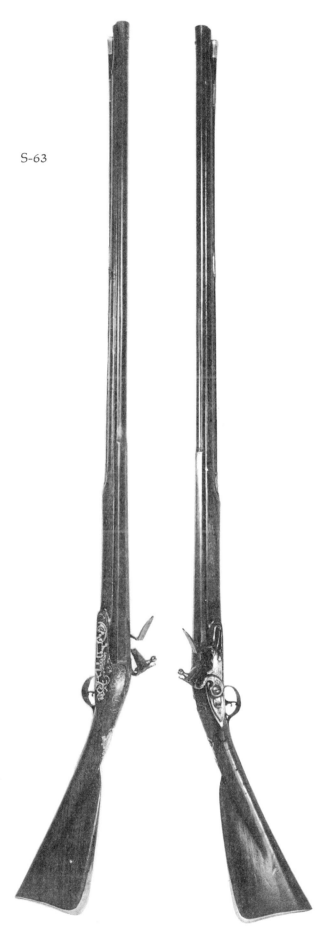

S-63

S-61

Spanish musket, circa 1750, brass-banded and similar to Germanic pieces except for the distinctive circular top jaw screw. Length: 5 feet.

S-62

Dutch wall gun, circa 1720. Wall guns and the later swivel guns were essentially very large muskets, intended as intermediary weapons between musketry and artillery. Such weapons were rested on the stud under the barrel when being fired. This piece weighs 25 pounds, and fires a 6 bore or .95 caliber ball. Length: 6 feet 3 inches.

S-63

Silver-mounted English fowling piece made by Thomas Ketland about 1775. The silver furniture and general styling are unusually beautiful and graceful. Although not a military piece, it is included as a fine example of a Revolutionary-period fowler. Length: 4 feet 7 inches.

EDGED WEAPONS

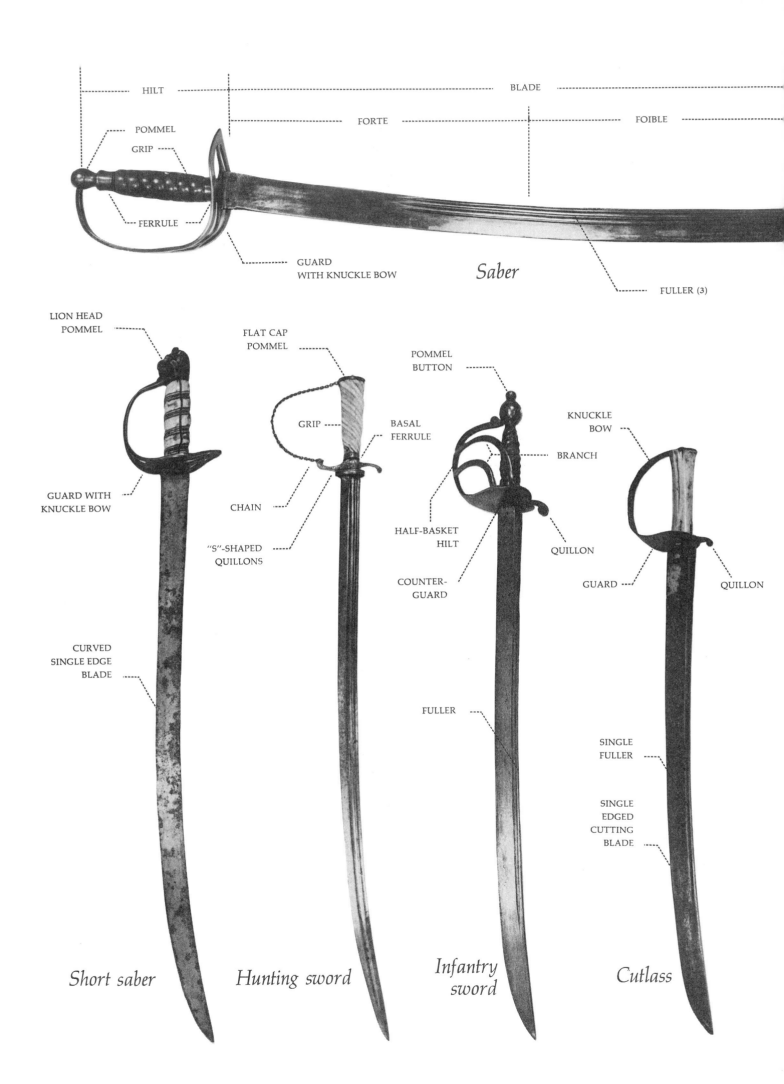

HILT   BLADE

POMMEL

FORTE   FOIBLE

GRIP

FERRULE

GUARD
WITH KNUCKLE BOW

Saber

FULLER (3)

LION HEAD
POMMEL

FLAT CAP
POMMEL

POMMEL
BUTTON

KNUCKLE
BOW

GRIP

BASAL
FERRULE

BRANCH

GUARD WITH
KNUCKLE BOW

CHAIN

HALF-BASKET
HILT

QUILLON

"S"-SHAPED
QUILLONS

COUNTER-
GUARD

GUARD

QUILLON

CURVED
SINGLE EDGE
BLADE

FULLER

SINGLE
FULLER

SINGLE
EDGED
CUTTING
BLADE

Short saber   *Hunting sword*   *Infantry sword*   *Cutlass*

NOMENCLATURE OF EDGED WEAPONS

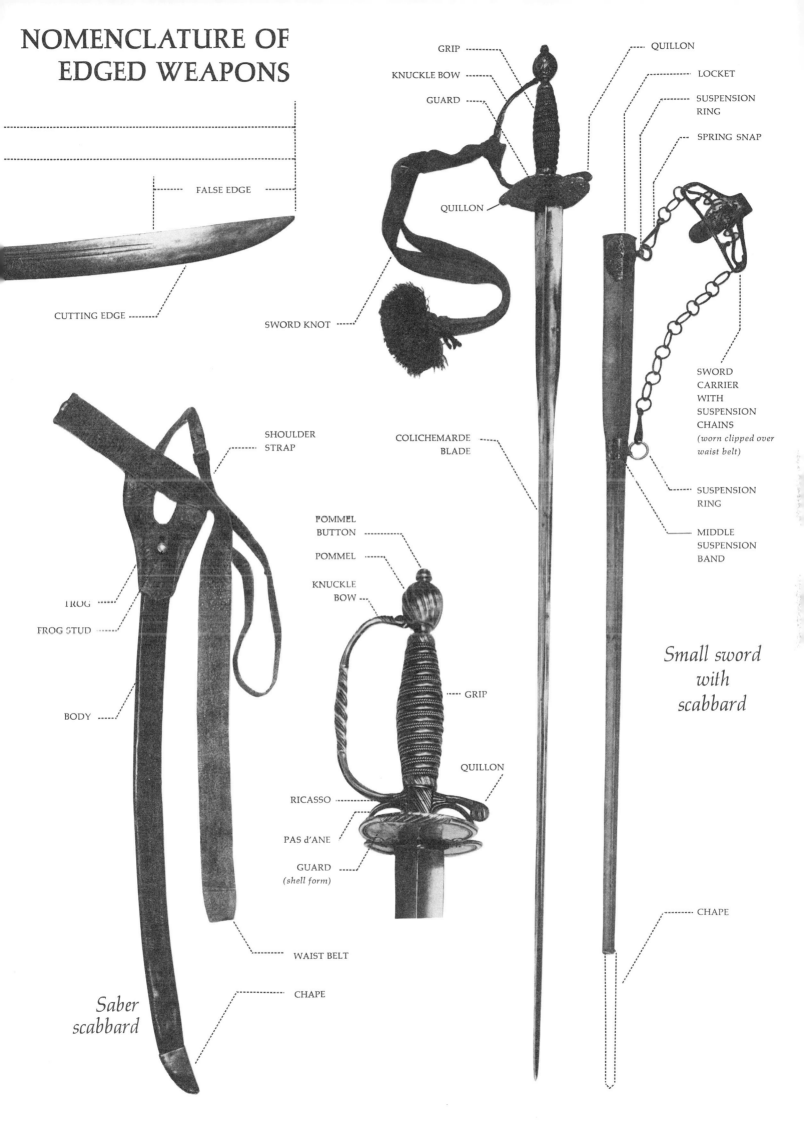

FALSE EDGE

CUTTING EDGE

GRIP

KNUCKLE BOW

GUARD

QUILLON

SWORD KNOT

SHOULDER STRAP

FROG

FROG STUD

BODY

POMMEL BUTTON

POMMEL

KNUCKLE BOW

COLICHEMARDE BLADE

GRIP

QUILLON

RICASSO

PAS d'ANE

GUARD
(shell form)

WAIST BELT

CHAPE

Saber scabbard

QUILLON

LOCKET

SUSPENSION RING

SPRING SNAP

SWORD CARRIER WITH SUSPENSION CHAINS
(worn clipped over waist belt)

SUSPENSION RING

MIDDLE SUSPENSION BAND

Small sword with scabbard

CHAPE

The edged weapons used by officers and enlisted men during the Revolutionary War fall into five general categories—small swords, sabers, hunting swords, infantry and artillery swords, and cutlasses.

SMALL SWORDS

The small sword was by far the most popular arm used by the officers who fought in the war. It originated in France during the latter part of the seventeenth century as a civilian dress or court sword for gentlemen. The degree of artistic embellishment and expert workmanship was usually proportional to the wealth and status of the owner. Many officers brought their civilian swords into military service with them, just as they brought along their personal pistols and shoulder arms.

Small sword blades were made in many shapes. The cross section was hexagonal at first, then diamond-shaped, and later triangular. During the latter part of the seventeenth century the colichemarde blade was developed. It had an unusually wide hollow triangular section at the hilt, which extended approximately one-fourth of the blade length. From this broad section, the blade tapered to an unusually sharp point, making this sword effective only as a thrusting weapon. The excessively broad forte section of the colichemarde blade gave added strength against breakage. Also popular for officers' small swords was the triangular-shaped single-edged blade, which had a constant taper from the hilt to the tip. This blade was essentially a cutting sword; however, the tip was double-edged for about 6 inches or more (called a false edge), thus making it both a cutting and thrusting weapon. Grooves, known as fullers, were usually cut into the blade's surface, to make the sword lighter as well as better balanced.

The decorations on the blade were in many forms, some having the British Royal Cypher or crown, panoplies of arms, patriotic inscriptions, and floral or geometric designs. Brass was the most common metal used in hilts, followed by steel, iron, silver, and on occasion, gold.

Small swords were usually carried in brown or black leather scabbards. Parchment scabbards made from sheep or goat skin were also widely used, particularly for the colichemarde blade. Fittings of silver, brass, or steel were usually found at the tip, middle, and throat of the scabbard.

One distinguishing feature of American-made small swords was their plain lines which were in contrast to the heavily chased and engraved metalwork on their European counterparts. They nevertheless bore a strong resemblance to the British sword, since many of the men who wore them before the Revolution in colonial America were in the service of the Crown.

The small sword, in addition to being an ornament of beauty, was also a formidable fighting weapon. Many officers wore their swords at all times, and in the absence of firearms, relied upon them as their only means of defense.

SABERS

The saber was undoubtedly the most important weapon carried by horse troopers or dragoons. Just as the bayonet was the deciding factor in battles between infantry units, the saber determined the outcome of many encounters between cavalry troops.

Early in the eighteenth century the heavy basket-hilted broadsword was very popular with horsemen. Later, the saber was shortened and a much simpler and lighter hilt was provided in the form of half-basket and stirrup-hilt types. Some had a straight blade, but the slightly curved blade was much more widely used.

Probably the most distinctive edged weapon made by American swordsmiths was the heavy saber. It was indispensable for mounted officers, and some infantry officers preferred it to the small sword. Heavy sabers were sturdy fighting weapons, and while not embellished with delicate artistic work as were small swords or hunting swords, they were very handsome pieces.

In both the British and American cavalry units it is very difficult to differentiate between sabers carried by officers and those carried by enlisted men. Frequently the colonel of a British cavalry regiment purchased identical sabers for distribution to his men, and often officers and enlisted men selected from the same supply. This was not standard procedure, however, and just as the pistols and shoulder arms of the officer were of a fancier grade, it would be safe to assume that the finer quality saber belonged to an officer.

In America, light cavalry officers, as well as enlisted men, used a conglomeration of sabers from many sources, and little uniformity can be found. The many surviving examples to be found today indicate that the saber was made in considerable quantity by American swordsmiths.

One very interesting type of pommel infrequently found on some sabers was the dog head. It appears to have been made for a few years just prior to the Revolution, and was possibly an adaptation of the popular lion-head pommel following the break with England.

The horse soldier's dependence on the saber is probably best expressed by a cavalry captain from Massachusetts named Epaphras

Hoyt who fought in the Revolution. In his *A Treatise on the Military Art*, published in 1798, he wrote:

It is generally agreed by experienced officers, that fire arms are seldom of any great utility to cavalry in an engagement, while they are drawn up in regiments, squadrons, or other considerable bodies: Indeed there is little hope of success from any who begin their attack with the fire of carbines or pistols; numerous examples could be cited from military history to show their inefficiency. It is by the right use of the sword they are to expect victory: This is indisputably the most formidable and essentially useful weapon of cavalry: Nothing decides an engagement sooner than charging briskly with this weapon in hand. By this mode of attack, a body of cavalry will generally rout one that receives it with pistols ready to fire.

Some officers carried a light saber that had a blade 27 to 30 inches long. The construction of these sabers was pretty much along the same line as that of the heavy saber, except for size. A typical short saber had a true knuckle bow; that is, a guard made from heavy sheet brass or steel to resemble a knuckle bow which divides as it turns up toward the blade, having a branch on either side and a transverse connecting bar at the midpoint where they cross the blade. The three branches come together on the opposite side of the blade, forming one integral piece.

Although shorter and lighter than the heavy saber, the short saber was a rugged fighting weapon. Because the blade was about four inches shorter than the heavy saber, it was less cumbersome to wear. The average height of the men who fought in the Revolutionary War was less than it is today, and the shorter men who fought on foot certainly must have favored the short saber.

HUNTING SWORDS

The hunting sword was worn by many high-ranking officers. This weapon, as the name implies, was designed for the hunt, and was never intended for personal combat. The blade length usually ranged from about 24 to 28 inches, and this, coupled with its light weight and exquisite appearance, made it appeal to officers, who wore it primarily as a symbol of rank. Its single-edged cut and thrust blade, either straight or slightly curved, technically classifies it as a saber. The grips were made from horn, bone, ivory, and occasionally wood. Usually they were carved in a sort of spiral pattern, and many of the ivory grips were stained a color. The guard was either straight or S-curved quillons. Some common forms of the pommel were the bird head, lion head, and flat cap, sometimes fancy and sometimes plain. The mountings were generally silver or brass, and a great number of them had a chain extending from the pommel to the quillon.

INFANTRY AND ARTILLERY SWORDS

Infantry swords issued to British troops were fairly well standardized, whereas the Americans used almost anything they could lay their hands on. At the beginning of the Revolution the American colonials were asked to bring along swords as well as shoulder arms. As the war continued, the United States gradually acquired a quantity of swords to issue its soldiers.

After the bayonet appeared early in the seventeenth century, the importance of the infantry sword began to decline steadily. The bayonet was not standardized in European armies until the beginning of the eighteenth century, and in America the adoption came much later. Before the war, a colonist serving in the militia had his choice of bayonet, sword, or belt ax, but by the time the Revolution began, many colonies had made the bayonet mandatory. Nevertheless, a number of men from militia units came into the Continental Army with their short cutting swords.

The two more standard British infantry swords were those of 1742 and 1751. Before the Revolution, England had shipped many of these swords to America to be issued to the colonial troops to fight against the French. When the Revolution started, many Americans armed themselves with these swords.

In the British, French, and American armies enlisted artillerymen carried the same swords as infantry privates. German artillerymen, however, had a special sword known as a *pallasch*. It had a straight double-edged blade about 29½ inches long, with a half-basket hilt of brass, smooth grips, stirrup-shaped knuckle bow, and langets on the quillon. The langets pressed against the scabbard locket and held the sword firmly in the scabbard.

Some militia units of the individual colonies began replacing the infantry sword with the bayonet, but many required both sword and bayonet throughout the Revolution.

About the mid-eighteenth century the French infantry sword had an all-brass hilt and double-edged blade, resembling a small sword of that period. Shortly afterward, the design became more military, with a 27-inch long blade not too unlike the British infantry sword. In 1767 several variations of the grenadier sword were standardized into a true briquet, with a slightly curved single-edged blade about 23 inches long. The all-brass hilt had a ribbed grip with stirrup-type knuckle guard and langet.

Both the French and British infantry swords began to fade from use by the 1760s, and in 1764 the French made the infantry sword obsolete except for the sergeant's and grenadier's. Grenadiers were originally seventeenth-century soldiers whose primary function was to throw grenades. Later they developed into a sort of elite corps.

The Hessian soldiers carried swords almost identical to the British 1742 pattern. In fact, many of the British 1742 swords were made in Germany. The special jaeger troops of the German infantry carried a straight double-edged sword with a blade 22 inches long. The brass hilt had a smooth grip with a rectangular knuckle bow and quillon. Officers of the jaeger troops carried a more elaborate version of this sword, which was a symbol of their having originally been hunt masters. It was 22 inches long in the blade, and etched with hunting scenes.

British enlisted troops, with the exception of sergeants, abandoned the sword during the outbreak of the Revolution. Generally speaking, the sergeants and grenadiers in all the fighting forces were the last enlisted men to stop wearing a sword.

CUTLASSES

The cutlass was a short sword carried by naval personnel. The relatively short, single-edged blade was fairly wide and sturdily constructed, and was either straight or slightly curved. With its false edge, it could be used for both cut and thrust. Because it was used aboard ship, where most fighting was done in close quarters, a large guard was necessary to afford maximum protection to the hand. The grips were usually made of wood, bone, or iron. The cutlass was severely plain, with little or no ornamentation.

SWORD CARRIERS AND HANGERS

Swords were carried by either waist belts or shoulder belts. Infantry soldiers usually wore the waist belt, a heavy band with a buckle in front, although some favored shoulder belts. Sometimes the belt had a double frog for carrying a bayonet. Shortly before the Revolution the British adopted the crossed-shoulder belts for carrying the cartridge box and bayonet. The British and French almost always made their belts of buff leather, but a shortage of leather forced the Americans to use linen and harness leather as well as buff. Both waist belts and shoulder belts were worn by American officers. The sword was almost always attached by a frog when carried on a shoulder belt. A frog was also used for attaching a sword to a waist belt, but other means were popular too. One device used two straps of different lengths, suspended from the belt, which engaged rings that were attached to metal fittings on the scabbard. Another used a metal hanger clipped to the waist belt. Two chains of different lengths were attached to the hanger, and a clip at the end of these chains snapped onto carrying rings affixed to the scabbard.

French cavalrymen and British dragoons carried their sabers on the waist belt, while the British horse and light horse troops and the American cavalry generally used the shoulder belt.

The following photographs show examples of the edged weapons discussed here.

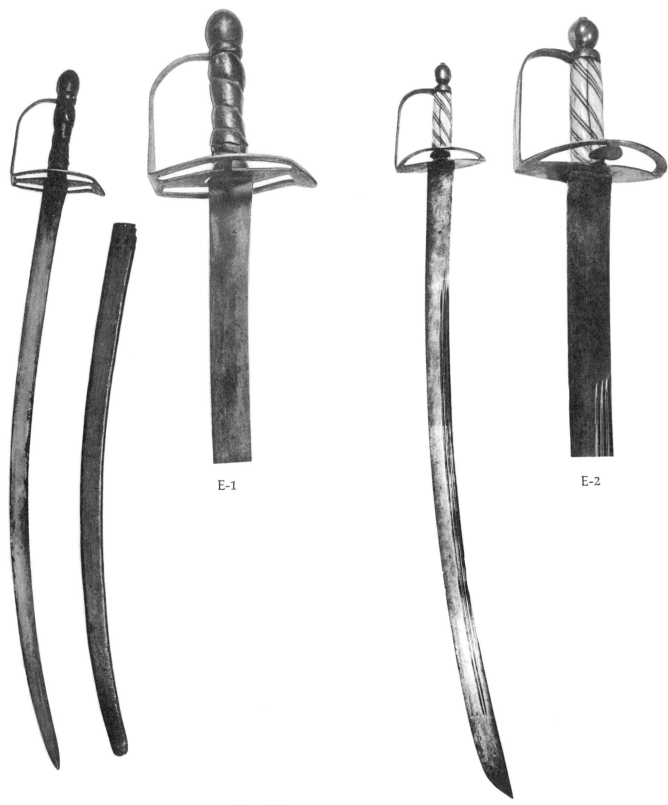

E-1

E-2

E-1   *American Revolutionary War saber with steel hilt and black leather-wrapped grip. This sword was made by Potter, and its original black leather scabbard is also shown.*
Blade length: 36 inches.

E-2   *American Revolutionary War saber with brass hilt and ivory grip.*
Blade length: 32½ inches.

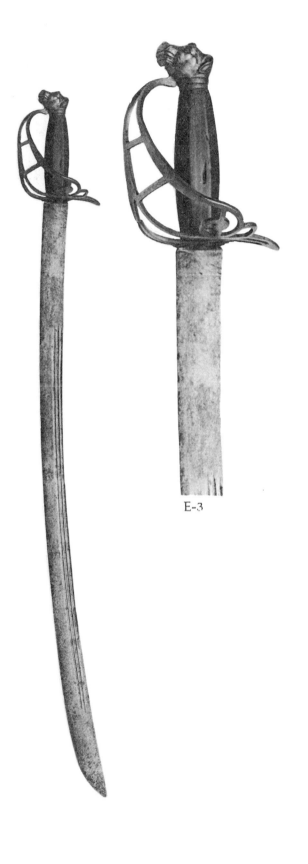

E-3

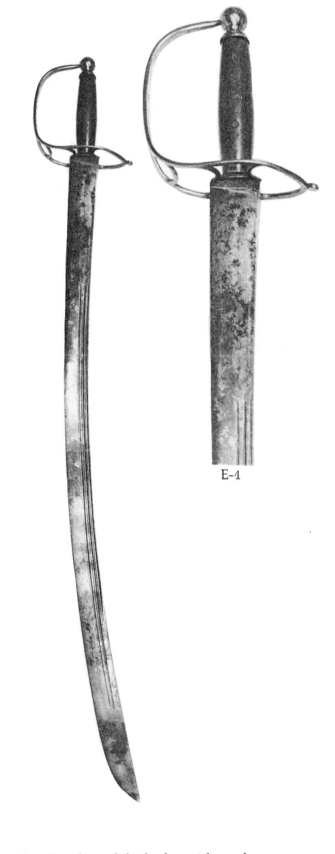

E-4

E-3   *Horseman's saber with dog-head pommel
and octagonal cherry grip.
Half-basket guard blade, unmarked,
with three fullers. Blade length: 34 inches.*

E-4   *American brass-hilted saber with maple
grip and three-fuller blade, circa 1775.
Blade length: 33 inches.*

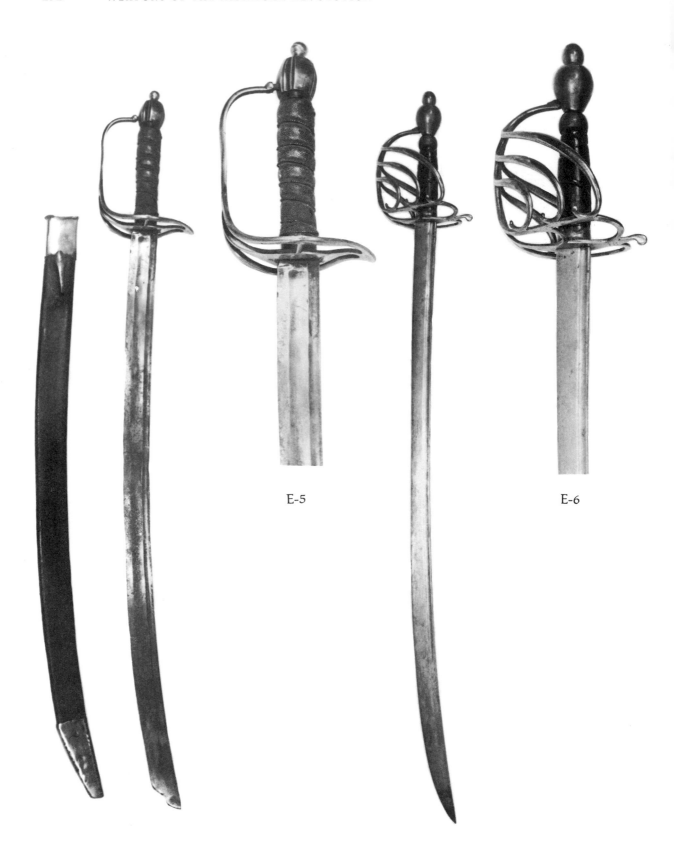

E-5

E-6

E-5   *Large British mid-eighteenth-century horse trooper's saber with brass hilt and sharkskin grip. The guard is marked "B/30." Blade length: 32 inches.*

E-6   *Steel-hilted grenadier or dragoon pattern sword with black leather grip, circa 1770. Blade length: 32 inches.*

E-7

E-8

E-7   *American saber with brass hilt,*
      maple grip, and three-fuller blade,
      circa 1775. It is complete with brown
      leather scabbard with tooled design,
      frog, and waist belt with shoulder strap.
      Blade length: 33 inches.

E-8   *American saber with steel stirrup hilt,*
      three-fuller blade, and black leather
      scabbard with brass fittings, circa 1775.
      A nut serves in lieu of the capstan rivet.
      Blade length: 33 inches.

E-9

E-10

E-9   *American saber with brass hilt and maple or cherry grip, and three-fuller blade. It is shown with its brown leather scabbard with hand-tooled design. Blade length: 33½ inches.*

E-10   *American or British saber with steel stirrup hilt, dark brown leather grip bound with wire, and three-fuller blade. It is shown with its brown leather scabbard, complete with frog. Blade length: 33 inches.*

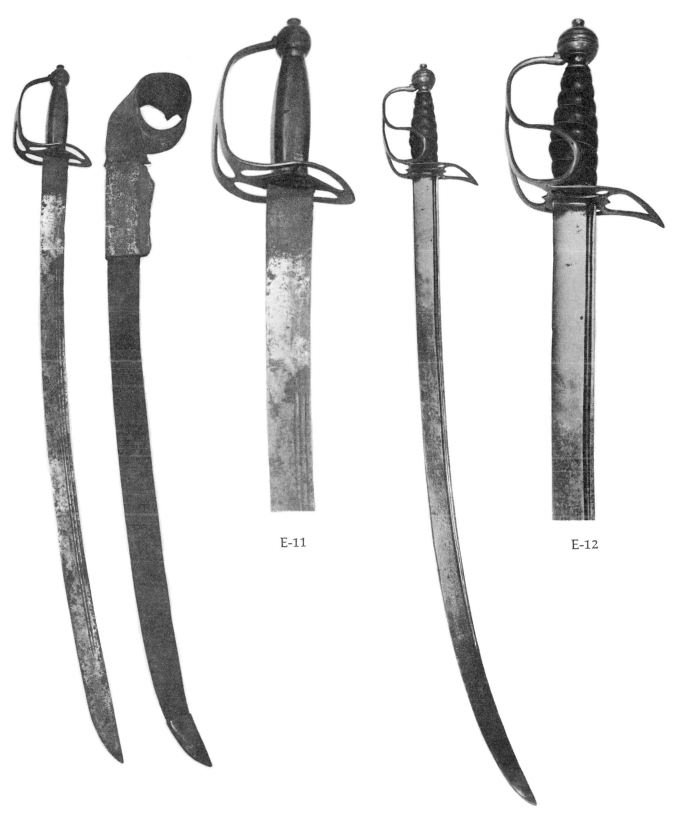

E-11

E-12

E-11   *American brass-hilted saber with maple*
grip and three-fuller blade,
complete with scabbard, frog, and a
portion of the shoulder belt, circa 1770.
Blade length: 34 inches.

E-12   *American brass-hilted saber with cherry*
grip and single-fuller blade, circa 1775.
Blade length: 34½ inches.

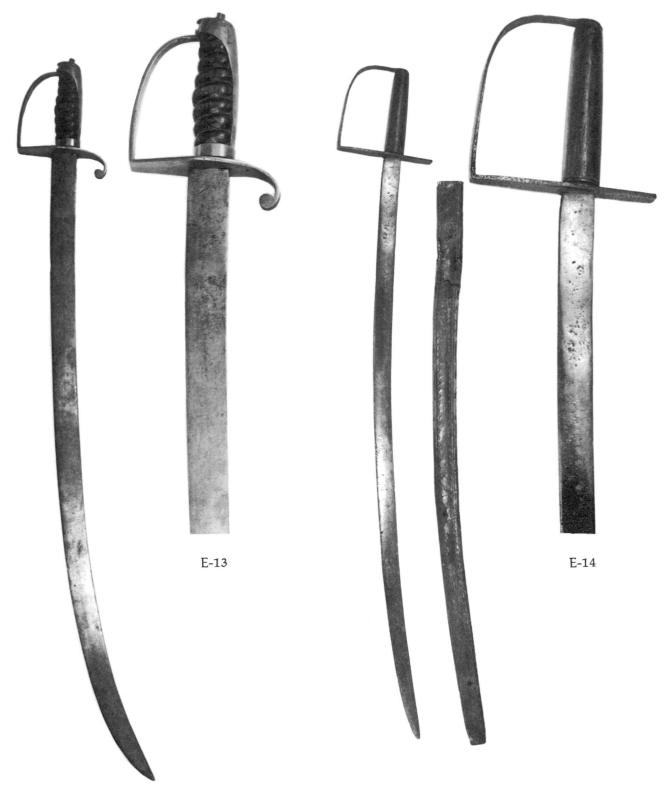

E-13

E-14

E-13   *American saber with brass stirrup hilt
        and cherry grip, circa 1775.
        Blade length: 34 inches.*

E-14   *Extremely plain American sword with
        walnut grip and steel "D" guard.
        The hand-tooled scabbard has a slotted
        piece through which a belt can
        be threaded. Circa 1770.
        Blade length: 31½ inches.*

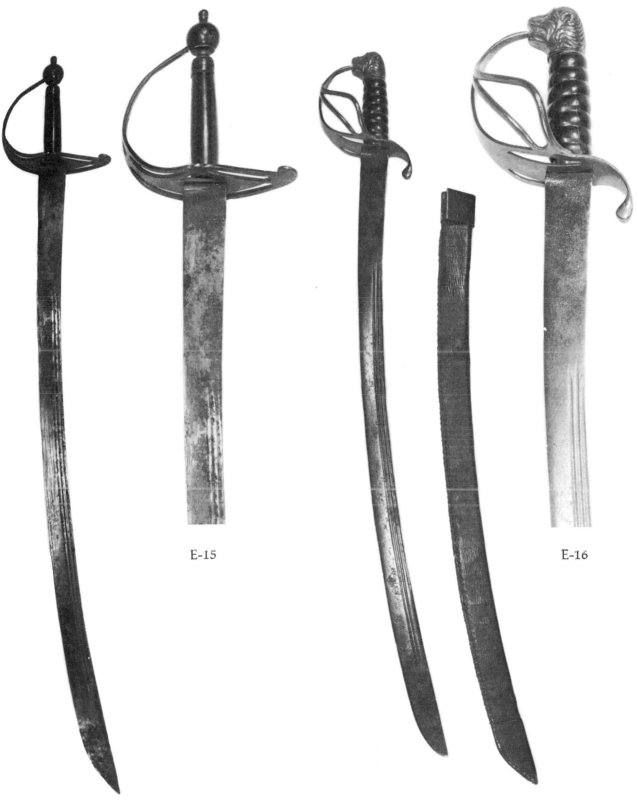

E-15

E-16

E-16 *American brass-hilted saber with lion-head pommel, cherry or maple grip, and three-fuller blade. It is shown with its black leather scabbard. Blade length: 32 inches.*

E-15 *American brass-hilted saber with maple grip, circa 1775. Blade length: 33 inches.*

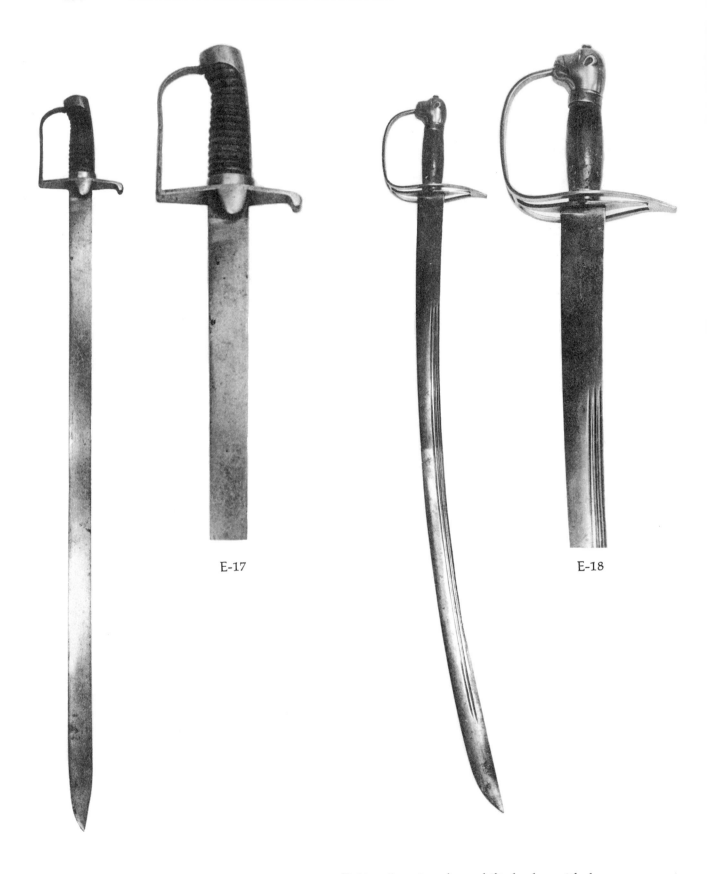

E-17

E-18

E-17   *British brass-hilted light dragoon saber*
        of the 1773–1788 pattern.
        Blade length: 36 inches.

E-18   *American brass-hilted saber with dog-*
        or lion-head pommel and three-fuller
        blade, circa 1775.
        Blade length: 33 inches.

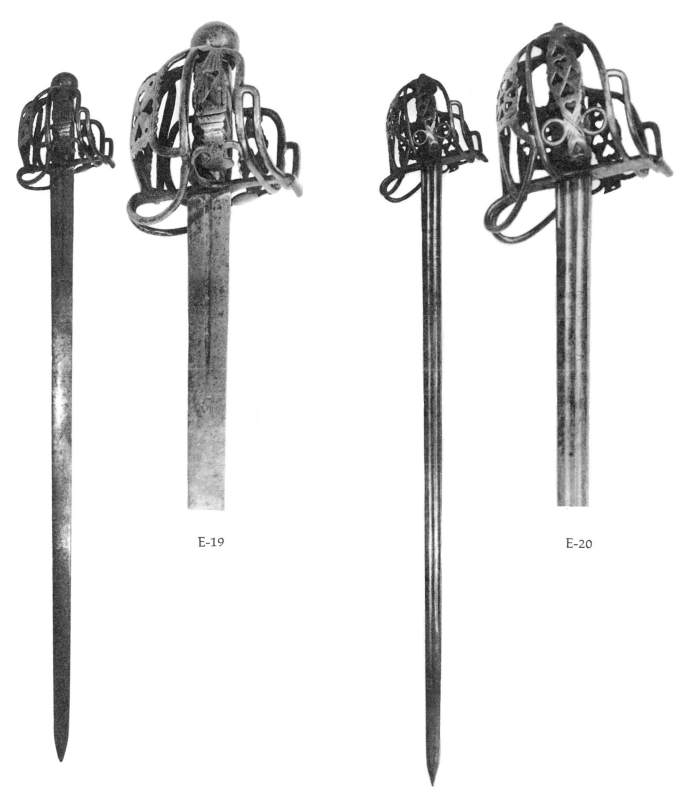

E-19

E-20

E-19   *British trooper's broadsword with*
double-edged blade, circa 1750.
This is the Scottish basket-hilt type
popular with the heavy cavalry during
the first half of the 18th century.
Blade length: 34 inches.

E-20   *Basket-hilted Scottish backsword*
with fishtail grip, circa 1760.
The blade is inscribed "Andrea Ferara."
Blade length: 35 inches.

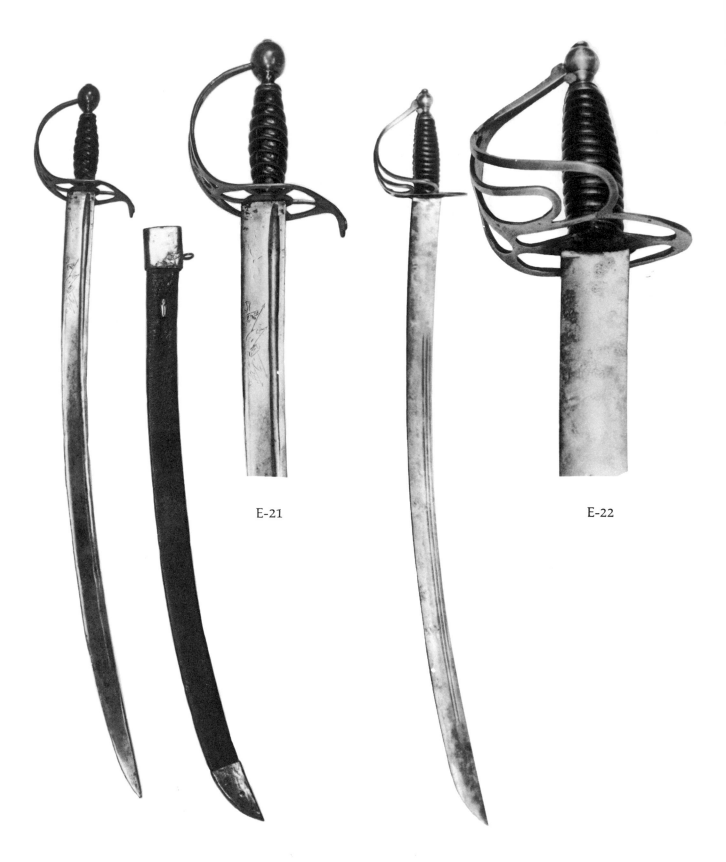

E-21

E-22

E-21   *American brass-hilted saber with cherry grip and single-fuller blade, complete with black leather scabbard with brass fittings. Blade length: 34 inches.*

E-22   *American officer's saber of the Revolutionary period with brass hilt and walnut grip. Blade length: 32½ inches.*

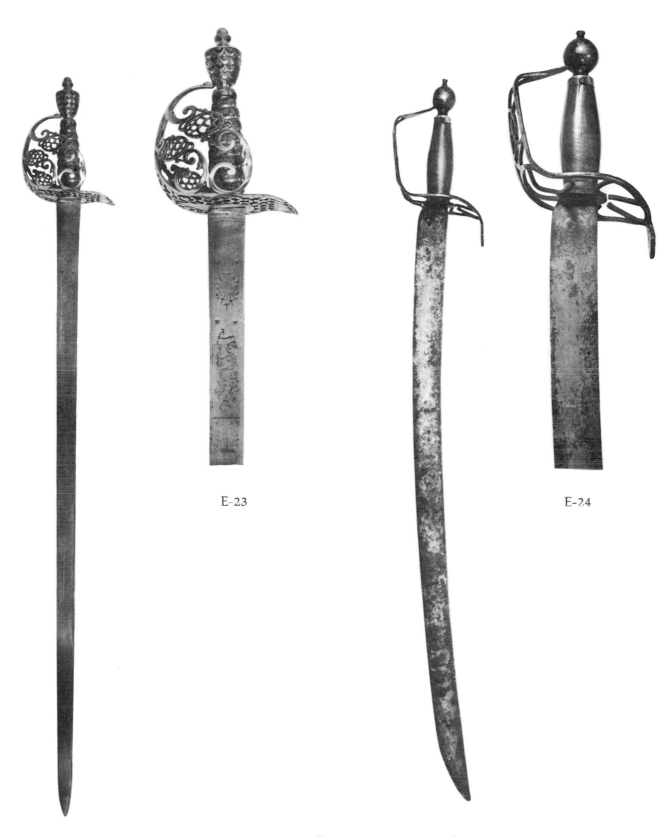

E-23

E-24

E-23 *British dragoon officer's steel-hilted*
saber of extra fine quality, circa 1760.
Blade length: 36 inches.

E-24 *American Revolutionary War sword with*
cherry grip and brass hilt.
The brass guard is in the shape of a
wagon wheel.
Blade length: 28½ inches.

E-25

E-26

E-25   *American short saber with brass hilt,
cherry grip, and single-fuller blade,
complete with black leather scabbard
with brass fittings, circa 1775.
Blade length: 26½ inches.*

E-26   *American or British short saber with
brass lion-head pommel and yellow
ivory grip, circa 1770.
Blade length: 27 inches.*

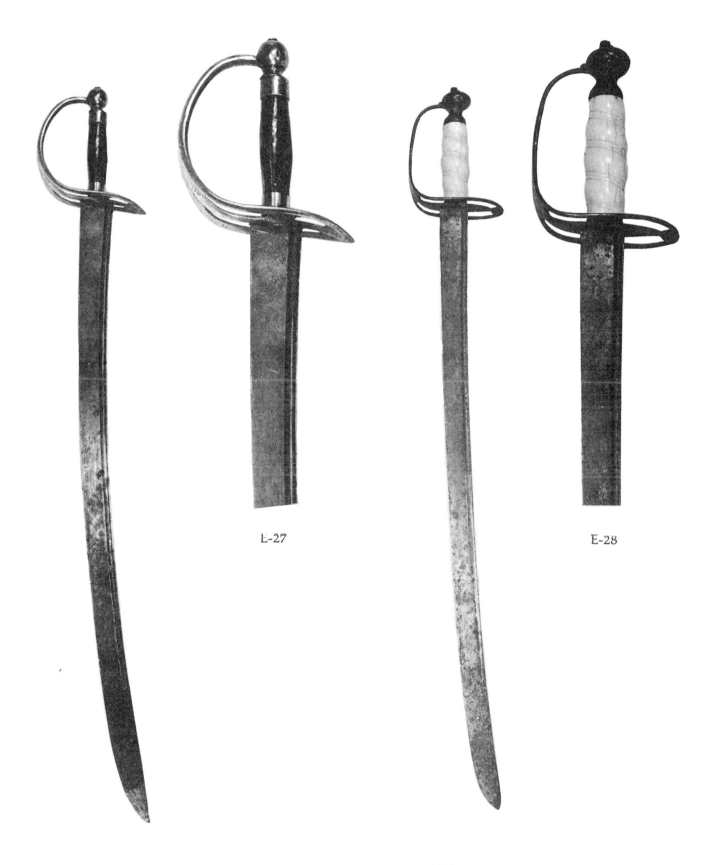

E-27

E-28

E-27   *American short saber with brass hilt and single-fuller blade, circa 1770.*
Blade length: 27 inches.

E-28   *Steel-hilted American short sword or saber with ivory grip and single-fuller blade, circa 1770.*
Blade length: 26 inches.

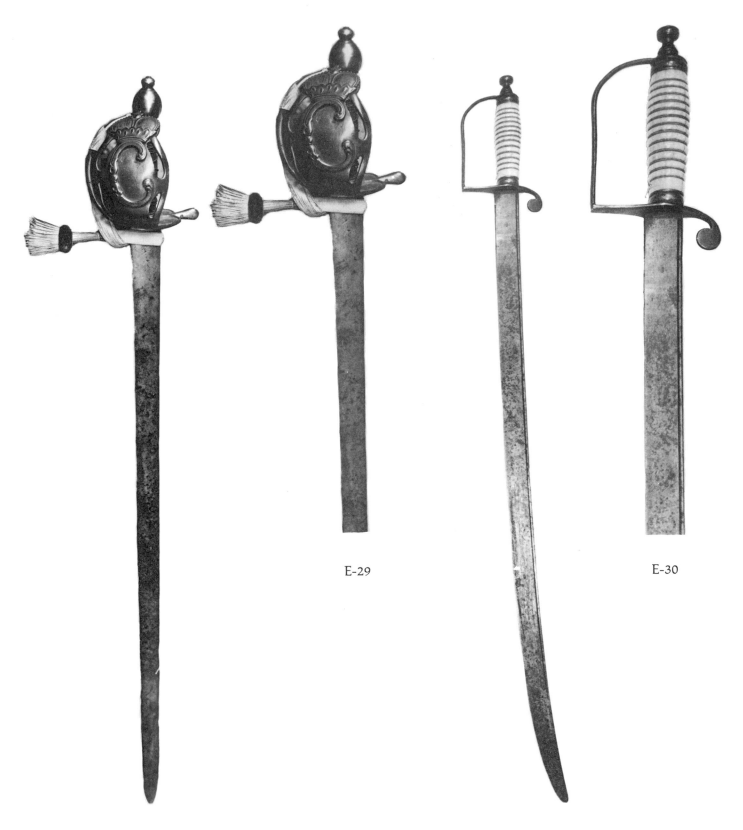

E-29

E-30

E-29   *German brass-hilted sword captured by
the Americans from a Hessian dragoon of
the Brunswick Regiment von Riedesel at
the Battle of Bennington, Vermont, in 1777.
Blade length: 36¾ inches.*

E-30   *American brass-hilted sword or small
saber with ivory grip and
single-fuller blade, circa 1775.
Blade length: 28 inches.*

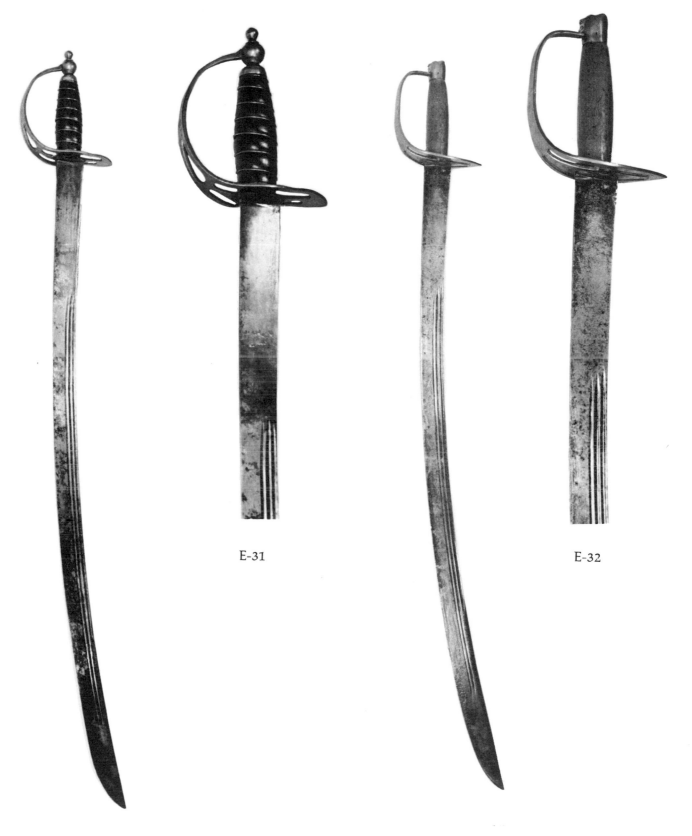

E-31

E-32

E-32   *American brass-hilted saber with*
maple grip and three-fuller blade.
The pommel is in the form of a crude
bird head. Blade length: 33 inches.

E-31   *American brass-hilted saber with*
wooden grip. Blade length: 32½ inches.

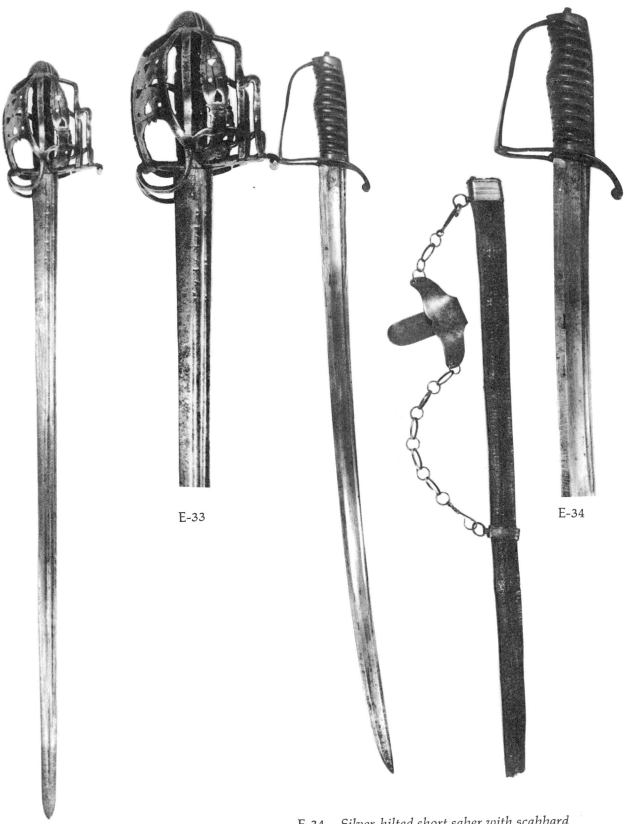

E-33

E-34

E-33   *Steel-hilted British cavalry backsword, circa 1740. Blade length: 34 inches.*

E-34   *Silver-hilted short saber with scabbard and carrier used by Lieutenant Alexander Kidd, who served in the 2nd Regiment of Ulster County Militia. Blade length: 25 inches.*

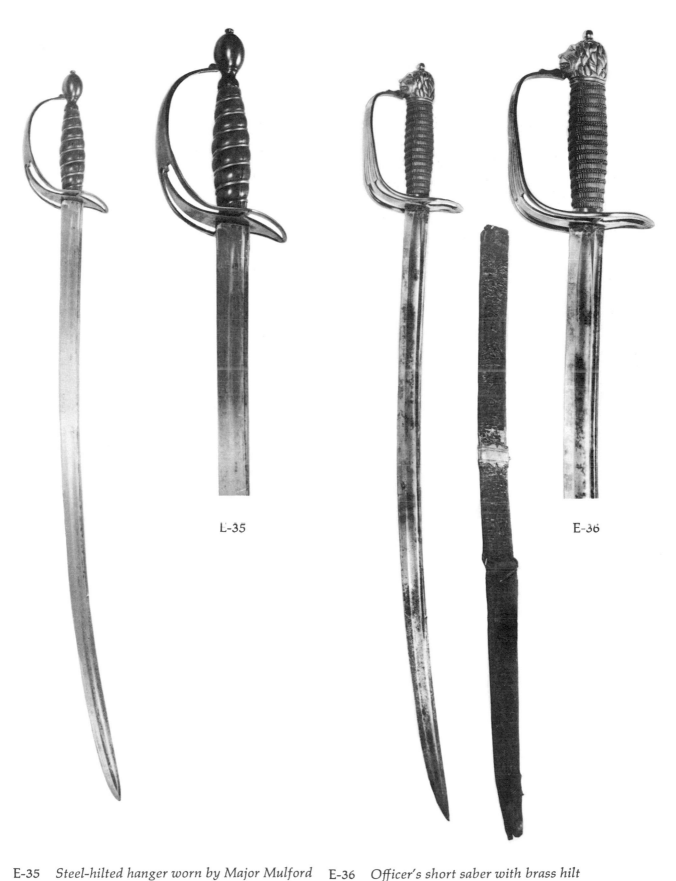

L-35

E-36

E-35   *Steel-hilted hanger worn by Major Mulford*
during the evacuation of Fort Ticonderoga,
July 6, 1777. Blade length: 26¾ inches.

E-36   *Officer's short saber with brass hilt*
lion-head pommel, shown with
leather scabbard. Blade length: 24 inches.

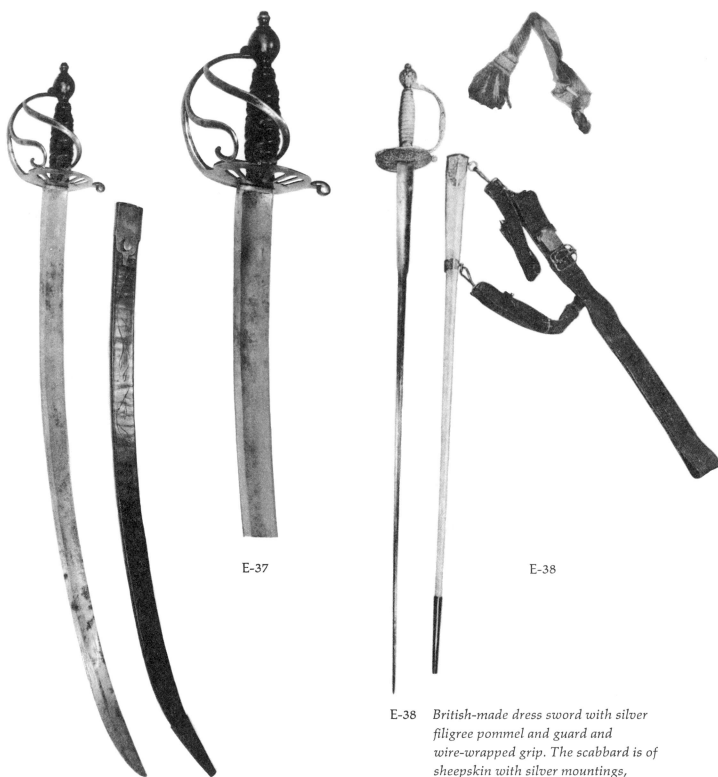

E-37

E-38

E-37   British or American dragoon
cavalry saber with steel hilt, circa 1760.
The leather on the scabbard has been replaced.
Blade length: 37 inches.

E-38   British-made dress sword with silver
filigree pommel and guard and
wire-wrapped grip. The scabbard is of
sheepskin with silver mountings,
and the green belt has silver fittings.
The sword knot is made of silver threads.
This is the sword believed to have been
worn by George Washington when he
resigned his commission in 1783 and
when he was inaugurated as President
in 1789. Blade length: 33½ inches.

E-39

E-40

E-39   *British steel-hilted rapier-like small sword with finely pierced hilt and slender colichemarde blade, circa 1770. The guard shows the design of the Maltese cross. Blade length: 31 inches.*

E-40   *English silver-hilted small sword, mid-eighteenth century, with boat guard and gadroon border. This sword has a cutting edge blade. Blade length: 32 inches.*

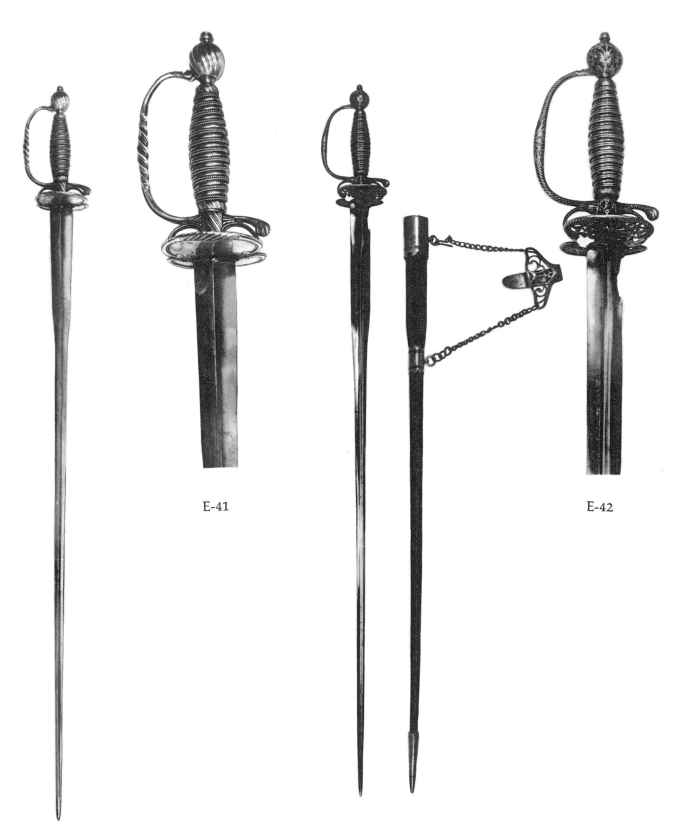

E-41

E-42

E-41   *British silver-hilted small sword with*
        double shell guard and colichemarde
        blade, hallmarked 1754.
        Blade length: 32 inches.

E-42   *British silver-hilted small sword with*
        shell guard and colichemarde blade,
        circa 1760. The black leather scabbard
        has silver fittings.
        Blade length: 33 inches.

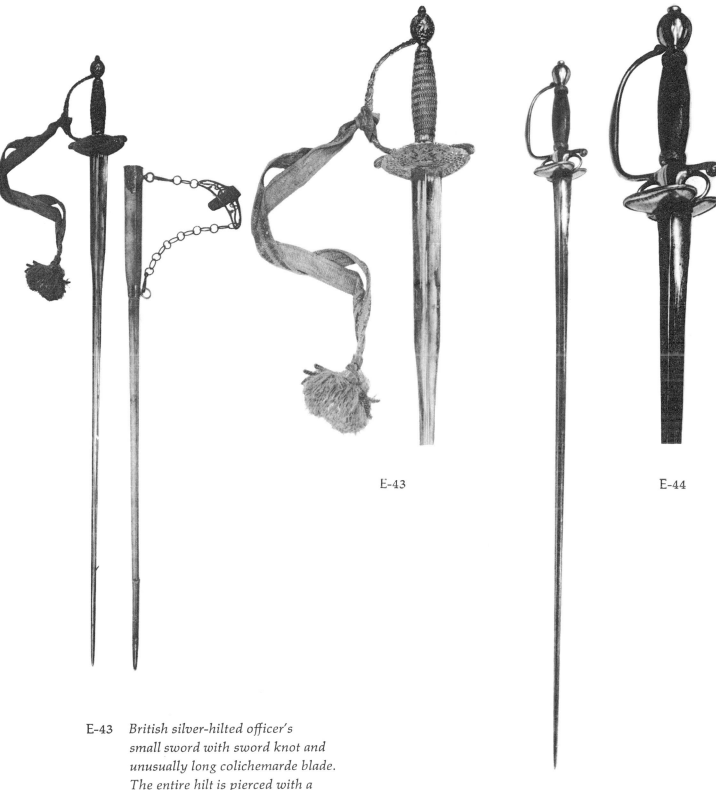

E-43

E-44

E-43   *British silver-hilted officer's small sword with sword knot and unusually long colichemarde blade. The entire hilt is pierced with a military motif, and the parchment scabbard has fittings decorated in a military style. The sword is hallmarked 1759 with the maker's mark "I.B." The guard is marked Beckett and St. James's. Blade length: 35 inches.*

E-44   *Brass-hilted small sword, probably American, with double shell guard and straight colichemarde blade, circa 1765. Blade length: 29 inches.*

E-45

E-46

E-45   *British steel-hilted officer's
small sword with colichemarde blade and
grip wrapped in silver wire.
The pommel and guard are pierced
with military trophies. It is shown
with its original parchment scabbard
with steel fittings. Circa 1760.
Blade length: 32 inches.*

E-46   *American steel-hilted small sword with
cherry grip and straight colichemarde
blade, circa 1770. Blade length: 27 inches.*

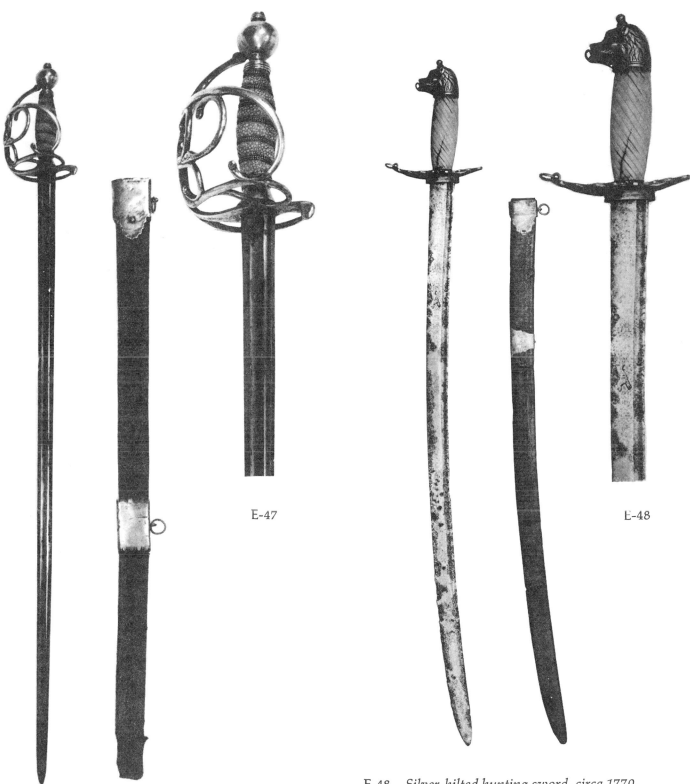

E-47

E-48

E-47　*British officer's small sword with silver basket hilt and white sharkskin grip, made by J. Crum and hallmarked 1755. Blade length: 32½ inches.*

E-48　*Silver-hilted hunting sword, circa 1770, made by William Moulton. The ivory grip was originally tinted green. It is fitted with an English blade bearing the running fox and the letter H, for the swordsmith Harvey. Blade length: 27½ inches.*

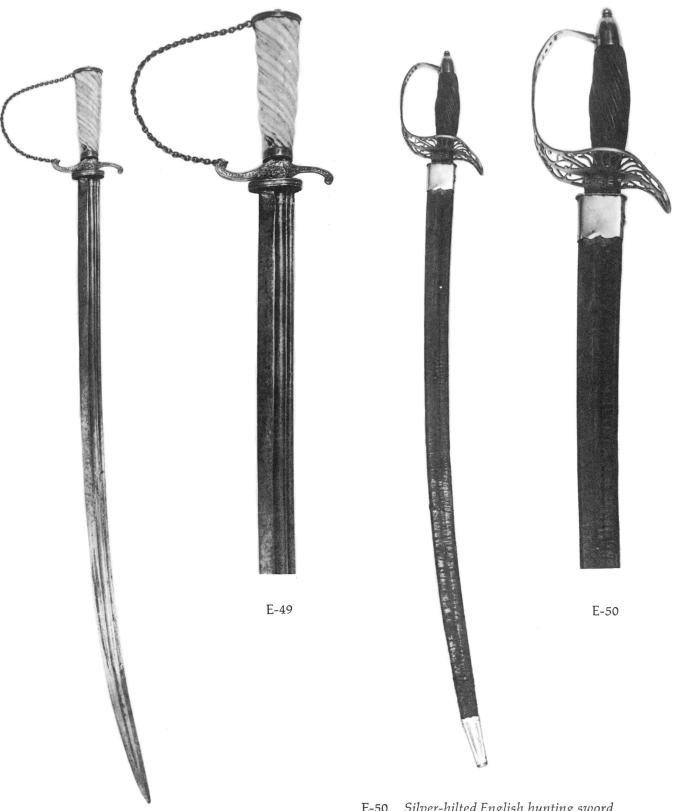

E-49

E-50

E-49   *Ivory-hilted hunting sword,
probably American, with "S"-shaped quillon,
circa 1770. Blade length: 28 inches.*

E-50   *Silver-hilted English hunting sword
with green grip and gracefully
pierced guard, complete with original
brown leather scabbard with silver
fittings, circa 1760.
Blade length: 27 inches.*

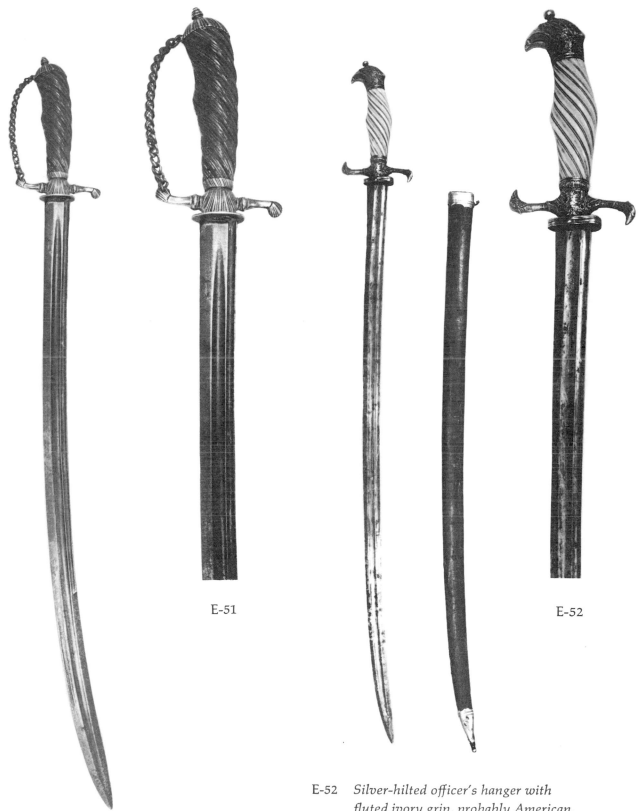

E-51

E-52

E-52   *Silver-hilted officer's hanger with fluted ivory grip, probably American, circa 1780. The carved eagle pommel is sometimes referred to as a "chicken eagle." Its original silver-mounted brown leather scabbard is also shown. Blade length: 28 inches.*

E-51   *British silver-hilted hunting sword, hallmarked 1774, with green ivory grip. Blade length: 24 inches.*

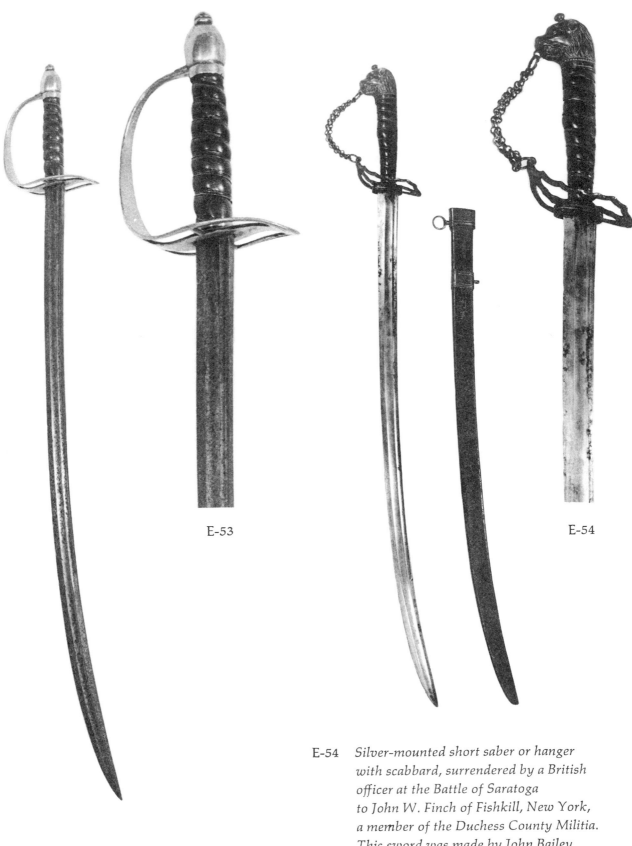

E-53

E-54

E-54 *Silver-mounted short saber or hanger*
with scabbard, surrendered by a British
officer at the Battle of Saratoga
to John W. Finch of Fishkill, New York,
a member of the Duchess County Militia.
This sword was made by John Bailey
of Verplanck's Point, New York,
who later moved to Fishkill.
Blade length: 25 inches.

E-53 *American officer's silver-hilted hanger,*
circa 1780. Blade length: 25 inches.

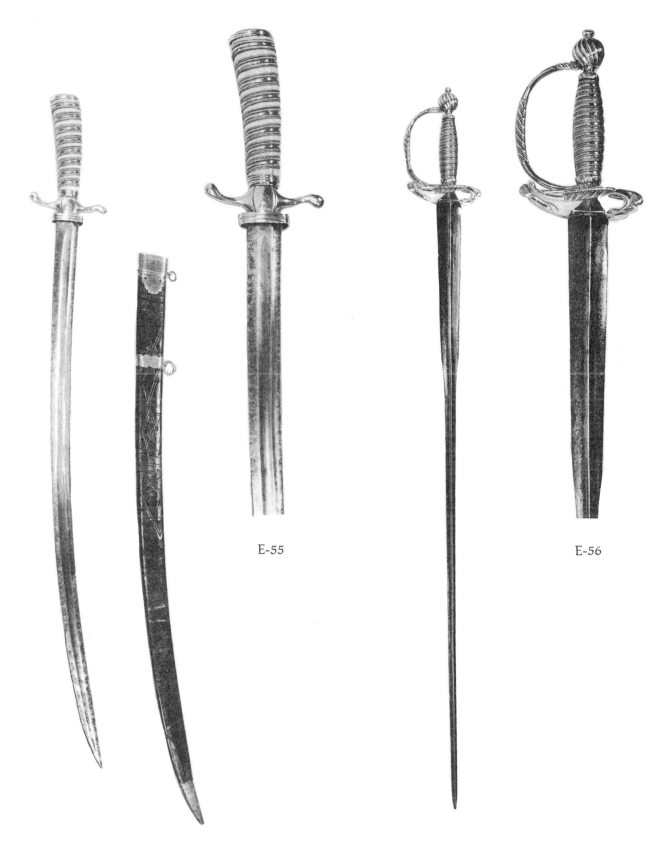

E-55

E-56

E-55   *Irish hunting sword with ivory grip and*
silver trim, made in Dublin by Bennett,
circa 1780. Blade length: 24 inches.

E-56   *British officer's dress sword*
with silver hilt and colichemarde blade,
made by John Wilkes and hallmarked 1762.
Blade length: 33 inches.

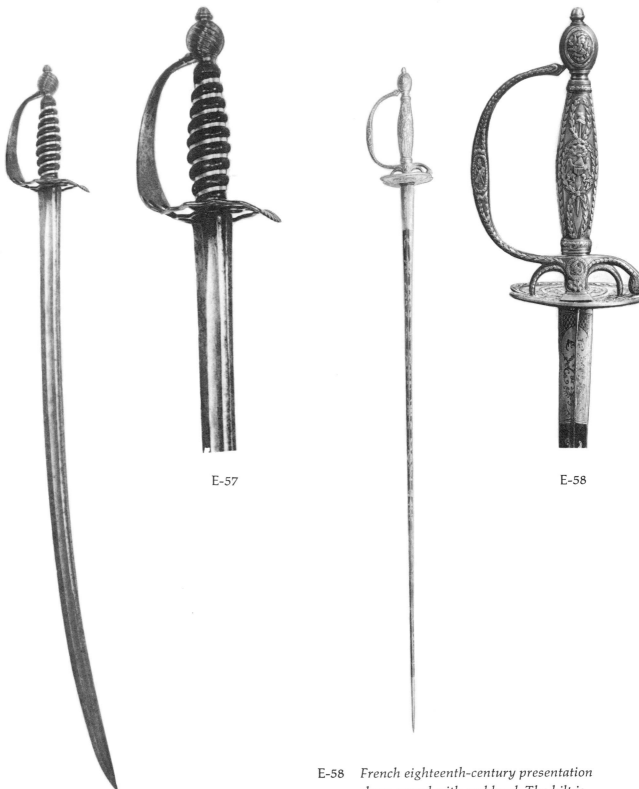

E-57

E-58

E-58   *French eighteenth-century presentation dress sword with scabbard. The hilt is inscribed "Congress to Col Willett Octr 11, 1777." The blade is inscribed "LIGER Fourbisseur De S. A. Msgr Le Duc de Chartre & Comte de Clermont Rue Coquilliere a Paris." Blade length: 32½ inches.*

E-57   *British officer's hanger, circa 1780, of the style popular in both Army and Navy. Blade length: 27 inches.*

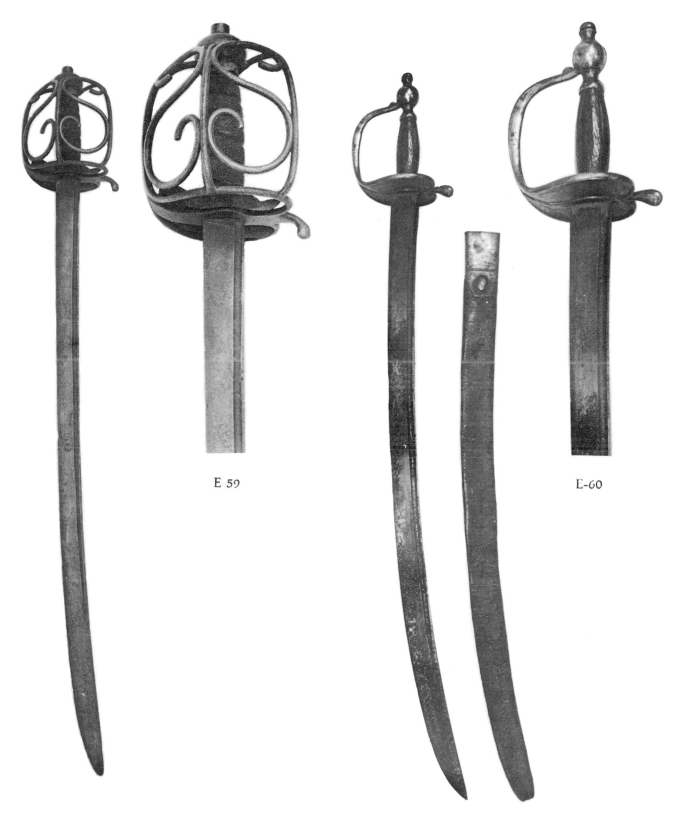

E 59

E-60

E-59   *Pre-1742 British hanger with iron hilt.*
Hangers of this type were carried by
grenadiers of the Royal Welsh Fusiliers
and other regiments of the period.
Blade length: 28 inches.

E-60   *British brass-hilted 1742 infantry sword,*
with wood grip and original black
leather scabbard with brass fittings.
Blade length: 28¼ inches.

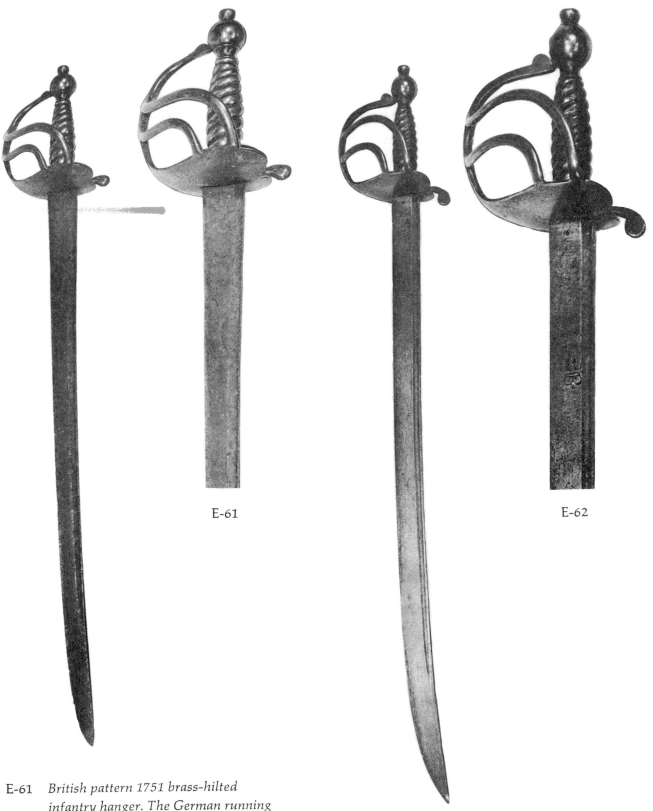

E-61

E-62

E-61   *British pattern 1751 brass-hilted*
infantry hanger. The German running
wolf is marked on the blade,
which was made in Solingen.
The underside of the guard is engraved
"M. Cheshire" and "Co/40."
Blade length: 24½ inches.

E-62   *British model 1751 infantry sword with*
all-brass hilt and single-fuller blade
marked "GR." Blade length: 24½ inches.

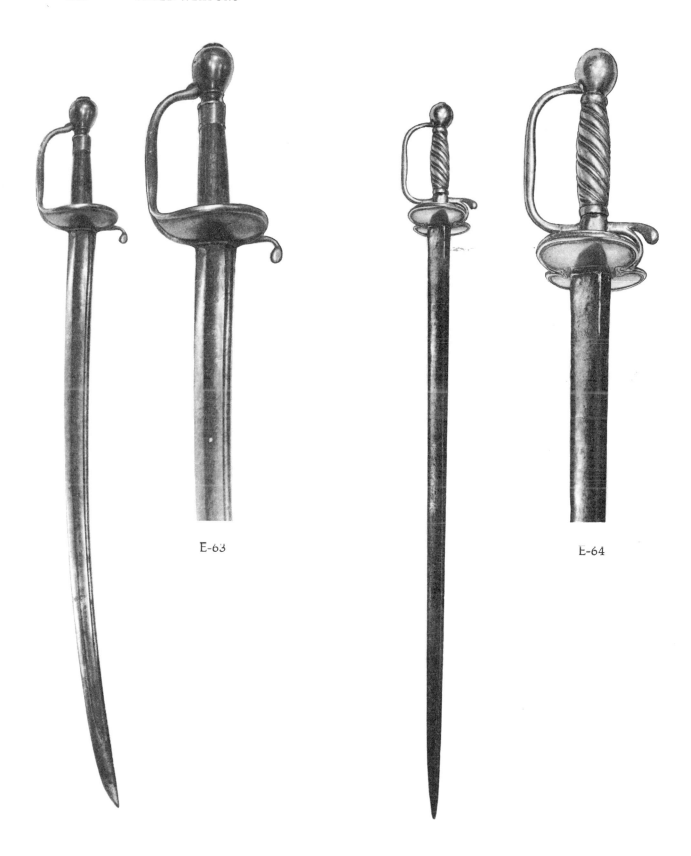

E-63

E-64

E-63 *Brass-hilted infantry sword,*
probably American, circa 1760.
The blade is engraved with a sun and moon.
Blade length: 23 inches.

E-64 *French brass-hilted infantry sword*
with brass grip, double clamshell
guard, and triangular-shaped blade,
circa 1750. Blade length: 29 inches.

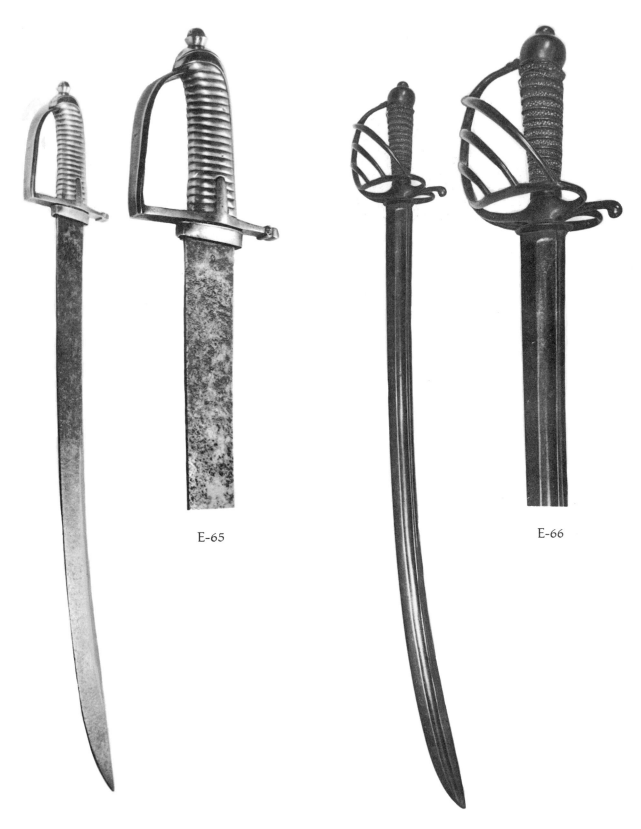

E-65

E-66

E-65 *French 1767 pattern brass-hilted sword or briquet. The blade is etched on one side "Artillery of Va." and on the other "Victory or Death." Blade length: 23 inches.*

E-66 *British sergeant's grade sword with steel basket hilt and sharkskin grip, circa 1770. Blade length: 27 inches.*

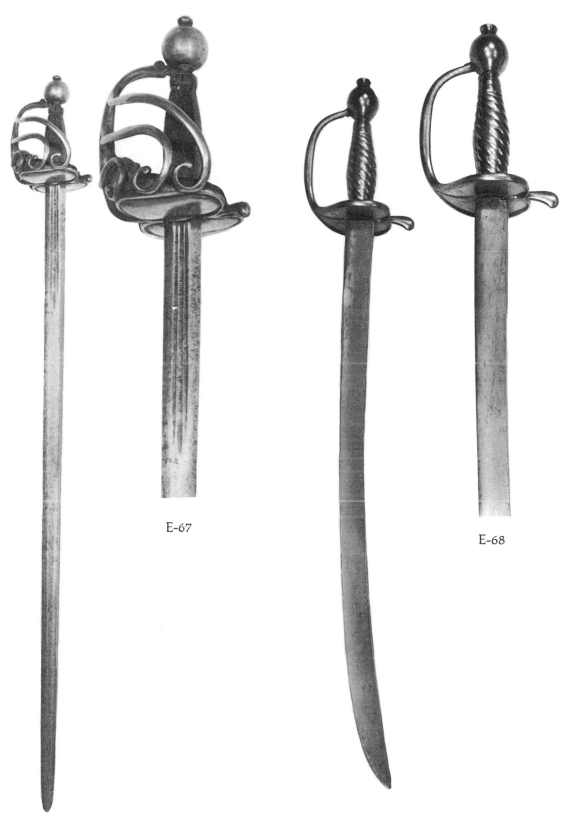

E-67

E-68

E-67   Short sword with brass hilt, circa 1760,
of the type carried by junior officers
in the French and Indian War.
Blade length: 31½ inches.

E-68   German infantry sword with unusually
massive brass hilt, circa 1740.
The blade is stamped with "FR" and crown,
for Frederick the Great.
Blade length: 23½ inches.

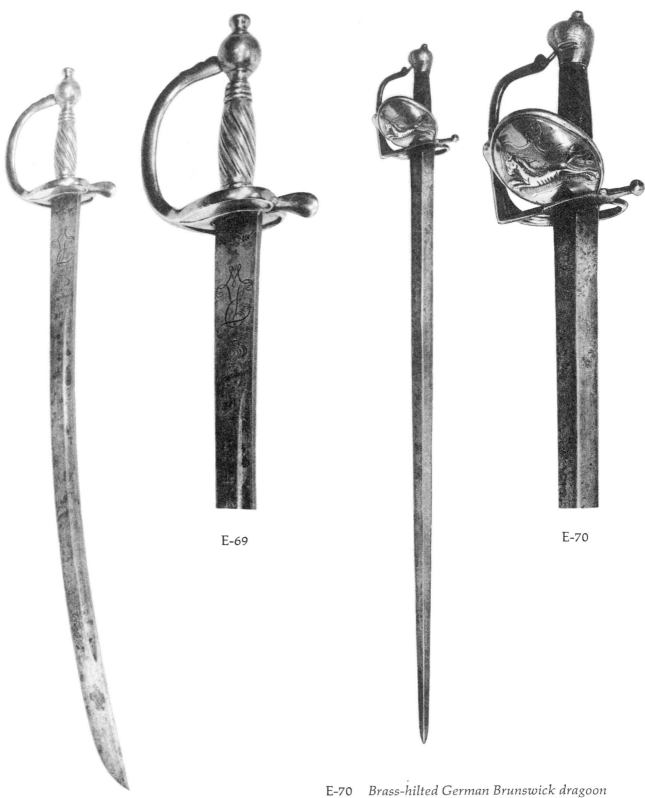

E-69

E-70

E-69   Mid-eighteenth century German infantry
        sword with all-brass hilt.
        The blade is marked with a crown and "FR."
        Blade length: 26 inches.

E-70   Brass-hilted German Brunswick dragoon
        private sword with double-edged,
        diamond-shaped blade tapering evenly
        from hilt to tip, circa 1760.
        The counterguard is embossed with the
        design of the Hanoverian running horse.
        Blade length: 30 inches.

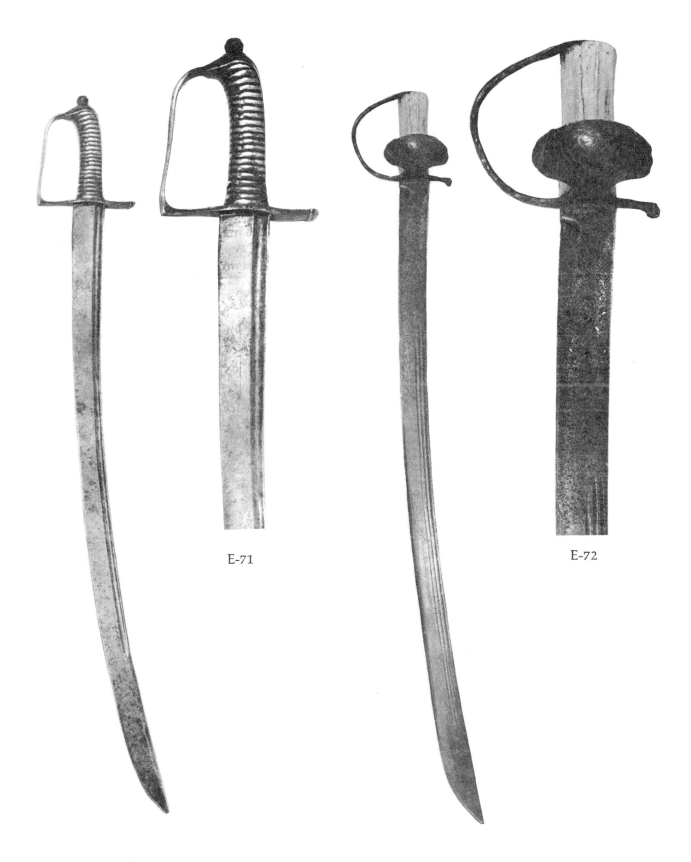

E-71

E-72

E-71　*German briquet with brass hilt.*
The blade is inscribed on both sides
"Vor Gott Und Das Vatterland."
Circa 1770. Blade length: 26 inches.

E-72　*Cutlass with shell guard and bone grip,*
circa 1740. The three-fuller blade has
the sun and moon engraving.
Blade length: 30½ inches.

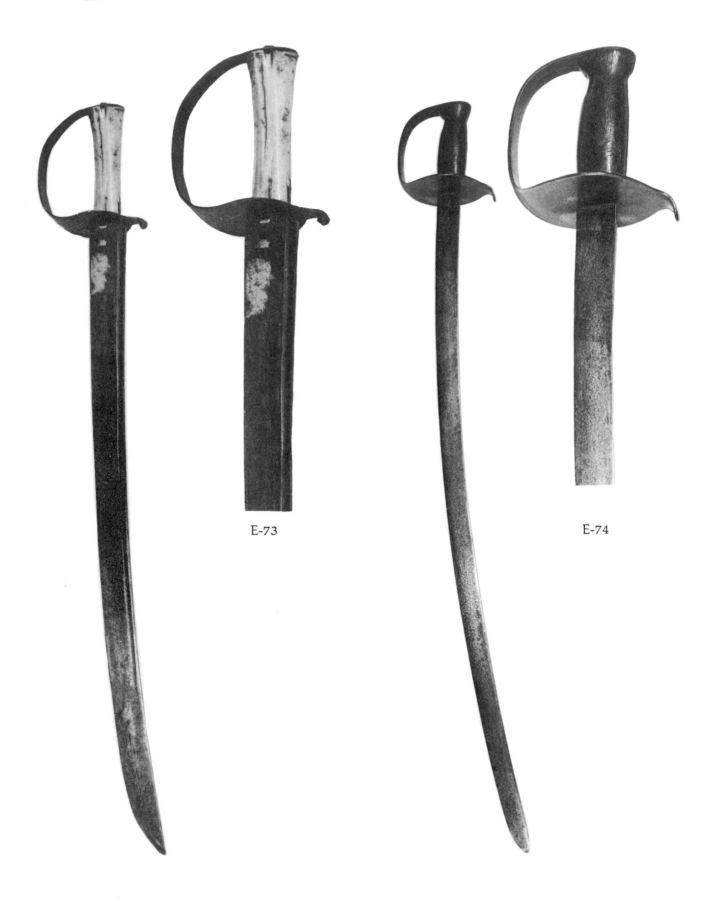

E-73

E-74

E-73   *Steel cutlass with bone grip. American,
circa 1760. Blade length: 23 inches.*

E-74   *Massive steel cutlass with maple grip,
circa 1760. Blade length: 34 inches.*

ENGRAVED POWDER HORNS

The first horns came to America from Europe, and many of these were made from tortoise shell or staghorn. Most American horns were made of cow or ox horn. To prepare such a horn for use, the first step was to saw off each end and then boil the horn in potash water. Next the tapered end was bored enough to make a spout, and the spout was fitted with a stopper. The base was fitted with a wooden plug, and the outside of the horn was scraped and treated with oil and pumice. The horn could then be left plain or decorated with engravings. Most American horns were homemade, but some were made by professional engravers. These were often stained with a yellow dye.

Engraved powder horns of the period 1750–1780 have great appeal, both from the point of view of historical interest and as a form of graphic art. A great difference is to be seen in the quality of the decorations, some having been done by their owners, strictly amateur artists, and others by professionals and given as gifts to soldiers.

When the American Revolution began, men brought with them their powder horns and other accoutrements as well as their weapons. The horn was an important part of a soldier's equipment, and was often used to express his sentiments of loyalty to the cause of independence or the Crown. Some interesting examples can be seen in the following rhymes found on powder horns of this period:

> "The Red Coat that steals this horn
>   Will go to hell so sure as he is born."

> "May the blossom of Liberty never fail
>   And the King and tirants never prevail."

> "My day's to come if God will lend
>   My King and Country I'll defend."

Many elaborately decorated map horns were made in England by professional engravers for British officers being sent to America. These horns served a dual purpose, as the engraving work was closely copied from contemporary maps, and though inaccurate by modern standards, they were a great help to their owners. The two most frequently found maps show the route up the Hudson River to Lake Champlain, and from the Hudson Valley to Lake Ontario through the Mohawk Valley, which was the waterway to the west. These map

169

horns had the location of the principal forts along the way engraved on them. Prior to the Revolution, horns owned by both Americans and British were often engraved with the British royal arms.

Powder horns were used whenever powder and bullets were carried separately. When the two were rolled together to make cartridges, these were carried in a pouch. Horns were used as long as loose powder was used by sportsmen. Metal powder flasks became popular around 1830, but horns continued to be used by many hunters.

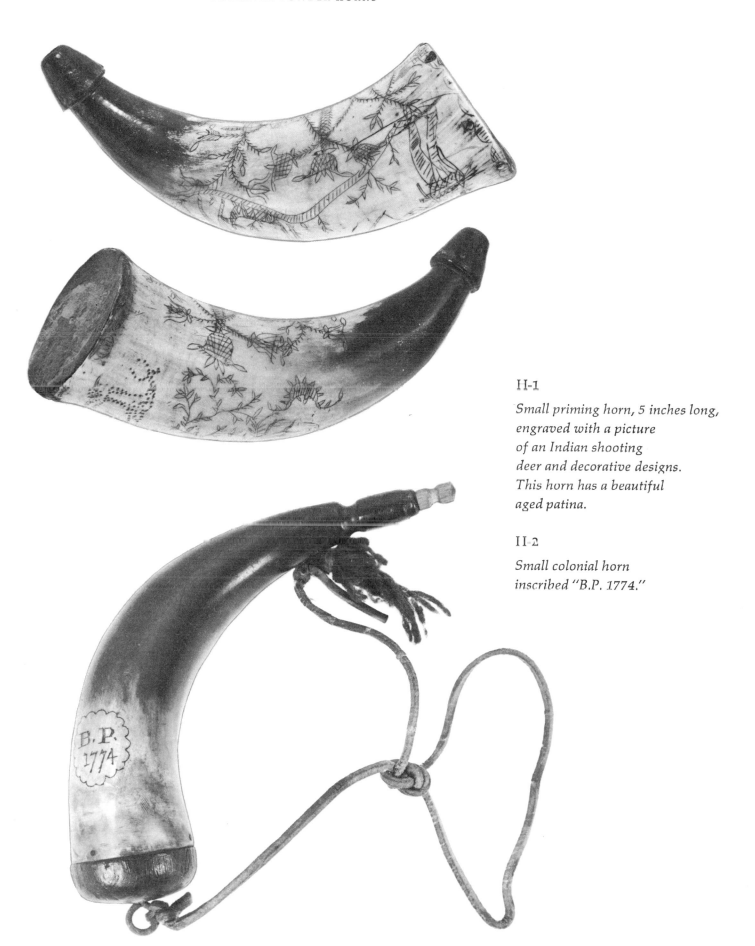

II-1

*Small priming horn, 5 inches long,
engraved with a picture
of an Indian shooting
deer and decorative designs.
This horn has a beautiful
aged patina.*

II-2

*Small colonial horn
inscribed "B.P. 1774."*

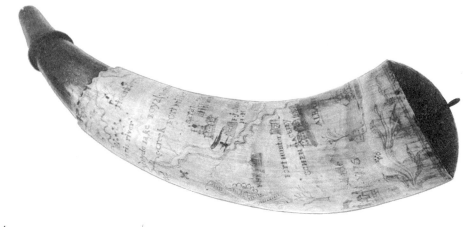

H-3

An American professionally engraved map horn with the inscription "Cap. Josiah Starr was at the taking of St. John's, Nov. 2, 1775."
Captain Starr was from Connecticut and served with Benedict Arnold during campaigns in Canada. He later attained the rank of colonel. The horn bears the names of forts from Albany up through the Hudson and Mohawk valleys.

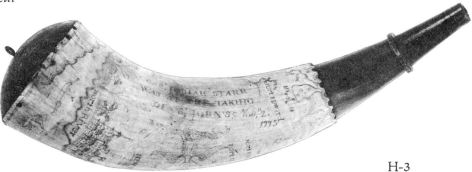

H-3

H-4

Engraved powder horn of unusually fine color. It was probably decorated by its owner, Jeremiah Howard, whose name appears on one side. The name "Brimfield" which appears on the reverse side, refers to Howard's home town in Massachusetts. The horn is dated 1774. Howard's name appears in Massachusetts Soldiers and Sailors of the Revolutionary War, *Volume III, which states that he belonged to Col. Joseph Thompson's Company of Minutemen, Col. Timothy Danielson's Regiment, which marched on the alarm of April 19, 1775.*

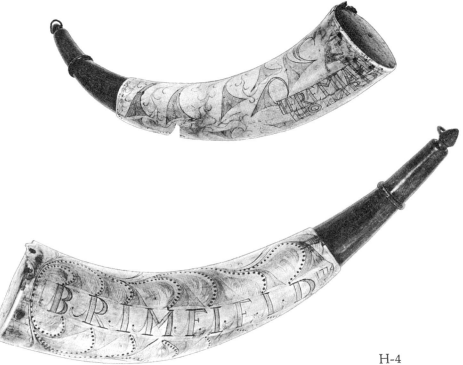

H-4

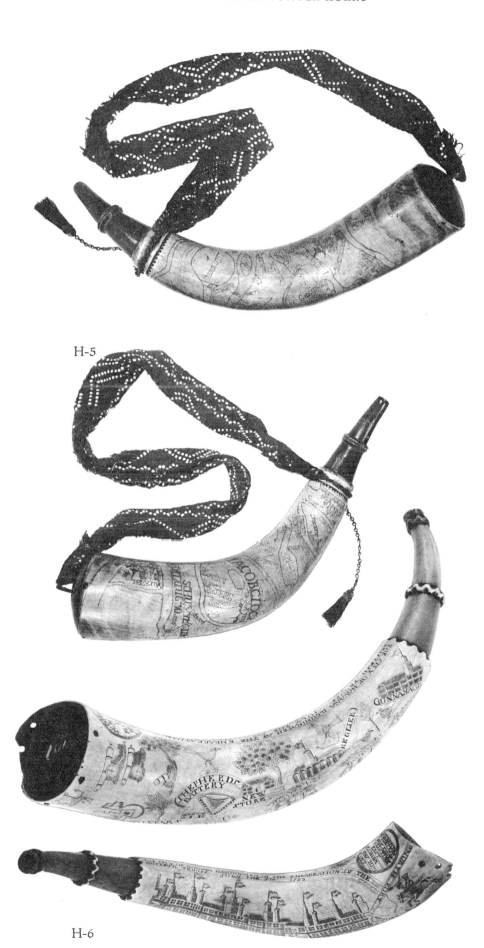

H-5

H-6

H-5

*Revolutionary War powder
horn with the original
beaded carrying sash and brush.
The horn is marked
"Jacob Clock 1779" and
"Fort Schuyler Aug. 10, 1779."
It has a map of New York,
showing villages, forts,
rivers, etc. This is an
unusually large horn,
about 17 inches long.*

H-6

*Cuba horn inscribed
"The city of Havana illuminated
at the embarkation of the
British troops, July the 7th 1763."
A view of the town is shown,
with six ships in the harbor.
Moro Castle, Apostles Battery,
and other important locations
are engraved on the horn.
Other engraving reads
"Yelverton Peyton, Capt.,
9th Regt. Foot, St. Augustine
East Florida, Jeny
(January) 30th, 1767,"
indicating that Captain Peyton
later served in the army
of occupation in Florida.
The exceptionally white
color of this horn is in
pleasing contrast to the
heavy black lettering and
bright red coloring.*

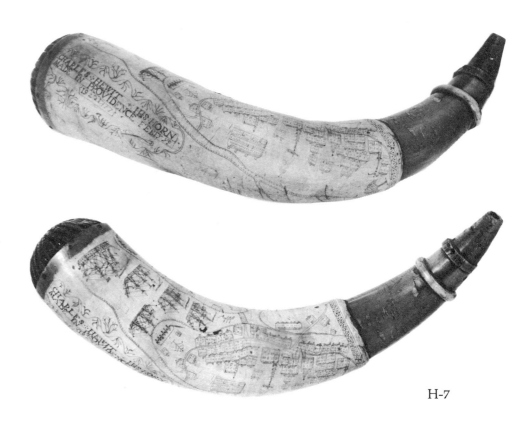

H-7

This horn is one of only two known that are engraved with the town map of Providence, Rhode Island. It is inscribed "Charles Hewit—his horn—made in Providence Febry. YE 19, 1777." The town hall and many of the churches and buildings carved into this horn are easily identifiable and still in use today. Five sailing ships are shown in the harbor. The large, multistoried building next to the inscription later became the home of Brown College, and is still standing on the university campus.

H-7

H-8

Engraved map horn with the British Royal Coat of Arms and the owner's name, S. Goddard, with the date 1761. The engraving is of the finest professional quality and includes the names of all the forts along the Hudson River from Albany to Lake George and Lake Champlain, and from Albany up the Mohawk River by Lake Oneida to Niagara.

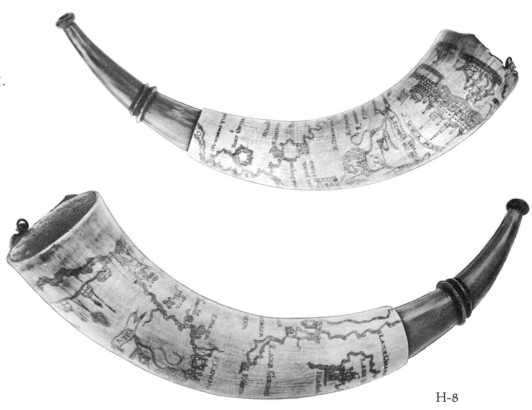

H-8

H-9

H-10

H-9

Typical example of a horn engraved by the owner himself, a type of military scrimshaw. It reads "Wilibe Lowell His Horn Made in Roxbury in the Year 1775—Liberty or Death—Apiel to Heaven." Directly below are the walls of a fort and a man, four cannon, and several muskets with fixed bayonets. Elsewhere on the horn is engraved a ship, some town buildings, and many horses.

H-10

Fine quality Cuba horn made in England and used by a British officer sent to fight with the English forces attempting to take Havana from the Spanish in 1762. This horn is beautifully engraved with warships, the English Royal Coat of Arms, various Cuban fortifications, and both mounted and foot soldiers.
Cuba was an important Spanish stronghold in this hemisphere, and the American colonial troops suffered heavy casualties in taking this island from the Spanish. This horn has acquired a beautiful brownish patina over the years.

H-11

This horn is carved with the typical New York colony war map showing the line of march for the Canadian expeditions, starting from New York City. Among the forts and towns shown are Albany, Schenectady, Saratoga, Fort Edward, Lake George, Ticonderoga, Crown Point, Oneida Lake, and Fort Ontario. The British Royal Coat of Arms appears on the reverse side. Although not dated, the horn is of the French and Indian War period.

H-12

Map horn made in England or Scotland circa 1755 and fitted with a sterling silver charging device. Although there is no name on the horn, its original owner can be identified by the coat of arms. These arms, Montgomerie and Eglington quartered, belong to the Earldom of Eglington, and therefore the horn is identified as the property of Archibald Montgomerie, second surviving son of Alexander, Earl of Eglington. Archibald Montgomerie was the Lieutenant Colonel Commandant in America in 1757 and during the succeeding years of the campaign in this country. He later succeeded his brother in the earldom.

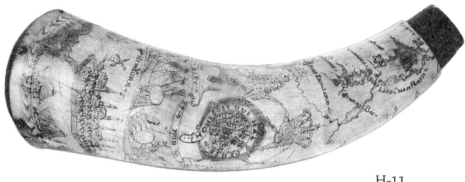

H-11

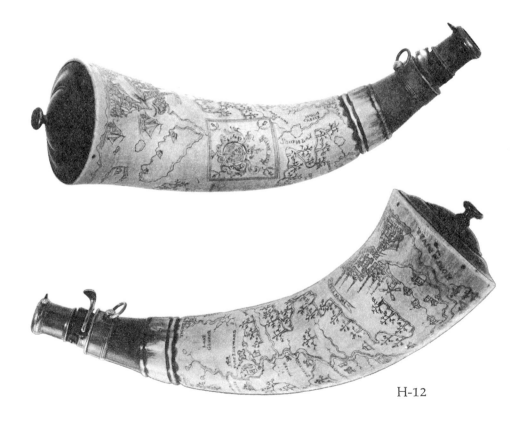

H-12

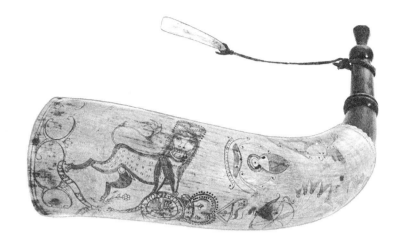

H-13

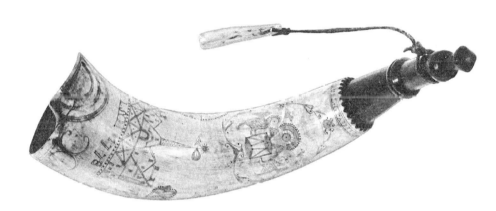

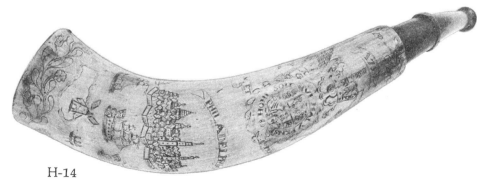

H-14

H-13

Powder horn with the name "Mr. Samuel Gravill" engraved around the top. At the bottom is depicted a village scene with "Kelso 1778" engraved below it, Kelso evidently being the name of the town. On the reverse side is the British Royal Coat of Arms. The extension at the base of the horn has two holes through which the carrying strap was threaded. The charger, or powder measurer, is made from the tip of an animal horn.

H-14

Dated 1750, this is one of the earliest map horns known to exist, and one of the very few decorated horns to have survived from before the French and Indian War (1755–1763). The engraving shows a view of the Delaware river, ships, and the town of Philadelphia, including the building now known as Independence Hall. An island in the foreground, probably Windmill Island, has since disappeared. Above the town is engraved "Philadelphia" and the British Royal Coat of Arms. The rest of the horn is decorated with scroll work, a man on horseback, and a hunter shooting at a deer.

H-15

H-15

Powder horn engraved
"JOHN BESSE HIS HORN CHARLESTOWN
CAMP IN MASSECHUSETTS BAY
NOVEMBER THE 6th 1775."
Besse enlisted twice in
a Massachusetts company
during the Revolution.

H-16

Powder horn engraved
"GILES REED'S HORN
TICONDEROGA NOV. 27, 1776."

H-16

H-17

H-17

Powder horn engraved
"Benjamin Hammond His Horn Nov 1768."
The designs engraved on
the rest of the horn are
typical of Pennsylvania
workmanship.

H-18

Powder horn engraved
"Noah Hall lieutinat His
Horn Made in Roxbury Camp{s},
y{er}, 1775 by Abimeleck Uncus 24
octob{r}." Uncus may have
been an Indian serving in
the army.

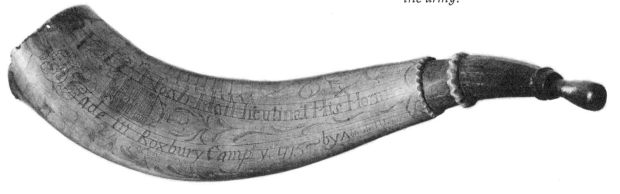

H-18

H-19

H-19

American powder horn engraved with a map showing the area from New York harbor up the Mohawk Valley, and inscribed "Petre Lot 1761."

ACCOU-
TREMENTS

POLE ARMS

Pole arms as weapons of war had been virtually abandoned by most European armies by the American Revolution. The halberd, pike, and spontoon had given way to the fusil and bayonet, though the halberd and spontoon were sometimes still carried as symbols of rank.

In early British regiments, the officers carried spontoons, and the halberd was the symbol of a sergeant in most European armies. In 1791 the halberd was officially abolished in England, but British troops sent out to America had already gradually abandoned it.

American-made halberds followed no uniform style, although many were copied from the British. Following the British regulations, they were required military items in all the colonies until the Revolution.

France officially gave up pole arms long before England, and so no French halberds were used in America during the Revolution.

The spontoon, though not officially abolished in England until 1786, had actually been given up some years earlier in favor of the light fusil.

American-made spontoons, like halberds, were made in many varieties. In 1778, a council of brigade commanders specified that spontoons for officers should have staffs six feet long, with the iron part one foot long. These standards met with General Washington's approval, and were made official. Washington, like many other American commanders, believed in the effectiveness of pole arms, and so America became the only country involved in the Revolution to use them to any great extent.

The American spontoon was intended as a weapon as well as a symbol of rank. This is evident from a passage in the General Orders given by Washington at Valley Forge in the winter of 1777:

As the proper arming of officers would add considerable strength to the Army, and the officers themselves derive great confidence from being armed in the time of action, the General orders everyone of them to provide himself with a half pike or spear as soon as possible —fire-arms, when made use of, withdrawing their attention too much from their men, and to be without either, has a very awkward and unofficer-like appearance.

183

General Anthony Wayne also advocated the spontoon as a weapon, and ordered fifty of them for use by his officers in the attack on Stony Point in New York.

The pike was the enlisted man's pole arm, and the navies of most countries used the boarding pike. Many contemporary records contain references to it. The American Army ordered pikes in large quantities for its soldiers. One argument for it was that its reach was beyond that of a bayonet. Probably its chief use was as a trench spear to defend fortifications.

Thus, by the Revolution all countries except America had virtually abandoned pole arms as weapons. A possible reason for their continued use is that firearms were scarce for American troops, whereas useful pole arms could be fashioned quickly and cheaply by any blacksmith.

SADDLE HOLSTERS

Pistols carried by a man on horseback, whether officer or dragoon, were almost always kept in leather holsters attached to the pommel of the saddle. The shape and size of the holsters conformed to the pistols that they carried. The holsters had flaps or covers that protected the pistol against the elements and prevented it from being jostled out of the holsters when the horse was in motion. Often these covers were decorated with such animal fur as bear or leopard skin, with cloth embellished with braid trim, or were plain leather. Ornamental metal caps in brass, pewter, and sometimes silver were often found on the muzzle end of these holsters. They were purely decorative, and many holsters had plain uncapped ends.

It is very difficult to state with certainty that a particular pair of holsters is definitely of the Revolutionary period, since it is unlikely that any abrupt change in styling occurred at the end of the war. Most saddle holsters carried an officer's pair of pistols, and as there was a wide variety of officer pistols to suit the individual taste, it would naturally follow that the holsters themselves would not be made to a uniform pattern.

Many American-made saddle holsters of the early nineteenth century have leather compartments at the top with tin inserts to accommodate four or five paper cartridges. However, it is not certain whether this feature is definitely post-Revolutionary.

Because of the deterioration of leather as a result of the passage of time, many saddle holsters have unfortunately found their way to the junk pile, and thus surviving examples from Revolutionary times are extremely scarce.

The following illustrations show examples of saddle holsters in use both before and during the Revolutionary War.

THE GORGET

During the second half of the seventeenth century the gorget made a definite change from being a part of the defensive armor to being an ornamental symbol of rank for officers. It is because of this change that it has survived long after other armor ceased to be worn.

At the time of the American Revolution, the gorget was regulation in the British army. It was either gilt or silver, depending on the color of the buttons and lace on the uniform, and was engraved with the King's Arms or the King's Cypher and Crown. The prevailing fashion in men's neckwear and collars dictated the various ways in which the gorget was worn, and probably influenced the changes that took place in its shape. From 1702 to around 1768 the gorget in the British army was worn suspended around the neck by a ribbon, and it was shaped like a fairly wide crescent. After 1768, it was worn fastened to the lapel or collar buttons, and its shape became more nearly round, with the shoulder ends closer together. After 1790, when a new style of coat collar was in fashion, the gorget was attached to the collar buttons, and the shoulder ends were pinched in so that they almost touched.

The French gorgets of the Revolutionary War period were gilt, with the Royal Arms of France in silver applied.

There were many variations in the design of gorgets worn by some of the Hessian officers. Generally, they were quite large and made of silver, with the arms of the principality from which they came in gilt and enamel.

Although never officially adopted by the Continental Army of the United States, the gorget was worn by some field officers during the Revolution. There was no uniformity in the design of American gorgets, since they were not regulation equipment. An interesting example is George Washington's gorget, shown in the following photographs.

The American Indians were attracted by the shiny, decorative gorgets, and many plain ones with no engraving were made as items of trade with the Indians.

Generally speaking, the gorget was no more than a symbol of rank for officers of all the armies participating in the American Revolution. As such, it has lingered on through the years, and while officially abandoned by the British army in 1830, it is still worn by some armies today.

THE BAYONET

The earliest bayonet, the plug bayonet, was first used in the mid-seventeenth century in England and France, and was merely a knife that fitted into the muzzle of a musket. Its obvious disadvantage was that the musket could not be fired while the bayonet was affixed.

By 1700 the socket bayonet had been developed. It had a cylindrical socket at the hilt that fitted around the barrel of the musket, enabling the soldier to fire while the bayonet was in position.

Blade styles varied, but the most popular was the sharply pointed spear type, with the blade usually triangular in cross section.

Identification of bayonets is much more complicated than that of firearms. The great interchangeability possible on early muskets increases the difficulty in pinpointing the date of manufacture, as does the fact that the development of the bayonet did not necessarily coincide with that of the weapons with which it was used.

The following bayonets represent the basic types used during the Revolution.

MILITARY HEADGEAR

The headgear most closely associated with the American Revolution are the tricorn hat and the cocked hat. The tricorn was a black felt hat, with a broad brim up to 5½ inches or more wide. The brim was turned up and attached to the crown at the sides and rear, forming a triangular shape, and worn with point to the front. This hat is chiefly associated with minuteman and militia units. A cockade made from a ribbon, usually black, and placed under the ties on the left side of the hat gave the wearer a military air. This hat, and its smaller version, the castor hat, which had a narrower brim turned up on the left side, were worn by riflemen in a variety of ways. Marines wore the castor hat bound with white tape and turned up on the left with a cockade.

The military hat was the cocked hat, so called because the front point was worn over the left eye and the hat was pulled down on the right side. The hat was worn in this position so that it would not interfere with privates carrying a musket at "attention firelock," straight up and resting on the left shoulder. Field grade and general officers apparently followed the civilian fashion and wore their hats with the point over the nose. This headgear had the brim pushed further against the crown than the tricorn. The brim was smaller and bound with tape. To prevent the front cock from squeezing to a point, a four-inch piece of whalebone was sewn into the hat there. In order to prevent the hat from falling off during exercises, two pieces of tape the color of the man's hair were sometimes sewn into the lining and fastened around the hair with hook and eye.

Many other types of headgear were worn during the Revolution. One of these is the boiled, or jacked, leather jockey-style helmet of the American dragoon. It was crested with fur or hair and frequently bound with turbans of various colored cloth or fur. Leather helmets of various styles were also worn by other troops, including British light infantry companies and regiments of Rhode Island and Delaware. British and French grenadier companies wore high fur caps with a metal plate in front. An interesting grenadier miter was worn by the German mercenaries. It had a high pointed metal front plate inscribed with the coat of arms of the German state from which the soldier came. A metal band went around the head and the back was cloth. The British light dragoon regiments wore an all-brass helmet turned up in front and decorated with various devices. For the British 17th Light Dragoons it was a skull and crossbones with the motto "Or Glory" lettered underneath. There is evidence that an American unit, Sheldon's 2nd Regiment of Light Dragoons, had all-brass helmets similar to the French dragoon helmet of the period. Indeed, they may have been imported from France.

Another form of headgear was the "Canadian" style fur hat, closely resembling the Daniel Boone look, except for its cloth top. Various stocking caps and canvas sailor caps were also worn.

A complete survey of Revolutionary headgear would fill a volume. What has been given here is merely a general idea of the more common style of head covering for the military man of this period. Within all the different types mentioned, there is much variation in detail.

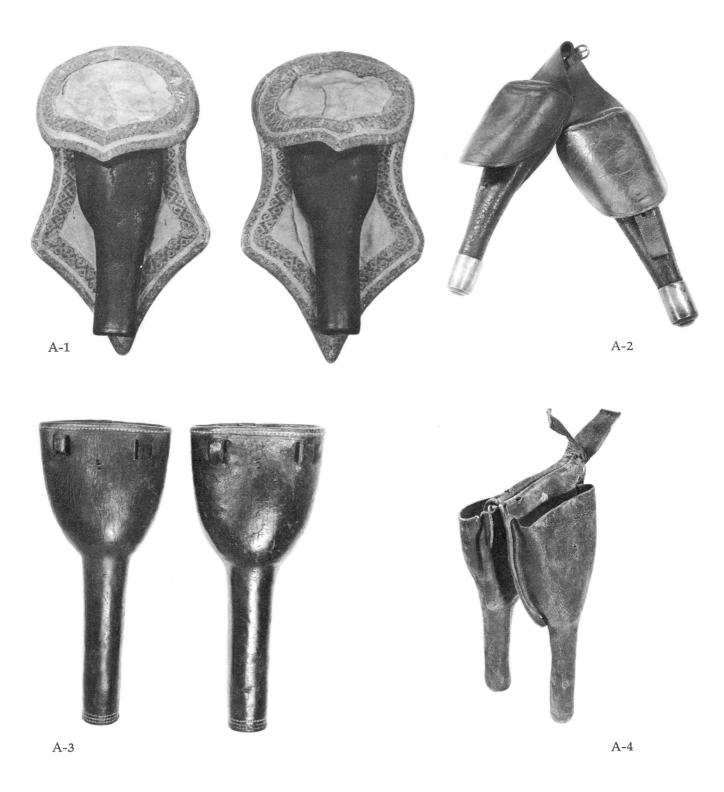

A-1

A-2

A-3

A-4

A-1   *Pair of black leather saddle holsters with fabric housings and covers, trimmed in scarlet braid. These were used by George Washington.*

A-2   *Pair of American black leather saddle holsters with brass caps, of the Revolutionary period. A geometric design similar to a sunflower is stitched on the cover flaps.*

A-3   *Pair of British black leather saddle holsters for flintlock pistols, circa 1750.*

A-4   *Pair of American black leather saddle holsters for flintlock pistols of the Revolutionary period. Covers are missing.*

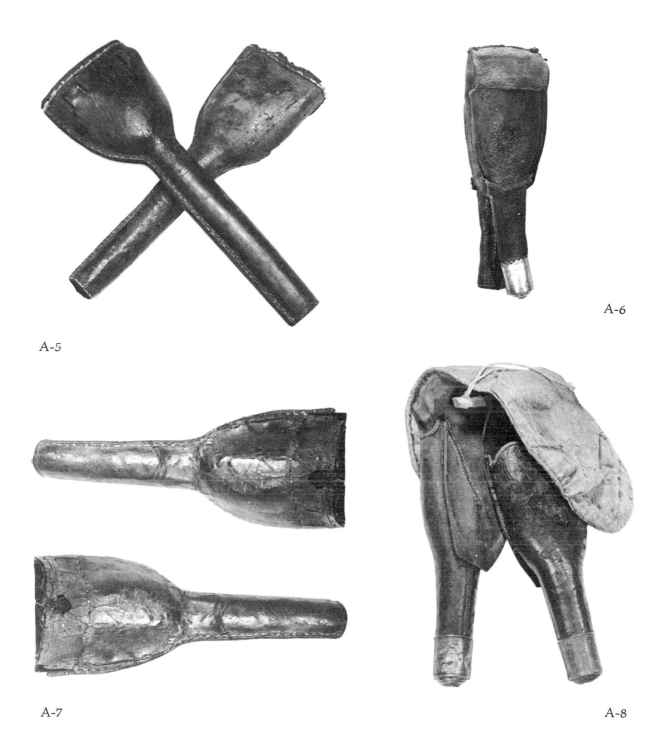

A-5

A-6

A-7

A-8

A-5   Mid-eighteenth-century British black leather saddle holsters made for
the heavy dragoon pistol with 12-inch barrel.

A-6   Pair of black leather saddle holsters with brass end caps, made around 1770.
One of the brass caps is missing.

A-7   Pair of mid-eighteenth-century British black leather saddle holsters for the
heavy dragoon pistol.

A-8   Pair of American black leather saddle holsters with brass end caps, of the
Revolutionary period. These are complete with their covers,
or flaps, made of bearskin; however, most of the fur is missing.

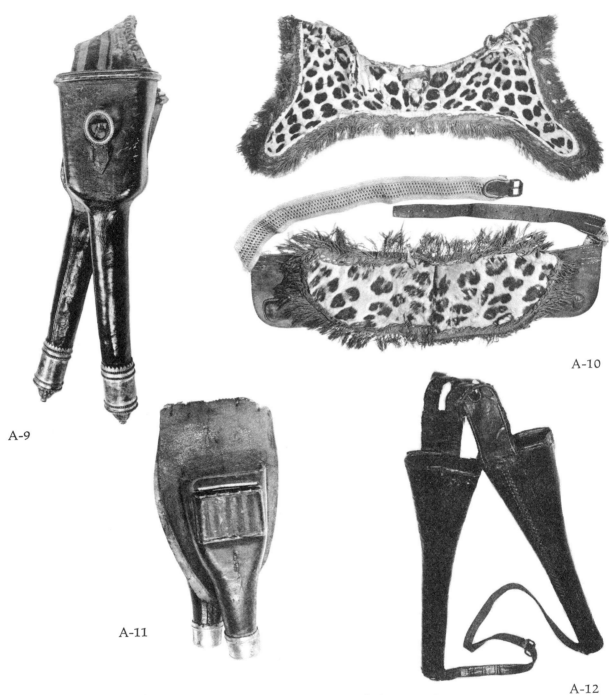

A-9   Pair of early eighteenth-century black leather saddle holsters with
        very decorative gilt end caps. These are probably German, and the fine
        quality is indicative of use by a high-ranking officer.

A-10   Pair of brown leather saddle holsters with leopard-skin covers,
        trimmed with red fringe. The leopard-skin pad prevented the holsters
        from chafing the horse.

A-11   American black leather saddle holsters with pewter caps and
        leather-covered tin storage compartment for cartridges. Possibly of the
        Revolutionary period or shortly thereafter.

A-12   Pair of early eighteenth-century black leather saddle holsters
        for long-barreled pistols. The strap affixed to the tips passed underneath
        the horse's body to prevent the holsters from flapping up and down.

A-13

A-14

A-15   A-16

A-13   *A grouping of pole arms, complete with their shafts. Shown left to right are:*
       an American halberd made in New England, over all length 8 feet;
       American pike, over all length 6 feet 9 inches; British spontoon,
       over all length 7 feet. All of these pole arms are mid-eighteenth-century.

A-14   *Detailed views of the heads of the pole arms shown on this page.*

A-15   *Mid-eighteenth-century American halberd. The iron blade retains*
       much of the original tinning, and the original pine shaft has been preserved
       except for the lower part, which is a restoration.

A-16   *Mid-eighteenth-century American halberds.*

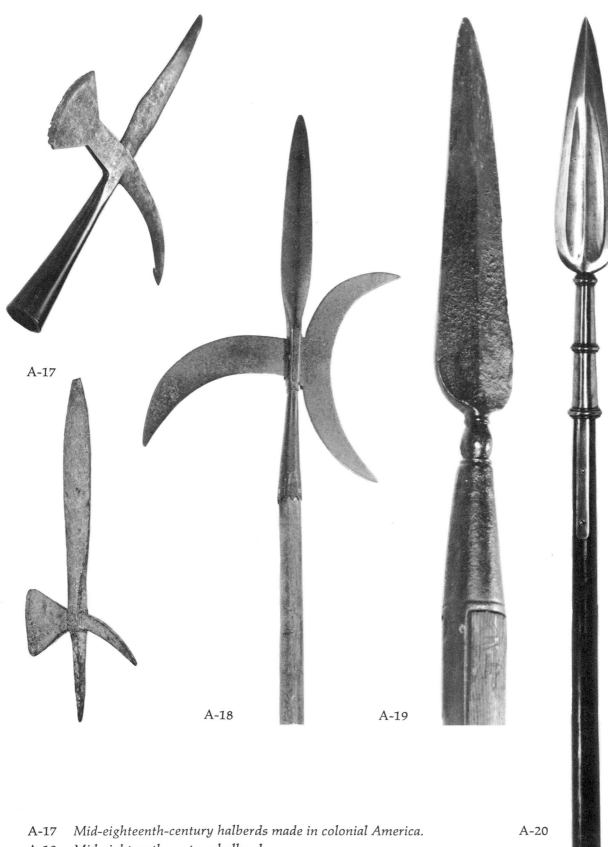

A-17   *Mid-eighteenth-century halberds made in colonial America.*

A-18   *Mid-eighteenth-century halberd,*
        believed to have been used by a Loyalist.

A-19   *Mid-eighteenth-century pike.*

A-20   *Early eighteenth-century British spontoon.*

A-21

A-22

A-23

A-21   *German Brunswick halberd engraved with*
        the Hanoverian horse, of the
        American Revolutionary period.

A-22   *Partisan, probably American-made*
        because of its crude workmanship.

A-23   *Massive mid-eighteenth-century American pole arm, the metal head*
        measuring 26 inches long by 3¾ inches wide. It is not known for what use
        this weapon was intended. The crossbar shown is a later addition.

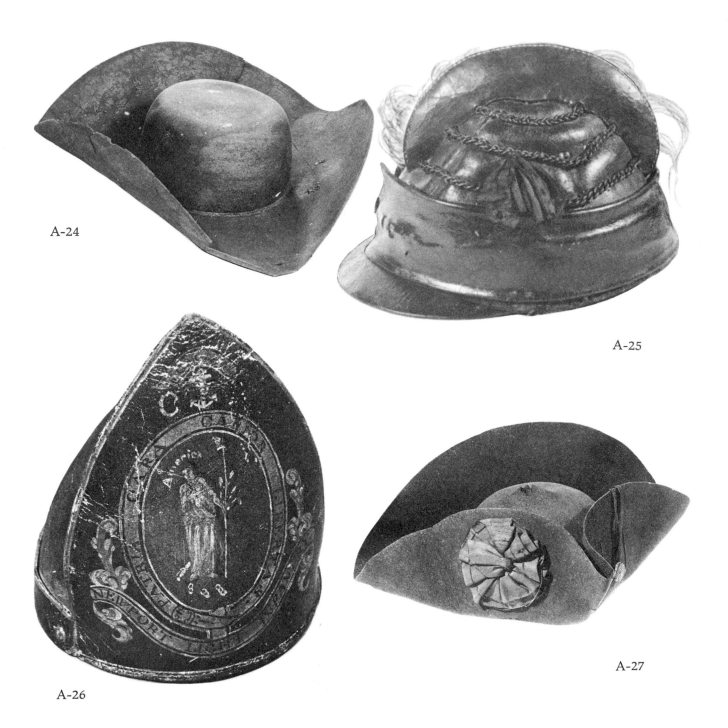

A-24

A-25

A-26

A-27

A-24   Black felt tricorn hat of the Revolutionary period.

A-25   American leather dragoon helmet worn by Captain Michael Titcomb of
Newburyport, who served from 1776 to 1779 in Washington's Life Guard.

A-26   Black leather hat of the Newport, Rhode Island infantry. Painted on the front
is a maiden, symbolizing America, breaking the chains of bondage.
Around this is the motto "Patria cara carior libertas" and "Newport
Light Infantry."

A-27   American cocked hat made of black felt with cockade on one side.
It was worn by Captain John Shethar (Connecticut) of the 2nd Continental
Light Dragoons,
1776–1780.

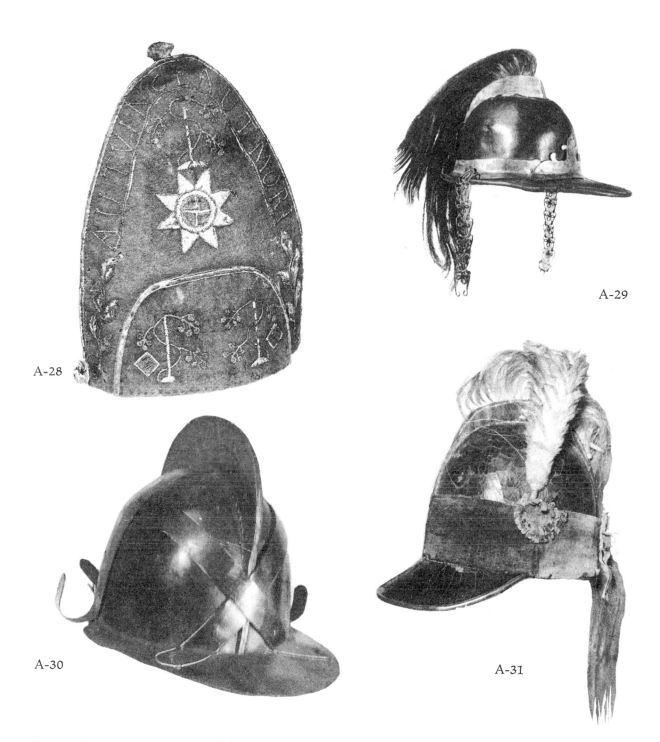

A-28   *American grenadier style hat made of coarse cloth with a red front and*
blue back. Crossed swords and muskets are embroidered at the back.
The hat is probably of Connecticut origin and may have been worn at the
Battle of Fort Griswold in September, 1781.

A-29   *American jockey-style dragoon helmet, circa 1778–1781, made of heavy leather.*
This hat has a brass band at the bottom, brass channel comb with horsehair,
ornamental brass link chinstrap, and pointed leather visor.

A-30   *American dragoon helmet, circa 1778, made of heavy leather. The three iron*
bands affixed to the helmet protect primarily against saber slashes.

A-31   *American dragoon helmet, circa 1778–1790, made of leather with horsehair*
crest and red muslin band at base.

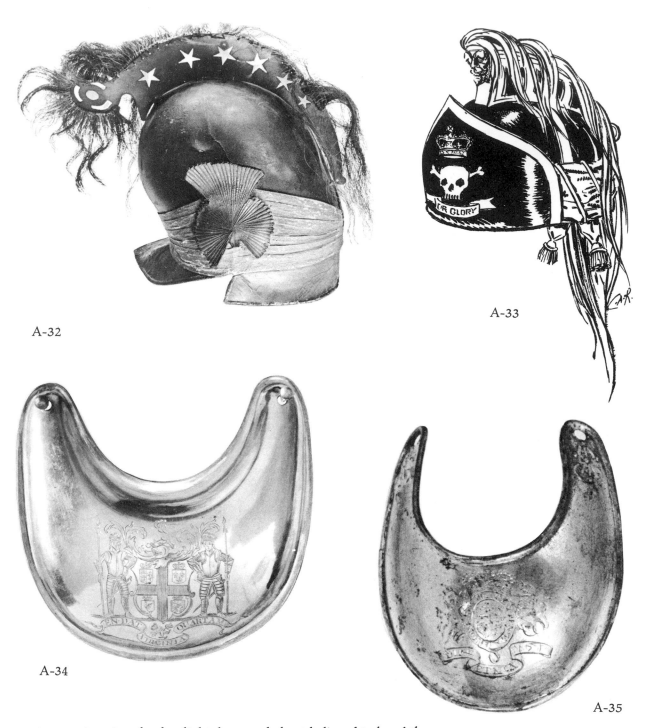

A-32

A-33

A-34

A-35

A-32   *American leather light dragoon helmet believed to be of the*
       Revolutionary period.

A-33   *Sketch of the brass helmet worn by the British 17th Light Dragoons.*
       The frontplate is painted black with white skull and crossbones and
       white scroll below, and the motto "Or Glory." The horsehair crest is red,
       and the red turban is held in place with white cording. Officer's
       helmets had silver cording and silver on the frontplate in place of white.

A-34   *George Washington's gilded brass gorget bearing the Colonial Arms of Virginia.*
       It shows a young girl and two men in half armor holding lances,
       with the motto "En dat Virginia quartam."

A-35   *Mid-eighteenth-century British brass gorget.*

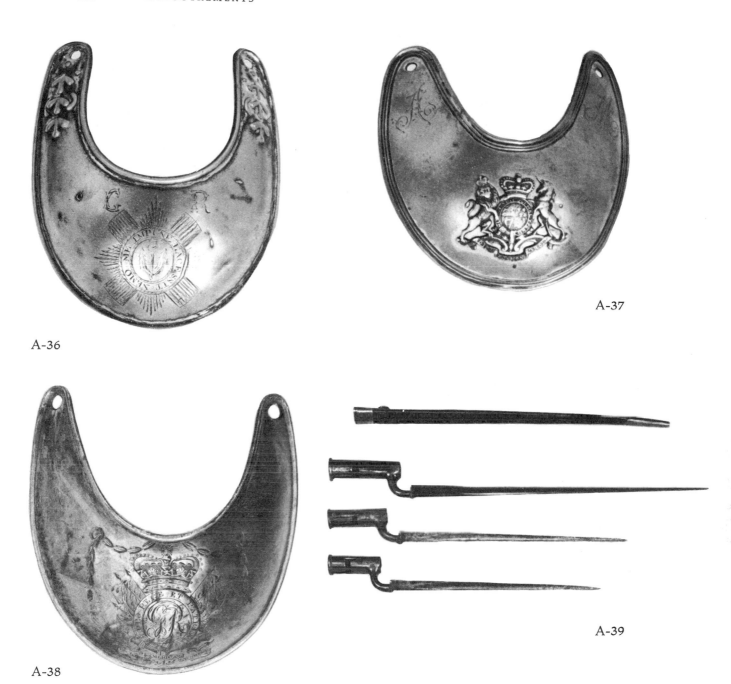

A-36

A-37

A-38

A-39

A-36   Officer's brass gorget engraved with the regimental device of the
         Scots Guards, circa 1760. Units of this regiment served in America during
         the Revolution.

A-37   Officer's gorget with the Royal Coat of Arms in silver applied, circa 1770.

A-38   Late eighteenth-century English gorget.

A-39   British bayonets.
         Top: Bayonet and black leather scabbard with brass fittings for the
         46- and 42-inch barrel Brown Bess muskets.
         Middle: Bayonet, dated 1779, for an officer's fusil.
         Bottom: Short bayonet for a carbine.

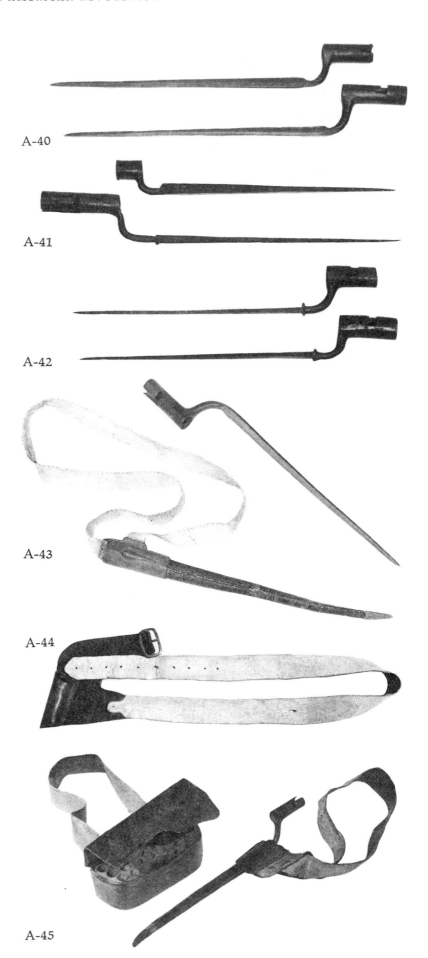

A-40

French bayonets.
Top: Bayonet for the model 1763
Charleville musket.
Bottom: Bayonet for the model 1746
Charleville musket.

A-41

American bayonets.
Two crude American bayonets.
The one at the top has an unusually
wide blade.

A-42

Hessian bayonets.
Two bayonets for Hessian,
or German, muskets.

A-43

American bayonet with black leather
scabbard and cloth carrying strap
of the Revolutionary period.

A-44

American-made infantry shoulder
sling belt of the Revolutionary
period, with double frog for short
sword and bayonet. The sling is
buff leather, and the frogs are
line-tooled black cowhide.

A-45

Crossed-belt set consisting of
black leather bayonet scabbard and
cartridge box with white
leather straps. The wooden insert
holds 24 cartridges.

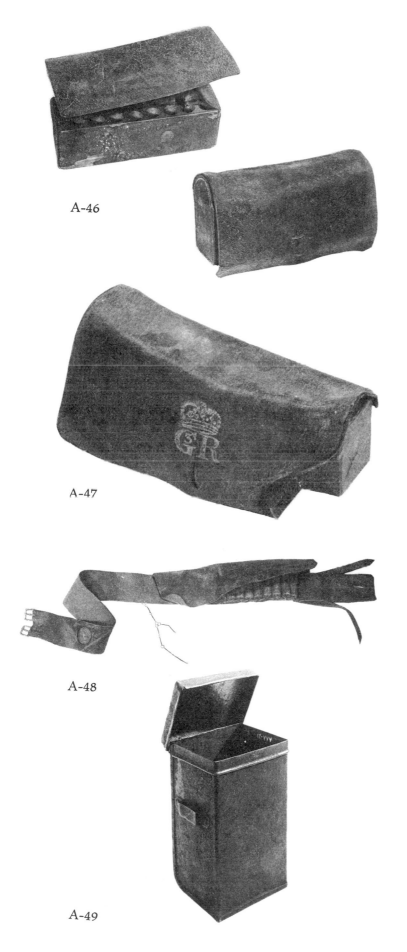

A-46

A-47

A-48

A-49

A-46

Black leather-covered cartridge boxes with wooden block drilled to accommodate 24 cartridges.

A-47

British waist cartridge box stamped with the Royal Cypher and Crown of George II. This box consists merely of a wooden block drilled to accommodate paper cartridges, with a leather flap nailed at the back of the block.

Λ-48

Black leather waist cartridge belt with tin inserts to accommodate 12 paper cartridges. The steel buckles are made with rollers. A pewter button and a pick and brush set with the brush missing are attached to the belt.

A-49

Revolutionary period American cartridge box or canister found in Schraalenburgh, now Bergenfield, New Jersey, with the date 1776 imprinted on the box. Several Revolutionary skirmishes took place in Schraalenburgh. Canisters of this type were used by colonial troops from Maryland and Delaware and possibly by others.

A-50

Leather waist-style cartridge box and tin cartridge box.

A-51

Brass bullet mold with maple handles to cast lead balls in four graduated sizes. The mold is marked with the initials J.M. for Josiah Miller, who worked in Connecticut during the third quarter of the eighteenth century.

A-52

Brass bullet mold with original maple handles for casting lead balls in four graduated sizes.

A-53

Eighteenth-century American soapstone bullet mold, probably from New England. Single matrix, with original hickory pins. The over all length is 3 inches.

A-54

Iron shot-and-swandrop mold . . . 24 shot and 2 swandrops, New England, eighteenth-century. There is an undecipherable maker's mark. The handles are finished like tight scrolls, similar to those found on the handles of betty lamps of that period.

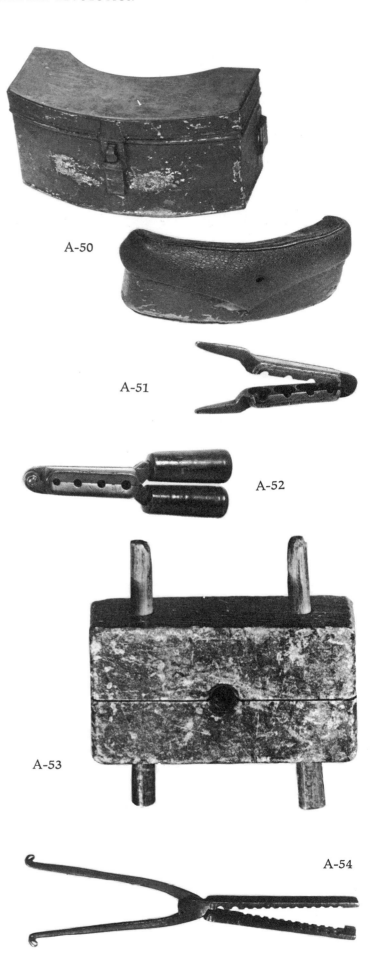

A-50

A-51

A-52

A-53

A-54

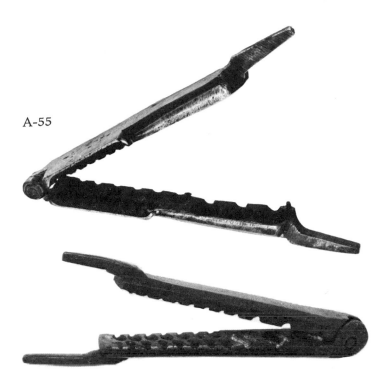

A-55

A-56

A-57

A-58

A-59

A-55

Brass game mold of colonial vintage. It casts three different calibers of musket balls, and fourteen small shots of three sizes for small game and birds.

A-56

Brass bullet mold for casting three musket-size balls of the same caliber, and also buckshot.

A-57

Brass bullet mold complete with handles for casting only buckshot. This mold is marked with the initials JM for the maker, Josiah Miller.

A-58

Brass bullet mold with maple handles for casting one ball and eighteen buckshot.

A-59

Iron bullet mold for casting four musket balls of the same caliber.

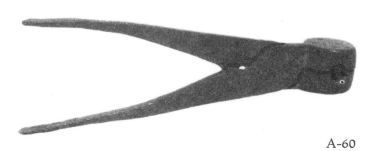

A-60

A-60

Iron single-cavity bullet mold.

A-61

Large brass mold, 14 inches long over all, for casting buckshot.

A-62

A group of brass bullet molds of assorted sizes.

A-63

French steel gang mold for casting .69 caliber lead balls.

A-61

A-62

A-63

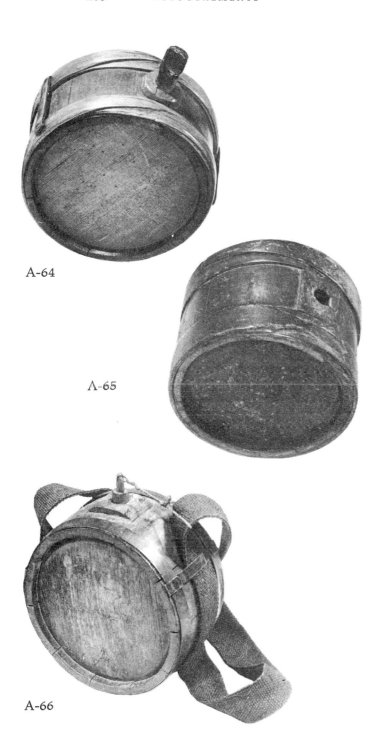

A-64

Λ-65

A-66

A-64

Wooden canteen with wooden hoops, circa 1770.

A-65

Wooden canteen with wooden hoops which are eyelet and buttonhole laplocked. This canteen has its original green finish and was made around 1760.

A-66

Revolutionary period wooden canteen with metal bands around the rims. The woven carrying strap is a later addition. The canteen is marked "U.S."

A-67

Barrel-shaped wooden rum keg, or canteen, with four hand-hammered iron hoops, circa 1770.

A-67

A-68

A-68

*Single-rim wooden canteen
believed to have been carried in the
American Revolution by a soldier
from Waldoboro, Maine.*

A-69

*Rum keg carried by soldier at
Battle of Bunker Hill.*

A-70

*Small wooden keg carried at
Battle of Bunker Hill.*

A-69

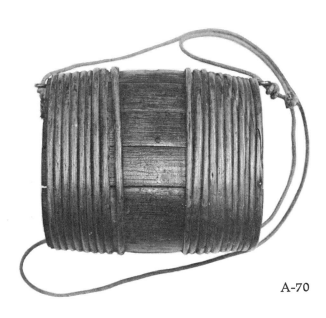

A-70

A-71

A-72

A-73

A-71

*Metal canteen carried by
Abraham Van Vlaack, Jr.,
Duchess County Militia, Fort
Constitution, New York in 1777.*

A-72

*A rundlet, or rum keg, of the
Revolutionary period.*

A-73

*Mid-eighteenth-century wooden
canteen with carrying handle.
Such relatively large canteens were
frequently carried to the fields
by colonial farmers. Due to the
shortage of almost everything,
it is possible that canteens like these
saw military service.*

A-74

*Revolutionary period brass mold with maple handles for casting plain pewter buttons. It is stamped with **the initials** J.M., evidently for the same Josiah Miller who also made bullet molds.*

A-75

*Brass mold for casting pewter **buttons** for the 1st Connecticut Regiment in the Continental Line.*

A-76

Brass button mold, probably made in New England.

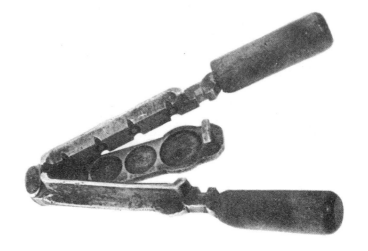

A-74

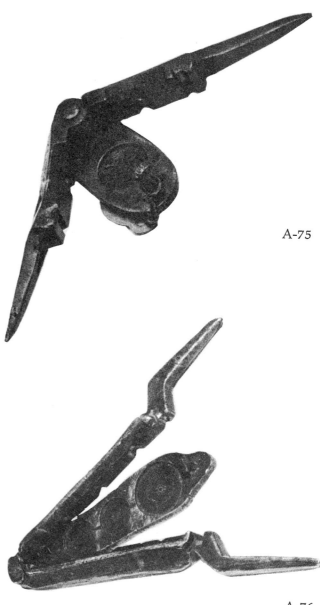

A-75

A-76

A-77

A-78

A-79

A-80

A-81

A-82

A-83

A-84

A-85

A-77

U.S.A. Continental pewter **uniform** button, 1775–1783.

A-78

American artillery pewter **uniform** button, 1775–1783.

A-79

Pewter uniform button of a New York regiment, 1775–1783.

A-80

Pewter uniform button of **the Royal** Regiment of Artillery, circa **1780.**

A-81

Pewter uniform button of the 10th Regiment, Massachusetts **Line,** 1777–1783.

A-82

Pewter uniform button of **Butler's** Rangers, 1777–1783. This **Tory** company was notorious for committing atrocities toward **civilians.**

A-83

Pewter uniform button of the British 38th Regiment of Foot, **which** served in America from 1775 to **1783.**

A-84

Pewter uniform button of the Royal Provincials, 1776–1783, a **Loyalist** corps with no distinctive **buttons of** its own.

A-85

Pewter button of the 3rd Massachusetts Line, 1779–1783.

A-86

Rifleman's belt ax of the Revolutionary period, from northern New York. The overall length is 16 inches.

A-87

Two sizes of belt axes of the type carried by many American soldiers, especially riflemen, during the Revolution.

A-88

Mid-eighteenth-century spike axes.

A-89

Pipe tomahawk, probably made in France around 1760. The head is inlaid with gold and silver.

A-90

Spike ax head, engraved "Liberty."

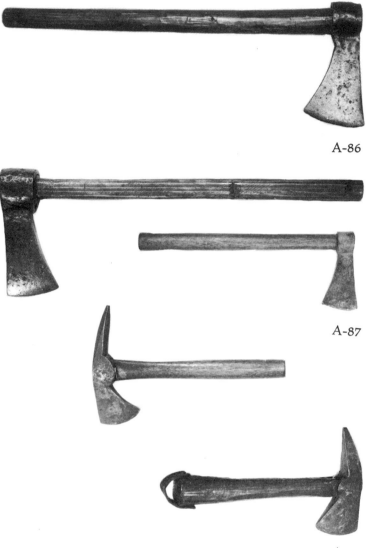

A-86

A-87

A-88

A-89

A-90

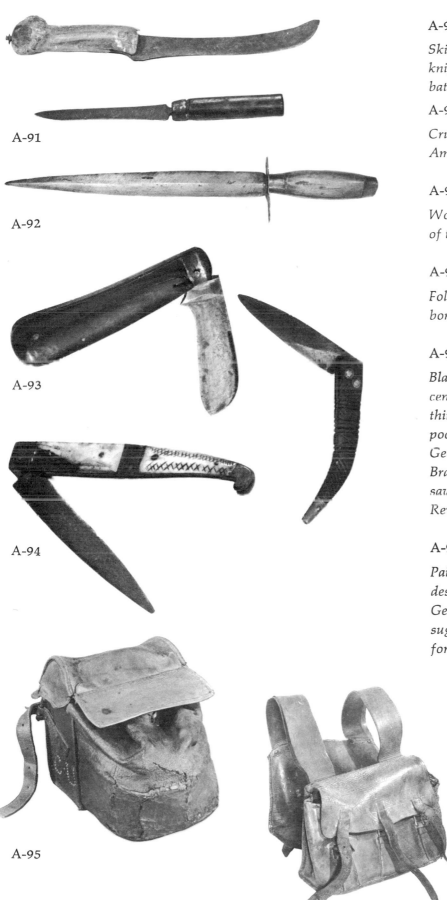

A-91

A-92

A-93

A-94

A-95

A-96

A-91

Skinning knife and a bone-handled knife found on the Saratoga battlefield.

A-92

Crude knife, the product of an American colonial blacksmith.

A-93

Wooden-handled jackknives of the colonial period.

A-94

Folding pocket knife with bone handles.

A-95

Black leather pack bag with center compartment framed in thin wood and collapsible front pocket. This bag was used by George Washington during Braddock's campaign, and possibly saw later service during the Revolution.

A-96

Pair of brown leather saddle bags, described in the public paper of George Clinton as being among the suggested list of accoutrements for horsemen in 1778.

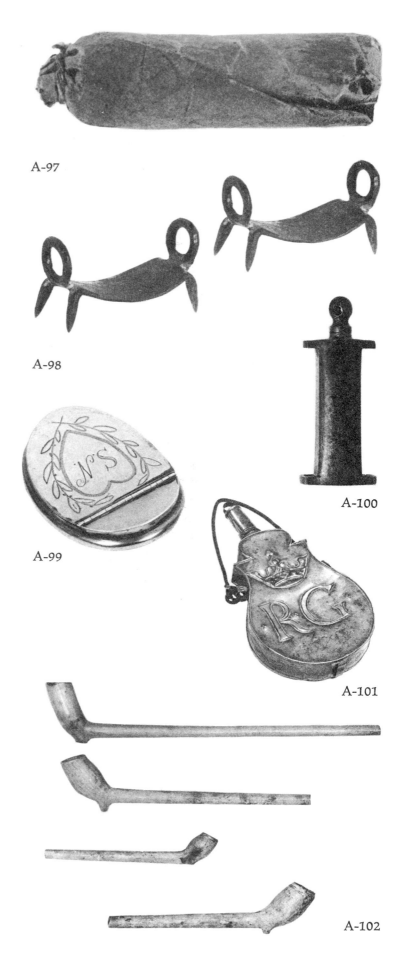

A-97

A-97

*Paper cartridge of approximately
.80 caliber, wrapped in brown paper.
This is the type of cartridge used
during the Revolution. A lead ball is
shown alongside the cartridge.
Soldiers usually bit off the end of
the cartridge, and poured the
powder down the barrel. Next came
the ball, and then the paper,
which was used as wadding.*

A-98

*Pair of steel ice creepers which
fastened to the shoes.*

A-98

A-99

Eighteenth-century brass snuff box.

A-100

*British sergeant's oiler, 4 inches
long, used to oil the flintlocks in
his squad, circa 1775.*

A-100

A-101

*Brass powder flask dated 1728,
and embossed with the crown and
"RG" for the Royal Grenadiers.*

A-99

A-101

A-102

Mid-eighteenth-century clay pipes.

A-102

A-103

A-105

A-103

Tooth extractors of the Revolutionary period.

A-104

Black leather wallet marked with owner's name, "Capt. James Armour," and dated 1775. Shown with the wallet are several coins and pieces of paper scrip of the period.

A-105

Hunting bag and powder horn carried by riflemen and some militia units. The horn is engraved "W. SMITH CAP. PECKS CO."

A-106

George Washington's Continental Army uniform, without military insignia, made of dark blue cloth with buff facings and plain gilt buttons. The waistcoat and knee breeches are of buff cloth. This uniform was presented to the United States government by George Washington Parke Custis, and is now displayed in the Smithsonian Institution.

A-107

Homespun linen hunting shirt, or rifle frock, worn by Abraham Duryea in the Battle of Long Island, August, 1776. Rifle dress with leather breeches was worn on field service during the Revolution by both officers and men.

A-108

Buckskin knee breeches of the Revolutionary period. Soldiers wore breeches of leather, wool, or linen with long home-knit stockings of white or gray wool. Some men wore long trousers of heavy white linen, white wool, or deerskin.

A-106

A-107

A-108

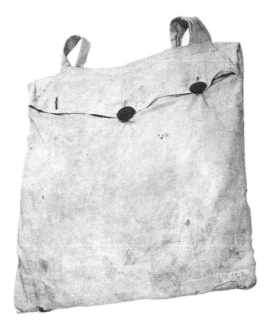

A-109

A-109

Homespun linen knapsack worn by David Uhl, a militia Captain, during the Revolution.

A-110

Black leather boot with with spur, possibly a postillion boot.

A-111

Epaulet of Lieutenant Robert Burnet of Captain William Stevens' 2nd Artillery Regiment, Continental Line. Red cloth with gold thread.

A-110

A-111

A-112

A message warning Connecticut that the American militia had been attacked at Lexington and that the British were on their way to Concord.

A-113

A grouping of nine enlistments in the 3rd Connecticut Line Regiment in Captain William Judd's company. All enlistments are dated during early 1777.

A-114

German newspaper clipping dated August 27, 1776, which was found in the patch box of the jaeger rifle shown in the shoulder arms section, photograph S-48. The article concerns an assassination plot against George Washington and several high-ranking officers on his staff.

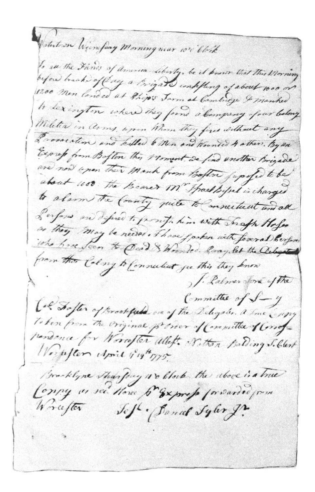

A-112

A-113

A-114

A-115

A-116

A-117

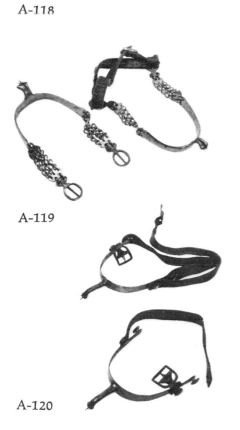

A-118

A-119

A-120

A-115

Powder measure.

A-116

Hand grenade found at
Fort Ticonderoga.

A-117

Four sizes of grapeshot.

A-118

Pair of silver spurs given by George
Washington to Lieutenant Thomas
Lamb at Valley Forge in
January, 1778.

A-119

Pair of brass spurs of the
Revolutionary period. It is almost
identical in construction to a pair of
silver spurs worn by George
Washington that are now preserved
in the Museum of the Mount Vernon
Ladies' Association.

A-120

Pair of silver spurs of the
Revolutionary period.

A-121

A-122

A-121

Camp knife and fork with horn inset on the handles. A unique feature is the interlocking design, which permits the two pieces to be joined as a pocket unit. This set was presented by George Washington to Lord Stirling.

A-122

Folding knife and fork set.

A-123

Small portable camp broiler used during the Revolutionary period.

A-124

Side drum of approximately Revolutionary period decorated with star device on dark green ground. The hoops are painted a muted orange-red, with overpainted decoration somewhat resembling marbleizing. Ropes and leather lugs are replacements.

A-123

A-124

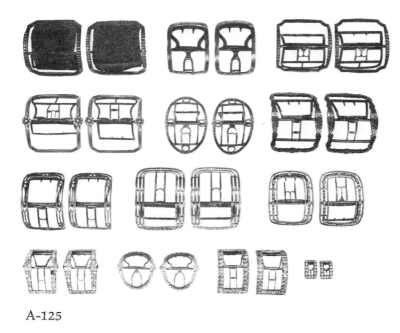

A-125

A-126

A-127

A-128

A-125

A grouping of eighteenth-century brass, steel, silver and paste shoe buckles. The small pair on the bottom row are knee buckles.

A-126

Eighteenth-century ten-sided wooden telescope with brass fittings, made by Dolland in London.

A-127

Small horns, about 3 inches long, used for carrying salt.

A-128

Eighteenth-century tin tinder box. Two types of steel strikers, together with a piece of flint, are shown inside the case. Also shown inside the case is a flat circular tin snuffer with a rolled tin handle in the center, used for snuffing out the flame. The lid has a candle holder built into its center. Finely shredded hemp, flax, or other forms of readily ignitable tinder were carried in the box. This produced a flame from the spark made by the flint and steel.

A-129

Eighteenth-century oval-shaped steel pocket tinder box with its original striker.

A-130

Steel pocket tinder boxes. The one on the right has the striker built as an integral part of the case.

A-131

Pick and brush set, possibly of the Revolutionary period. The pick was used for clearing the vent of a flintlock weapon, while the brush served to remove residue from the powder pan.

A-132

Revolutionary mess kit made of wood covered with leather, and lined with green wool. The interior is divided into fourteen compartments and contains a tray with nine compartments. It is equipped with the following: 4 tin pots with detachable wooden handles, 6 tin plates, 3 tin platters, 2 knives and 4 forks with black handles, gridiron with collapsible legs, 2 tinder boxes, 8 glass bottles with cork stoppers, 2 glass bottles for pepper and salt with pewter tops.

A-129

A-130

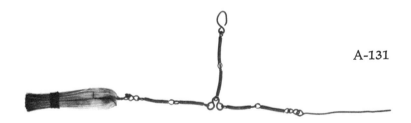

A-131

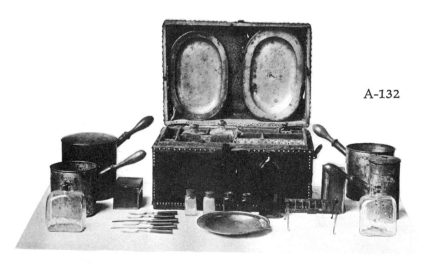

A-132

A-133

A-134

A-135

A-133

British match case worn by grenadiers on their cartridge box belt. The history of the match case goes back to the days of matchlock weapons when they were carried to protect the lighted end of the match. Later, grenadiers used them to protect the match used to light the fuses on grenades. They remained as a distinctive feature of the grenadier uniform even after they ceased to be used for that purpose.

A-134

British brass cartridge box plate of the 1st Regiment of Foot Guards.

A-135

Brass crossed-belt plate worn by Butler's Rangers during the Revolution. This was an infamous band of Loyalists who terrorized the settlers of upper New York and Pennsylvania. Their exploits even caused protests in England, and at the end of the war they fled to Canada.

A-136

A-136

Mid-eighteenth-century waist belts
for carrying the small sword.
One is brown leather and the other is
made of a black woven material.
All of the metal fittings are steel.

A-136

A-137

Straight razor with horn handle
made in England by John Shepherd,
about 1770. The blade is engraved
with maker's name.

A-137

ACKNOWLEDGEMENTS

The hard work associated with writing a book of this type is more than offset by the gratification experienced through others giving so freely of their time and effort. I would like to take this opportunity to express my appreciation to the following people for their assistance:

Stephen V. Grancsay, Curator Emeritus of the Metropolitan Museum of Art, who wrote the foreword and offered useful suggestions concerning the manuscript

Hermann W. Williams, Robert L. Miller, Robert Klinger, and Henry I. Shaw, Jr., who reviewed the manuscript in behalf of The Company of Military Historians

Clyde Risley, who provided all of the artwork and much information on headgear and equipment used by the horse soldier

Henry Bedlivy, for all of the photography in this book except the few photographs that came from museums and several individual collectors

Geoffrey P. Jenkinson and Lewis H. Gordon, Jr., who read the manuscript and made many valuable suggestions

Robert Held and his publisher, Harper & Row, Publishers, Inc., who gave me permission to reproduce the sketches drawn by Nancy Jenkins Held showing the steps in loading and firing a flintlock pistol

Glode Requa, who has shared with me over the past seventeen years his extensive knowledge of Colonial weapons

Major Kenneth C. Miller of Washington's Headquarters, Newburgh, New York, who offered kindness and cooperation in making arrangements for the items in the museum to be photographed

William S. Cornwell, who furnished the detailed information on canteens

My wife, Jean, who did the typing and correspondence, and performed countless other chores in connection with the book.

WARREN MOORE

221

PICTURE CREDITS

I would like to thank the museums, historical societies, and individuals listed below who permitted items from their collections to be photographed for this book. For the sake of simplification, the following legend has been used to designate the photographs: **P**—Pistols; **S**—Shoulder Arms; **E**—Edged Weapons; **H**—Engraved Powder Horns; **A**—Accoutrements.

Bergen County, New Jersey, Historical Society: **A**-49.
Chemung County Historical Society, Elmira, New York: **A**-69, 70.
Essex Institute: **A**-25.
Massachusetts Historical Society: **A**-34.
Metropolitan Museum of Art: **E**-58; **A**-38.
Morristown, New Jersey, Historical Park: **S**-23.
Mount Vernon Ladies' Association: **E**-38; **A**-1, 95, 118, 121.
New York Historical Society: **E**-29; **A**-27, 28, 135.
Niagara County Historical Society, Lockport, New York: **A**-68.
Smithsonian Institution: **P**-24, 29; **S**-22; **A**-106, 132.
Washington's Headquarters, Newburgh, New York: **E**-34, 35, 36, 54, 65; **A**-17, 18, 19, 24, 50, 71, 90, 91, 94, 105, 107, 108, 109, 110, 111, 115, 116, 117, 122, 123.
West Point Military Academy Museum: **P**-1.
Peter Blum: **E**-23, 31, 32, 33, 37, 55, 56; **H**-15.
Frank Burggraf: **A**-63.
Ed Charol: **S**-45, 52, 53, 54, 59; **A**-26, 47, 62, 76, 101, 133.
William S. Cornwell: **A**-72.
Wayne Daniels: **S**-4, 5, 61, 62; **A**-44.
Paul Doniger: **S**-12; **E**-22; **H**-17; **A**-86.
Lewis H. Gordon: **P**-55, 56, 58, 67, 68, 72; **S**-2, 3, 14, 17, 20, 25, 26, 30, 31, 33, 38, 43, 44, 51; **E**-19, 53, 57, 59, 67; **H**-18; **A**-36, 37, 100.
Stephen V. Grancsay: **S**-48; **E**-48; **H**-19; **A**-15, 114.
William H. Guthman: **S**-6; **E**-1, 2, 24; **A**-16, 21, 32, 112, 113, 134.
Geoffrey P. Jenkinson: **P**-7, 9, 12, 16, 18-23, 31, 40-44, 46, 51, 52, 70, 71, 76; **H**-16.
Waverly P. Lewis: **A**-29, 30, 31.
Ed Marron, Jr.: **P**-63, 64.
George C. Neumann: **S**-32.
John R. Phillips: **H**-9.
Glode Requa: **P**-54; **S**-8, 9, 50; **H**-5.

222

Clyde Risley: **E**-8; **A**-6, 77-85, 96.
Dr. Norman Schaeffer: **P**-10.
John Watson: **S**-39, 47; **A**-20.
Wester White: **S**-11, 15.
Hermann W. Williams: **E**-3; **A**-55, 75, 124.
Paul J. Wolfe: **A**-53, 54.

BIBLIOGRAPHY

Bird, Harrison K., Jr., "Early American Cavalry Helmets," *The Bulletin of the Fort Ticonderoga Museum*, V (July, 1940), Nos. 5-6.

Blackmore, Howard L., *British Military Firearms 1650–1850* (London: Herbert Jenkins, 1961).

Blackmore, Howard L., "Henry Hadley, Foreigner, and Four Pairs of His Pistols," *The Connoisseur Magazine*, October, 1957.

Blair, Claude, *European and American Arms* (New York: Bonanza Books, 1962).

Bolton, Charles Knowles, *The Private Soldier under Washington* (New York: Charles Scribner's Sons, 1902).

Calver, William Louis, and Bolton, Reginald Pelham, *History Written with Pick and Shovel* (New York: New York Historical Society, 1950).

Carey, A. Merwyn, *English, Irish and Scottish Firearms Makers* (New York: Thomas Y. Crowell, 1954).

Chaffers, W., *Hand Book to Hall Marks on Gold and Silver Plate* (New York: Charles Scribner's Sons, 1907).

Cornwell, William S., "The Museum's Collection of Military Canteens," *Bulletin of the Rochester Museum of Arts and Sciences*, 1964.

Dean, Bashford, *Metropolitan Museum Studies*, Vol. I, Part 1: American Polearms.

Dillin, Captain John G. W., *The Kentucky Rifle* (York, Pa.: Trimmer Printing, 1959).

Englehardt, A. Baron, "The Story of European Proof Marks," *Gun Digest Treasury* (Chicago: The Gun Digest Company, 1961).

Ferguson, James, *Two Scottish Soldiers* (Aberdeen, Scotland: D. Wyllie and Son, 1888).

George, J. N., *English Pistols and Revolvers* (Onslow County, N.C.: Small-Arms Technical Publishing Company, 1938).

George, J. N., *English Guns and Rifles* (Plantersville, S.C.: Small-Arms Technical Publishing Company, 1947).

Glendenning, Ian, *British Pistols and Guns* (London: Cassell, 1951).

Grancsay, Stephen V., *American Powder Horns* (Philadelphia: Ray Riling Arms Books Co., 1965).

Held, Robert, *The Age of Firearms* (New York: Harper & Row, 1957).

Lewis, Waverly P., *U.S. Military Headgear* (1960).

Oakes-Jones, H., "The Evolution of the Gorget," *Journal of the*

Society of Army Historical Research (London), March, June, and December, 1922.

Pell, Stephen, "The Gorget; As a Defense, As a Symbol, and as an Ornament," *The Bulletin of the Fort Ticonderoga Museum*, IV (September, 1937), No. 5.

Peterson, Harold L., *Arms and Armor in Colonial America* (Harrisburg, Pa.: The Stackpole Company, 1956).

Peterson, Harold L., *The American Sword 1775–1945* (Philadelphia: Ray Riling Arms Books Co., 1965).

Rogers, Colonel H. C. B., *Weapons of the British Soldier* (London: Seeley Service & Co., 1960).

Rogers, Colonel H. C. B., *The Mounted Troops of the British Army* (London: Seeley Service & Co., 1959).

Sawyer, Charles Winthrop, *Firearms in American History* (Boston, 1910).

Webster, Donald B., Jr., *American Socket Bayonets, 1717–1873* (Ottawa: Museum Restoration Service, 1964).